2006

W9-ABG-735

BORDERING THE FUTURE

BORDERING THE FUTURE

The Impact of Mexico on the United States

John A. Adams, Jr.

PRAEGER

Westport, Connecticut
London

Library of Congress Cataloging-in-Publication Data

Adams, John A., 1951–
   Bordering the future : the impact of Mexico on the United States /
   John A. Adams, Jr.
     p. cm.
   Includes bibliographical references and index.
   ISBN 1-56720-637-9 (alk. paper)
   1. United States—Foreign economic relations—Mexico. 2. Mexico—Foreign
economic relations—United States. 3. Mexico—Economic conditions—1994–
I. Title.
HF1456.5.M6 A33 2006
337.72073—dc22   2005032301

British Library Cataloguing in Publication Data is available.

Library of Congress Catalog Card Number: 2005032301
ISBN: 1-56720-637-9

First published in 2006

Praeger Publishers, 88 Post Road West, Westport, CT 06881
An imprint of Greenwood Publishing Group, Inc.
www.praeger.com

Printed in the United States of America

The paper used in this book complies with the
Permanent Paper Standard issued by the National
Information Standards Organization (Z39.48-1984).

10 9 8 7 6 5 4 3 2 1

To John and Calvin

CONTENTS

Tables and Figures   ix

Preface and Acknowledgments   xi

Introduction   1

1 Agriculture: Tierra y Libertad   17

2 La Frontera: The Border and Immigration   41

3 Black Gold: Energy Dynamics of Mexico   61

4 Mexico versus China   77

5 Maquilas, Technology Transfer, and Trade Corridors   99

6 Focus on the Future   121

Notes   127

Bibliography   149

Index   165

TABLES AND FIGURES

TABLES

1-1	Mexican Agriculture Imports to the United States	24
1-2	U.S. Agriculture Exports to Mexico	25
1-3	World Sugar Supply and Utilization, 1999–2003	32
1-4	Chronology of CFTA and NAFTA, 1989–2008	33
1-5	U.S. Agribusiness and Food Processing Industry in Mexico	35
2-1	U.S. Border Demographic Characteristics (SMSAs)	45
2-2	U.S.–Mexico Border Treaties, Agreements, and Operations, 1848–2005	47
2-3	Border SMSA Population, 1970–2010	50
2-4	Hispanic Immigrant Population Remittances Sent Home	51
2-5	Factors Accounting for Illegal Immigration Surge since Mid-1960s	54
2-6	Border Arrests by Sector, FY 2002–03	57
3-1	Mexico's Petroleum Refineries	65
3-2	Western Hemisphere Oil Capacity	66
3-3	Global Oil Production Forecast	67
3-4	Natural Gas Production and Net Imports	68
3-5	U.S.–Mexico Border Electrical Power Interconnections	69
3-6	Services Permitted Under MSCs	72
4-1	Top Ten Mexican Multinational Firms	82

4-2   Comparative Economies   85

4-3   Comparative World Economic Rankings   87

4-4   Top Ten China Exports, 2003   89

4-5   Mexico: Peso-Value, 1900–2006   91

5-1   Maquiladora Industry: Top Ten Sectors, 2004   101

5-2   Maquila Industry Economic Indicators, 1999–2009   102

5-3   U.S.–Mexico Trade, 1996–2003   104

5-4   2003 U.S. Trade with Mexico   105

5-5   Components of an Intermodal Transportation Corridor   115

5-6   Maquiladora Industry Top 10 Companies in Mexico, 2005   118

6-1   Critical Threats to Mexico and U.S. Vital Interests   124

FIGURES

1-1   Growth of U.S.–Mexico Agricultural Trade since
        the Late 1970s   19

1-2   Integration in the North American
        Cattle and Beef Industry, 2004   31

1-3   U.S. Average Tariff, 1789–2005   34

2-1   Rio Grande Watershed   49

2-2   United States–Mexico Border   59

3-1   Demand for Natural Gas by 2010   70

3-2   Burgos Basin Region   74

4-1   U.S. Imports from Nonindustrialized Countries   94

4-2   Where America Worked: 1800–2001   97

6-1   Total Population Projection for the U.S.–Mexican
        Border Region   122

PREFACE AND ACKNOWLEDGMENTS

THIS BOOK IS my responsibility alone, yet I could not have completed it without the timely assistance and counsel of many friends and associates both in the United States and Mexico. A look into the United States–Mexico relationship has jelled in my mind for a number of years, and was propelled in late 2001 as world events seemed to take the spotlight off Mexico and off the United States–Mexico relationship. Over the past three to four years, with the lone exception of rising concern over illegal immigration, little attention has been directed either to Latin America in general or Mexico in particular. The brief visits by President George Bush with President Vicente Fox are largely the function of Bush's background from Texas—Mexico's largest trading partner within the United States. In large measure the spread of democracy throughout the hemisphere, with the exception of a couple of outdated and aging enclaves, and the rise of open markets and free trade have proven a significant boost to the economies and stability of the region. Mexico and NAFTA are a prime illustration for the argument that economic reform and open markets can generate political liberalization.

Geoffrey Garrett, in a recent December 2004 article on globalization in *Foreign Affairs* captured the essence of current priorities: "The problem today is that U.S. policymakers have more pressing things on their mind than Latin America's economic woes. Bailing out Mexico made sense in the years following the Cold War, when traditional security issues receded into the background. But since the September 11, 2001, attacks, achieving political goals through economic means has been given a much lower priority than the war on terrorism."

Nevertheless, the United States has pushed in recent years for bi- and multilateral trade accords to stimulate additional open markets and free trade in the Americas and has continued with a broad array of agreements and new ventures. NAFTA has forever altered the cross-border relationship with Mexico. The concern for safety and security on the borders of the United States is indeed a key element of the war on terrorism. Yet, clearly the post-9/11 focus of the United States south of the border has waned. Understandably, there are levels of priorities and security concerns in today's global environment, and among them Mexico's impact on the United States need not be underestimated or overlooked.

Since Mexico is our closest Latin American neighbor and primary trading partner, the cross-border relationship needs to be carefully monitored and nurtured. The post-9/11 global events do in fact have tremendous implications for regional security and a growing—though not always acknowledged or understood—interdependence between the United States and Mexico. The issues at hand are old, new, and ongoing—immigration, cross-border commerce, water rights, drugs, the development of energy resources, hyper–border urbanization, and crime— and are all areas I have watched evolve up close over the past three decades.

In my attempt to understand and assess the impact of these and other issues that will affect the future of the binational interaction, I am thankful to a number of individuals who over time, some without their knowledge, have helped shape the observations contained herewith.

J. Michael Patrick, Director of the Texas Center at Texas A&M International University has been both friend and sounding board for this project, along with the assistance of Parr Rossen and Flynn Adcock of the Center for North American Studies at Texas A&M University, Harold Hunt of the Real Estate Center also at Texas A&M, and John Kolmer, NAFTA Trade Specialist at the Turner Center for Entrepreneurship. Robert McKinley at the University of Texas at San Antonio along with Robert Harrison at the Center for Transportation Research in Austin provided excellent assistance in their areas of expertise as well as comments on early drafts.

For the evolving perspective on United States–Mexico relations and the dynamics of the border region I gained key insight from many, including Dan Griswold of the CATO Institute in Washington D.C.; John Christman, in Mexico City, a principal with Global Insight, a leader in the evolution of the maquiladora industry and analyst of Mexican political policy; and from former U.S. Ambassador to Mexico and author of *The Bear and the Porcupine* Jeffrey Davidow. Timely input from Daniel B. Hastings, Jr.; Louis Perez; Michael Yoder, U.S. Counsel in Nuevo Laredo; Rene Gonzalez; Don Michie of El Paso; and the energetic mayor of Laredo, Betty Flores, was invaluable for understanding the dynamics of the border region.

Longtime mentor Henry C. Dethloff provided helpful comments on the manuscript and the larger issues at hand. Also helpful at numerous stages of this project were Ron Kapavik, John Keck, David Perez, Lilia Torres, Arturo Garcia, Yvette Medina, Alberto Magnon, Memo Trevino, Guadalupe Martinez, Tom Moore, Tres Hendrix, Ralph Biedermann, and David Cardwell. A very special thank you is extended to Martha Huebner for her timely diligence and patience in reviewing the manuscript in its many drafts.

And as always, a very special thanks to Sherry, Calvin John, and John III for their patience and encouragement.

John A. Adams, Jr.

INTRODUCTION

Of all that extensive empire which once acknowledged the authority of Spain in the New World, no portion, for interest and importance, can be compared with Mexico.

—William H. Prescott, October 1, 1843

THIS WORK ATTEMPTS to discern trends and evaluate the dynamics that will mold the Mexican economy and relationship with the United States during the next two decades. At the dawn of the twenty-first century, Mexico is once again at a major crossroads. Changes in the basic fabric of the Mexican nation during the recent past provide a foundation for a broad assessment of future trends. Because the beginning of a new century is such a defining moment, it is particularly appropriate to reflect on the indicators and trends that are most likely to determine United States–Mexico relations in the foreseeable future.

This is a new era and a new Mexico, with new economic and political challenges. Cooperation between two nations that share a two-thousand-mile common border is constantly tested through a process of trial and evolution. Binational interaction is key to regional security and trade, as is urban and economic development along the border—all are critical elements to enhancing a stable and prosperous cross-border relationship. The topics and indicators amassed here present both obstacles and opportunities. Our two nations are different at the core—each one's origins, religious emphasis, social policy, political evolution, immigration attitudes, cultural icons, and cuisine have few direct parallels except for the fact of proximity that allows each nation access to the other.

One example of conflicting attitudes is the opposing view of history. Over the past two hundred years historical events have done more to shape the mindset of Mexico and its politics and attitudes toward the United States, than have those same events shaped U.S. perceptions of our southern neighbor. While this is at the core of political positioning for many in Mexico, very few

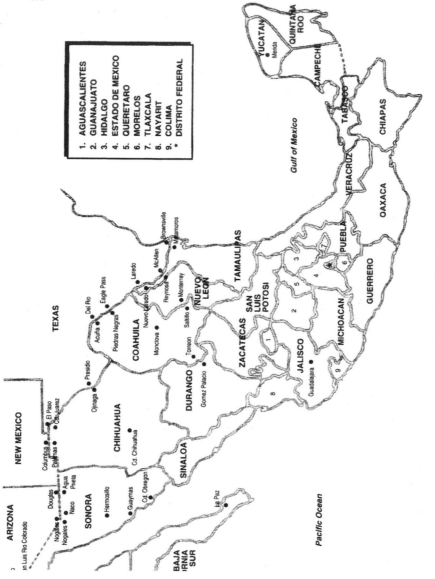

Source: Twin Plant News.

Americans (that is, North Americans) have taken that history into consideration. Thus, I have singled out a number of key topics that have the ability to create peril if unattended, but are, if attended to, the keys to a prosperous future. The primary issues and indicators include agriculture, immigration, border affairs and interactions, energy, enhancement of industry, political stability and the rise of more democratic government in the era following PRI dominance, and the global competitive challenge to Mexico's status quo—all of those will determine the course of Mexico's future and well-being as well as its impact on the United States for decades to come.

This is not a new school of innovative investigation. In the past there have been numerous studies that have addressed this same theme. A viable prediction of the future of Mexico and its potential growth was offered at mid-century by Howard F. Cline in *The United States and Mexico* (1953), where he concluded:

> The transference of population [26 million in 1950] from low-grade skills in the countryside to higher-paying jobs in nascent industry has not been the only augury of the future. Equally as important has been a large-scale, long-term attempt to interweave the two aspects of the industrial revolution, urban and rural, and to bring them into the same definite relation to each other. . . . [I]t is clear that Mexico has embarked on yet a new phase of an old Revolution.[1]

The United States–Mexico relationship was also part of an extensive 1969 twenty-nation hemispheric presidential study, *The Rockefeller Report on the Americas*, to assess concerns of "anti-U.S. trends" that could impact what was termed an "increasingly dependent" region.[2] And in the late 1980s, The Center for the Study of Foreign Affairs released a broad statistical and sectoral review edited by George W. Grayson, entitled *Prospects for Mexico* (1988) followed by a monograph by David Barkin on the changing structure of the Mexican economy, *Distorted Development: Mexico in the World Economy* (1990). Two British authors were among the first to provide a broad global glimpse into the twenty-first century: Paul Kennedy in *Preparing for the Twenty-First Century* (1993) and Hamish McRae in *The World in 2020: Power, Culture and Prosperity* (1994). Countless other prognostications will surely follow. There is reason to believe that early in the twenty-first century the dynamics of the new social, economic, and political environment developing in Mexico will have global ramifications. And in the process, the United States will be most affected.[3]

During the decade of the 1990s, Mexico was transformed as no other rapidly emerging nation. The growth of Mexico, along with the advancement of the country on the world scene, was affected by a dynamic series of political, social, and domestic economic events. In the aftermath of the economically stagnant 1970s and 1980s, all of Latin America, and particularly Mexico, endeavored to launch a new era of stability, democratic reform, and economic growth. The challenge to open a once closed insular economy—dependent on a series of bankrupt fiscal policies and a xenophobic regime reliant on import substitution—in the face of political and social pressures resulted in policies and external plans that did not always match the political and economic realities of a growing nation.[4]

The attraction of foreign direct investment, and the development of an aggressive industrial policy coupled with the completion of a broad number of multilateral trade agreements ushered in a new era of commerce and dependence on the whims of global economic partners. In contrast to efforts to become more competitive globally, Mexico faces today a broad array of domestic challenges that have significant implications for the future of the nation. Among the most pressing are immigration issues, followed by the need to provide social services to a population that daily becomes both larger and younger. And there is the need to address narcotic trafficking, to improve the development and management of natural resources, primarily oil and gas, and to institute meaningful land reform that enhances the ability to foster a productive agricultural sector. In sum, Mexico is one of the most fascinating and complicated emerging nations in the world. In a world economy that is becoming more integrated and "connected," the future course of Mexico has grave regional and global overtones with broad political, economic, and social implications.

Mexico during the latter part of the twentieth century began a transition that introduced a new generation of politicians, economic development strategic planners, "free" trade entrepreneurs, and globally minded industrialists. The technocrats of the Salinas and Zedillo era worked to distance themselves from the past and to place Mexico on the global stage. But these efforts were not without their problems. They, along with the institutions and organizations represented, carried much—if not all—of the same baggage and limited vision that had shaped events in Mexico for nearly a century. By the mid-1990s, Mexico, with a population approaching 100 million, became a significant factor in world economic events. The implementation of the North American Free Trade Agreement (NAFTA) in 1994–95 was a seminal event for both Mexico and its neighbors—as was the crash of the peso in late 1994 and the "tequila hangover" that followed both in Mexico and throughout the region. The NAFTA accord was one of over forty bi- and multinational trade agreements targeted to open the Mexican economy. In addition to becoming the darling of investors worldwide, the economy—dubbed the "Mexico Miracle"—of the growing nation demonstrated the promise and possibility of avoiding some of the past economic instability that had repeatedly hampered growth, created political instability, and slowed the gradual course to a more democratic framework.[5]

WHAT IS PAST IS PROLOGUE: *SI DIOS QUIERE*

Looking to the future of Mexico over the next two decades comes at a time when Mexico is again at a major intersection in its history. While the pre-Columbian legacy of Mexico is rich in lore and history, the arrival of the European influence in the early 1500s marked the transition from the ancient world of regional Indian nations to a colonial phase that gave rise to the roots of the modern Mexican nation. Quite by chance, yet most notably, the first two decades of each century over the past five hundred years have proved a pivotal transition point in the history of the Mexican nation, and the current era is likewise fraught with promise and peril:

1500–21 Consolidation and zenith of the Aztec empire in the Valley of Mexico followed by the arrival and conquest of Mexico by Conquistador Hernán Cortés, 1519–21.

1600–20 Emergence of New Spain (Mexico) as a prized colonial possession due to vast silver exports to the Spanish Crown—silver that would provide wealth and coinage for monarchs and merchants worldwide.

1700–20 The Bourbon dynasty replaces the rule of the Hapsburgs in Spain; entrenchment of the Spanish colonial system and laws; roots of exploration and attempts at occupation of the Rio Grande region.

1800–21 The Independence Era launched by Hidalgo and Morelos and concluded with freedom from Spain in 1821 under the presidency of Agustín de Iturbide; and on the northern frontier of Mexico the first major effort to set the boundary with the Adams-Onis Treaty of 1819.

1900–20 Until 1910 the high mark of the Don Porfirio Díaz era to "modernize" the Mexican economy, the gold standard was adopted in 1905, and in late 1910 the violent rejection of the past via a nationwide Revolution to redefine the direction of Mexico and the drafting of the Constitution of 1917.

2000 Election of the first non-PRI president in nearly a century—Vicente Fox—on July 2, 2000.

That this pattern of significant events early in each century, both at home and abroad, will continue between now and the year 2020 is quite apparent, given the dynamics of domestic, regional, and global events set in motion during the latter portion of the twentieth century. It is from this broad historical backdrop that Mexico will both influence and be affected by significant domestic, regional, and international events well into the future. Thus, a brief review of the cornerstone events of Mexico's colorful past is critical to a fuller understanding of future possibilities.

Discovery

While Columbus flirted with Mexico's coastline in the late 1490s, it was left to adventurer Hernán Cortés to bring the Old World to the New. While we should be ever mindful that the rich heritage of Mexico predates the arrival of Cortés at Veracruz in 1519, the image, transformation, roots of the national identity, and contemporary perspectives on Mexico dated primarily from the Spanish arrival and the exploratory era brought about by Christopher Columbus and those that followed shortly thereafter. Whole volumes have chronicled this period in world history and described what was referred to as the New World, or the "Americas." Both north and south were first discovered, then conquered and occupied by the first wave of Europeans. And of the vast new found regions most affected, Mexico found itself at the center of both European colonial expansion and religious zeal, as well as worldwide political intrigue. These rivalries were largely brought about due to the tremendous wealth of Mexican silver that filled the coffers of Europe, affected the monetary standard worldwide, and financed the warring rivalries among the nations—both at home and in the colonies.[6]

For two decades prior to the arrival of Cortés at the gates of Tenochtitlán, the seat of the Aztec empire and the current day site of Mexico City, the leadership of the Aztec empire was headed by the emperor chief, or *tlatoani*, "he who speaks." Moctezuma, an emperor who embodied both the earthly and spiritual command of the empire, was keen on the transition of his nation. He had envisioned for some time that change "from afar" would descend upon his powerful valley empire. Noted Mexican historian Enrique Krauze captured the concerns and essence of the last Aztec emperor:

> The melancholy Moctezuma had carried the burden of a fatalistic vision of history that—through a series of dreams, prophecies, and bad omens—had foretold the fall of the empire.... [a] kind of cosmic fear possessed the emperor. Could Cortés be none other than the mythical Quetzalcoatl [supreme god], the founder of the great Toltec civilization ... returning to claim what was his.[7]

The lore and history of these concerns and premonitions were dramatically fulfilled. The vast city-state presided over by Moctezuma rivaled any in the world at the time. The vast Aztec empire on the eve of the European arrival was held together via a series of warrior and intraregional commercial alliances. The capital city with its temples, luscious gardens, vast market areas, and houses, as well as canals and causeways, built among a series of islands and lakes in the Valley of Mexico was bigger than all but a few contemporary European cities. City services, trade connections, urban infrastructure, and technology were well ahead of their time. Upon the first sight of Tenochtitlán, Cortés and his men marveled at the expansive magnificence and "enchantments" of the tremendous city that rose from the water. Tenochtitlán, according to the invading Spaniards, was hailed as the inland "Venice of the New World."[8]

During the late fifteenth and early sixteenth centuries the Nahuatl-speaking Aztecs, descendants of the ancient Olmecs and Toltecs, dominated a web of friendly and unfriendly Indian nations that encompassed much of the current length and breadth of Mexico and stretched from the Rio Grande into present-day Central America. While historically the Aztecs were a nomadic warring nation, they had settled into a more stationary rural and urban commercial lifestyle, ever mindful of the need to maintain both a strong defensive posture as well as trading alliances with their tribal neighbors. Tenochtitlán was the political, religious, and commercial heart of the empire. Those outlying tribes that could not forge commercial alliances and peacefully trade were conquered to prevent concentration of hostile forces or disruption of trade corridors throughout the region. The Aztecs used human sacrifice as both a religious practice and a means to scare and dominate rival tribes. By all accounts, at the time of the arrival of the Spaniards, the Aztec nation was a resourceful, dominating, and thriving regional empire. The classic volumes of the *History of the Conquest of Mexico* concluded by William H. Prescott in 1843 still today represent the most intriguing coverage of this period in Mexico's history. The meeting of the Old and New World was a defining moment in recorded history. And contact with the Spanish conquistadors in 1519–20 marked the end of the Aztec nation.[9]

The siege and conquest of the Aztec empire by Cortés was completed in late 1521, and according to many Mexicans even today, marked the first in a long string of hostile "foreign" invasions of Mexico. With the Spanish conquest began the transfer of the Hispanic influence over the entire region, known as the Vice-Royalty of New Spain. The process, actually a series of conquests, would last nearly one hundred years. The vast lands claimed by Spain proved both hard to manage and defend, and included present-day Mexico, parts of Central America as well as large portions of the four southwestern states of California, New Mexico, Arizona, and Texas. The Aztec nation ceased to exist, and nearly all recorded documents of the great civilization, at the insistence of the Catholic Church, were systematically destroyed. Ancient temples, homes, aqueducts, and any structures deemed important to the conquered were razed. The Spanish began at once to introduce European religion, products, and culture. The power and seat of the Spanish colonial government would remain on the site of Tenochtitlán, newly christened as Mexico City, built on and from the rubble and stones of the fallen Aztec temples and buildings. The Spanish occupation was harsh. All pre-1520 regional Indian commercial ties were completely eradicated as the Spaniards imported a broad array of new fruits, grains, and vegetables, as well as beasts of burden. Horses, donkeys, and cows, along with chickens, swine, sheep, and goats, would gradually be assimilated. The Indians had a difficult time adjusting to their new lords. European diseases, such as smallpox, did more to kill and conquer the Aztec nation than all the armies of Cortés. The Indian population dropped in dramatic fashion from over 10 million in 1520 to about 1 million in 1530. New commercial practices, the Catholic religion, large-scale ranching, and the Spanish colonial system, as well as the total domination of the Indian population, hallmarked the first three centuries of Spanish rule.[10]

Livestock and agricultural products were introduced primarily for domestic consumption within the viceroyalty. By the first decades of the 1600s, the commodity that dominated the focus of New Spain was the mining and production of silver. While the search for riches had dominated the motives of the early conquistadors, none of them or the Spanish Crown, had envisioned the magnitude of mineral wealth in Mexico. Although Cortés opened the first colonial silver mines in the mountains of Taxco in 1525, the first large deposits were actually discovered in 1546 at Zacatecas. However, it was not until 1600 that the extent of the wealth of Mexican silver was realized. In addition to filling the treasury of Spain, coinage of Mexican silver into Spanish silver "pesos" or "pieces of eight," became an internationally valid means of exchange and redefined not only the rivalries in European markets but also the commercial exchange patterns throughout the world. Spain, by using the silver and gold riches of the Americas, became the first "globalized" economy with commercial ties with over half the globe. An estimated 80 percent of all exports from New Spain were silver. The mining has continued for over four centuries. And today, Mexico remains the leading producer of silver in the world.[11]

Furthermore, in addition to silver, Mexico has a vast amount of other strategic natural resources. Precious metals, along with a host of other natural resources (most notably petroleum) have defined both the wealth of the nation to this day as well as the degree of foreign intrigue surrounding the exploitation of this natural prosperity. Natural and renewable resources are key to the future of Mexico. Water is another resource—along with the agricultural patterns—that will determine the course of the quality of urban life, interaction with the consumer markets of North America, and industrial development. For example, a sustained unyielding drought in northern Mexico during the 1990s along with increased cross-border irritation over water usage and rights of the Rio Grande have created, and will continue to create, future friction and thus have broad implications on United States–Mexico relations. Notwithstanding, Mexico's path to independence and nationhood, as well as the cost to develop this vast wealth of natural resources, comes at a price. The country has been ever dependent on a steady infusion of foreign direct investment and more recently the inflow of worker remittances to harvest its resources, open new businesses, build homes, and expand its infrastructure. It is the ownership, efficient extraction, and management of these very natural resources that have had, and will continue to have, a profound influence as Mexico defines its domestic strengths and global positioning between now and the year 2020.

Era of Independence

The dominant rule of Spain in Mexico would not begin to diminish until the early 1800s when Europe became embroiled in the Napoleonic wars. During the first two decades of the nineteenth century, Mexico was torn between the rule of an absentee nation and domestic unrest as different factions within Mexico plotted to break away from the Spanish yoke. The turmoil was a direct result of three centuries of colonial social stratification based along racial lines, wealth, and position advocated by the viceregal government and leaders in both the church and commercial sectors. Both the society and the power structure of New Spain were segmented into a number of often well defined, yet overlapping, social distinctions. Of these groups, three segments were very prominent. The first were the "peninsular Spaniards" or European-born native sons (very few Spanish women emigrated to New Spain) known as the *peninsulares* or *gachupines*.[12]

Regardless of their ability or training, the peninsulares automatically filled most of the key positions within all sectors of society of New Spain. This practice greatly aggravated Mexican-born Spaniards known as Creoles. While many Creoles had some Indian blood, most were registered as Spaniards, incurring all the obligations to support the Spanish crown, pay taxes, and abide by the law of the viceroy. Yet they had little or no access to leadership, religious, or governmental positions. Notwithstanding, one critical segment of the economy dominated by the Creoles was the vast ranching operations. These Creole landed gentry would prove pivotal in the gestation of the revolution against Spanish rule. The third major social segment was those born of Spanish-Indian parents, known as mestizos. While a rapidly growing segment of the colony, mestizos at the time of the independence movement fared little better than the native Indians (composed of groups that spoke over one hundred indigenous languages and dialects), assuming jobs as farmers, artisans, laborers, and domestic workers. The road to the revolution within New Spain was marked by rival endeavors to balance the inequities of a three-hundred-year-old closed colonial rule and a highly stratified society.[13]

By 1810, commercial, social, political, and religious factors intertwined to cause a small village priest, Miguel Hidalgo y Cotilla, to incite open revolution and demand independence from Spain. While known as the "father of Mexico," his cry for freedom or *grito de independencia* to redress the social and political system that gripped Mexico turned violent. Factional groups lined up behind those in support of the Spanish, and those against the large landed estates, as well as those who wanted broader freedom for the Indian population. Hidalgo's call to arms, "death to the gachupines," unleashed a wave of pent-up frustration. After months of fighting and failing to capture Mexico City, his movement briefly stalled. Fearing capture, he attempted to flee to the United States but was captured and executed. In September 1811, a young Yucatan priest, José María Morelos, stepped forward to champion the uprising that included over two hundred priests and thousands of their Indian followers. Morelos was able to accomplish what Hidalgo had started; he, more so than any other figure in Mexican history, represented "the dilemma of Mexico, a country in permanent tension between deep seated tradition and inescapable modernity."[14]

A decade of revolution and destruction weakened Mexico both economically and socially. Efforts at recovery as an independent nation resulted in further unrest and the eventual drafting of the Constitution of 1824, which for the balance of the century pitted the federalist (strong central government in Mexico

City) against the Centralist faction, which desired a decentralized structure of governance. In the meantime, two significant developments in the United States would be critical cornerstones of change for both nations. First, the Monroe Doctrine outlined the limits of European intervention to be tolerated by the United States in Latin American affairs, and second the Adams-Onis Treaty of 1819 (following the Louisiana Purchase by Thomas Jefferson) helped set in motion the Manifest Destiny designs embodied in the expansion of the United States to the Pacific Ocean in what is today known as the Southwest.

The decade of internal civil war devastated the economy and uprooted the rural and urban population alike. Oddly enough, Mexico City was little touched throughout the turmoil. Not until the emergence of a royalist general, Agustín de Iturbide, in 1820–21 did the fighting stop. The tradition of authoritarian/centralized/imperial government in the hands of the few was to continue as a direct carryover of the pattern established by the sixty-three viceroys that ruled New Spain from 1521 until 1821 when independence was declared. From this struggle to separate from Spanish rule the Mexican nation was born. However, the swift end of the revolution for independence in 1821 was only the beginning, as deep-seated apprehensions rooted in Mexico's colonial and revolutionary past influenced the nation's course well into the twenty-first century:

> Though Iturbide had won the day and Hidalgo was widely despised at the moment of independence, history would eventually remember the fiery priest as the father of Mexico. It was Hidalgo's movement that embodied the aspirations of the nation as a whole, not those of just one class. But Hidalgo also terrified Mexico with the consequences of releasing those aspirations. That ambivalence continues to manifest itself in the way Mexico views its subsequent revolutionary heros: Villa, Zapata, and even today as subcomandante Marcos. Revered in spirit and feared in historical apparition, Hidalgo remains a contradictory symbol of both hope and horror. In 1821, the scepter of power had crashed through the first level in the social pyramid. And because of the terrible vision that Hidalgo held forth, it stopped right there.[15]

During the decades following the 1821 revolution, the Mexican nation looked to hold its national identity and dismantle all association with Spain. Many of the old peninsulares were expelled from Mexico, the colonial system dismantled, and the power of the church challenged. The countryside was in waste, and the production of silver, the prime source of wealth, came nearly to a halt during eleven years of unrest. The course of independence proved difficult as the country gradually reverted to a centralized government and authoritarian rule (which was constantly changed by regional strongmen known as caciques and caudillos) that gradually intensified by the latter part of the century. Successive Mexican governments were frustrated by foreign intervention, government debt, and low productivity nationwide. For the next three decades the new nation turned to a dashing and often controversial figure who would be president of the emerging Republic of Mexico eleven different times—Antonio López de Santa

Anna. During Santa Anna's years in and out of the presidency, Mexico lost or sold half of the territorial lands it had held in 1821. Following "Mr. Polk's War" with Mexico (1846–48) and the rise of Manifest Destiny, the United States was fortunate to acquire territory that in time would become the current boundaries.

By mid-century, Mexico turned to the only pure-blooded Indian president in the nation's history—Benito Juárez—who struggled to lead and define the national development of his country. Many observers and historians feel that before Juárez died of a heart attack in 1872, he presided over the only brief period of real (but limited) "democracy" in Mexico. The winds of change once again gripped Mexico. Beginning in 1876, through the personage and iron fist of Don Porfirio Díaz, Mexico would experience thirty-five years of bittersweet stability, foreign intrigue, industry and infrastructure enhancement and the rise of pent-up frustrations among those left out of this wave of limited prosperity.[16] The goal of the Díaz administration was to modernize Mexico and thus attract massive foreign investment for all areas of the Mexican economy. Both U.S. and European investors amassed vast holdings in the railroad, mining, banking, and manufacturing sectors. By late 1910, elements of unrest, not unlike those that were challenged by Hidalgo and Morelos a century earlier, again boiled over.[17]

Twentieth-Century Mexico

Vocal political opposition in Mexico has always possessed a keen appreciation for symbolism and timing. For Díaz, at the pinnacle of his power and mindful of the traditional Centennial observance of the "Grito" by Hidalgo, the year 1910 ushered out the old and opened the way for a new (and more nationalistic) wave of Mexican political activism. The flames of change were fanned by a new generation of desires and concerns to once again address the course and meaning of Mexican society. In this vein, the 1910 Revolution was more than sheer madness and bedlam, it was a search for direction within a complicated, multifaceted nation. A strong nationalistic theme slowly emerged— "Mexico for Mexicans"—that endeavored to break away from (or at least diminish) foreign domination, address the distribution of land, harness natural resources under government control, and rekindle a patriotic spirit. The first two decades of the 1900s blended the forces of change and newfound industrialization brought in by the Díaz administration. The elements of a fragmented society sought to redress centuries of ills with one more dramatic move. The outcome of the 1910 Revolution—marked by a decade of hostilities—was the gestation and foundation of the political and psychological framework for Mexico for the balance of the twentieth century.[18]

Economically, during much of the twentieth century, Mexico was on a roller coaster course marked by varying swings in growth, monetary policy, and stability. Antiforeign sentiment carried over from the revolution resulted in a more closed economy as well as limits on foreign investment/ownership. New laws created the "49 percent" foreign ownership and investment rule to ensure Mexicans would have a majority stake in all domestic commercial interest. Foreign investment was welcomed, but only to the extent it remained secondary to Mexican control. Buoyed by Articles 27 and 28 of the Mexican Constitution of 1917, natural resources were to be the "providence of the people," that is, owned by the central government. Further covenants empowered the state to expropriate and redistribute large landed estates. The initial high water mark in returning Mexican control to the Mexican economy came in March 1938 when President Lázaro Cárdenas issued a "Decree of Expropriation" that resulted in the nationalization of all foreign-owned operations in the oil and gas sector—an event still observed today. Henceforth, all "discovery, extraction, storage, refinery and distribution of products of the petroleum industry" would be conducted and controlled by the Mexican government and by Mexicans.[19]

In the decades that followed, a vast array of commercial and noncommercial sectors were brought under the aegis of the government, including port facilities, mining operations, banking, economic development, land distribution, and agricultural planning. Bordering on a socialist/managed economy, Mexico suffered because these nationalized activities proved costly, lacking in new technical innovations, and generally unprofitable. In time, the Mexican oil industry dominated the domestic economic and political decision process; thus, increased reliance on oil created a false sense of security that would extend from the 1920s through the 1980s. Overdependence on oil, which at its zenith accounted for over 70 percent of governmental revenue, proved to be a fragile base on which to build an economy. Massive petroleum reserves fueled nationalistic notions that Mexico was insulated from outside pressures allowing the political leadership to unwittingly isolate the nation. Turning to an import-substitution-industrialization (ISI) policy in the 1960s and 1970s to further limit foreign intrigue, Mexico allowed both its industrial base and competitiveness in a progressively more globally linked world to be compromised. The emergence of a single all-powerful political and patronage structure in Mexico during the early 1920s had much to do with these events.

From this wellspring of often violently opposing views of the revolution and the emergence of centralized governmental dominance of economic policy was crafted a new constitution. A governmental structure was created that relied on stability and power in the orderly (yet often times manipulated) procession and transfer of political power by a dominant political party, the Partido Revolucionario Institucional (PRI). During the balance of the century, opposition political parties had only a minor, but always vocal, influence on the direction of the nation. The legacy of the PRI, one of the oldest continuously-in-power political parties in the world, is that, for good or bad it transcended the elements of turmoil (oftentimes using disruption) to confine Mexico to a rather jaded sociopolitical evolution. One vestige of this dominance, for example, resulted in the emergence of the all-powerful Imperial Presidency—the *sexenio* that, although limited to a single six-year term, passed down power and patronage that fostered an allegiance among the party loyalists seldom seen in any nation. The central government in Mexico City, working through state governors and mayors at the local level, wove a web of political clout. While such patronage was often manipulative, it was also for Mexico a perverse stabilizing force.

Not until the mid-to-late 1990s, did the power of the PRI begin to wane. Pressure from both within and without Mexico built for greater democratic reforms and a broadened political base, one open to opposition parties and ideas that countered the PRI-controlled government machine style politics. Radical devaluations of the peso were blamed on manipulation and a lack of economic control by the PRI. Via a system of well-timed job and housing programs, grain and fertilizer disbursements, and infrastructure projects, the PRI-controlled central government could reach down to the people during election periods and control the desired outcome long after a number of opposition candidates filled the ballots. The often-cited questionable election of Carlos Salinas over Cuauhtémoc Cárdenas in 1988 (in the face of defeat) demonstrated the PRI machine at its zenith—election eve computers suddenly malfunctioned, ballots were lost, and the final outcome was not known for days. Salinas merely announced victory. Shortly after the election, the ballots were burned, thus preventing a recount. Gradually, opposition parties gained greater favor and political access (most notably the moderate PAN and leftist PRD) to the massive bureaucracy at all strata of the government, from Mexico City to the smallest village that had long paid homage to the PRI. With this last vestige of the PRI "machine" politics, the ancient patrons of the party known as *los dinosaurios* began their gradual slide from power.[20]

Quite possibly, observers of Mexico in the early 1990s, and particularly foreign investors bullish on the outcome of the North American Free Trade Agreement (NAFTA), were overly optimistic. However, while the optimism was well-founded, the ability of Mexico to "deliver," given the changing internal dynamics as well as external worldwide pressures that they oftentimes had no control over, was limited. Mexico briefly fell short of the much-touted economic "miracle" when the overheated peso crashed and was hastily devalued in late December 1994. The resulting currency crisis, or "Tequila Hangover," sent shock waves through the financial sectors of the major developed nations as well as emerging markets worldwide. A bailout program of $50 billion, an amount larger than the cumulative total of all previous Mexican debt initiatives in the twentieth century, was devised by the U.S. Department of the Treasury and the International Monetary Fund (IMF) to rescue and halt not only the specter of a major economic crash in Mexico and a potential "dominoing" financial disruption worldwide. Mexico by 1996–97 had become the benchmark case for other nations seeking to prevent or diminish the pitfalls of both rapid growth and currency instability.[21]

It was due to the trauma of the fourth major and a dozen smaller currency disruptions in two decades (1976–94) that Mexico proved itself very resilient to both external and internal factors. Like many emerging nations, Mexico has been caught in the web of major expectations based on hypergrowth, a growth that is often misunderstood and has complicated domestic issues. Mexico is no longer a third-world country, but instead is a vibrant, newly industrialized, emerging nation whose economy has global ramifications. The contemporary industrial growth, direct foreign investment, and market factors are all too often overshadowed by a legacy of turmoil rooted deep in the evolution of the Mexican nation. To the pleasant surprise of many observers, the rapid economic recovery in the wake of the 1994–95 currency crisis was based on a number of factors including a well-tooled industrial base able (as never before in Mexico's history) to export quality products. This generated much needed hard currency, as well as the increased confidence of foreign financial markets. During the final decade of the century, Mexico was second only to "emerging" China in attracting foreign direct investment. And China, in time, would evolve as a growing thorn of irritation to Mexico.[22]

In this modernization process, Mexico will not be moved to turn to its past heritage, but instead hopes to forge a new direction globally. Nevertheless, while Mexico is increasingly an urban nation, the historical social and political roots of a broad base of the population lie in the countryside. For example, the socioeconomic forces of the struggle for land, rising urbanization, agricultural issues, and access to water are an integral part of Mexico's past and its future. Land reform issues have dominated all levels of Mexican society and politics for five centuries. By the 1990s, issues of productivity of the progressively smaller farm plots within the *ejido* system were redefined during the Salinas administration. And debt relief for farmers was brought to the nation's attention during the national banking crisis by a vocal debtors' group known as the El Barzón movement, as well as rural landowners' blockage of the proposed site for the new international airport east of the capital in mid-2002. These events also have a linkage with growth and immigration issues that increasingly involve the United States.[23]

In terms of Mexico's external affairs, the overwhelming, and much mentioned determinate is, and will long continue to be, its proximity and relationship with the United States. No examination of either the past or the future of Mexico can be complete without an assessment of its relationship with the United States. The colossal neighbor to the north, as one author noted, has been both "distant" and pivotal to the emergence of Mexico over the past two centuries.[24] The roots and evolution of the United States–Mexico relationship—which include immigration, drugs, border infrastructure, commercial trade, environmental concerns, water rights, and labor issues—are crucial to the future of Mexico, and have long been a concern of the United States. Thus, to profile the dynamics and challenges of the next two decades of the new millennium in Mexico requires a constant reflection and understanding of forces and events since the arrival of Hernán Cortés in the New World. Mexico is ever mindful of its history; thus it should not be a surprise that past and future events are at times linked in the minds and culture of all Mexicans.[25]

Oddly enough, the miraculous economic successes of the Salinas-Zedillo era (in spite of electioneering and the December 1994 currency crisis) and the steadily growing number of public revelations regarding the manipulation by the PRI were the eventual undoing of the party, as evidenced by the midterm congressional and regional elections in July 1997 and the PAN victory in the presidential election of 2000. Opposition parties controlled over 35 percent of the key elected positions by 1997–98 and had made tremendous inroads at all levels of government. The irony of progress (political as well as economic) is that it cannot proceed without change, even in such well entrenched political institutions as the PRI. The neoliberal technocrats of the PRI, many times much to the dissatisfaction of aging party hard-line "dinosaurs," may have unwittingly established not only the groundwork for a diversified emerging global economy but also indirectly encouraged the demise (or at least the reduction) of their century-old power base due to two key factors that will set the stage and usher in the twenty-first century in Mexico: first, measured economic success both at home and abroad broadened the scope and magnitude of Mexico's role globally; and, second gradual democratic reforms to open the economy allowed them to have Mexico hailed as a "miracle."[26]

FOCUS ON THE FUTURE

These observations and projections are based upon a tremendous amount of data, as well as forecasts by a cross section of government agencies (foreign and domestic), and the analysis of academics and industry sources. Agencies such as the International Monetary Fund (IMF), the Organization for Economic Cooperation and Development (OECD), and the World Bank (IRBD), facilitate the economic integration of the global economy and will exert more influence over all emerging nations. This shift in emphasis by the "global" financial oversight agencies became increasingly evident after the Mexican currency crisis in 1994–95. Mexico held firm in its efforts to address the causes of the peso devaluation and thus became a model for nations in similar straits. The meltdown and currency crisis of the 1990s in Russia and Thailand (as well as Argentina in 2002) was not handled as effectively as Mexico faced its problems. While Mexico was on a path of growth and economic diversification, Russia by the early twenty-first century awoke to an economy that was reduced to half the size of that of the old Soviet Union in the late 1980s.[27]

This projection of key trends and growth patterns in Mexico for the next two decades, derives in good measure from recent developments. The assessment of certain observations and trends will require more than just the recent state of affairs. Raw data and numerical forecasts do not diminish or overlook the nonquantifiable forces such as cultural and social dynamics. Mexico has been misunderstood and misjudged by outside (or inside) observers who view momentary events in Mexico as solid evidence of major change or a new national direction. A prime example was the euphoria over the oil boom in the

1970s that heightened Mexican and worldwide expectations with often un-realistic conclusions and hopes that were dashed with the OPEC oil crisis. The second case concerns the 1994 jubilation over NAFTA and economic growth (equated with stability) in Mexico that many—up until the day prior to the December 20, 1994 devaluation—felt would never slow down. This resulted from a combination of the media hype of the "Mexican Miracle," along with the Salinas-Zedillo governments' projecting an attitude (in the face of de-clining economic indicators) that in some sense Mexico was too big to fail or crash. From 1993 to 2004, U.S.–Mexico total combined cross-border trade increased some 200 percent, from $82 billion to $267 billion. By the turn of the twenty-first century, the Fox administration stressed a new era of opti-mism and growth—only to be stalemated by a sluggish economy, antiquated energy sector, and a divided Congress. These events and other topics and trends will be examined in light of their future relevance and impact.[28]

Mexico's future is a study in contrasts. Never underestimate Mexico. As a major industrializing nation, Mexico will prove a key barometer among na-tions. And, most significantly, the future of Mexico is not viewed in a vacuum but, more so than ever, hinges on its relationship not only with the United States, but also with the world at large.

The essence of the United States–Mexico interaction was vividly captured by a longtime observer of the dynamic binational relationship, Sidney Wein-traub:

> The United States has reason to value its southern neighbor. The border needs no military defense. Mexican principles are in the Western tradition and pose no deep conflicts with those of the United States. Cooperation exists—even if at times it is less than ideal on either side—on water, environmental, drug, and other problems. The two economies have become increasingly linked through investment and trade. . . . The U.S. stake is high in how Mexico deals with its economic problems and confronts its political structure.[29]

Thus, no project of this magnitude is taken lightly. For over three decades I have conducted business in Mexico and have been an avid observer of this nation in transition. These activities and association with countless Mexican companies and their executives proved indispensable to these conclusions. Its people, culture, and perspectives are critical to all those who come in contact—either directly or indirectly—with Mexico. In an earlier volume, *Mexican Banking and Investment in Transition* (1997), I explored the course and role of the financial dynamics of the Mexican economy, and in the process of my research identified a number of significant future possibilities. I have often noted that any attempt, especially by an outsider looking in, to explore the depth of issues regarding Mexico is at best a work in progress. Thus, delving into the future of Mexico is merely an attempt to gauge a challenging range of possibilities and examine the various factors and forces that will affect the near future.

1

=▭~◊~▭=

AGRICULTURE: TIERRA Y LIBERTAD

More public-sector investment in rural Mexico is necessary to provide employment and to create the infrastructure that can make the farm sector more competitive. Similarly, improved state services are essential, especially in education, to insure that the basic needs are met and to improve the productive capacity of Mexico's farmers and workers.
— Tom Barry, *Zapata's Revenge*

My administration is protecting our farmers, helping them become more efficient, and ensuring that they have equal conditions—and I stress, equal conditions—as those of our major competitors.
— Vicente Fox

ONE OF THE greatest challenges for Mexico at the onset of the twenty-first century will be how to feed its growing urban population. The irony of Mexico is that this vast territory, which once boasted a highly productive agricultural sector, no longer can fully meet its day-to-day domestic food demands. Furthermore, the demographic changes over the past century, and most notably since the 1950s, have transformed the Mexican populace from a fragmented rural agrarian society to a nation that is daily more urban and less agricultural in tone. In spite of the fact that Mexico has four times as many farmers as the United States and at the large commercial level these farmers are better subsidized than their American counterparts, Mexico today is a net importer of foodstuffs.[1]

Over the past two decades there has been a high degree of economic integration throughout the North American market. Mexican agricultural production and food companies account for a reported 6 to 8 percent of the nation's gross domestic product (in real terms closer to 5 percent) and about 20 percent of manufactured output—falling short of both domestic demand and growth. Historically, since 1982 Mexican agriculture has annually accounted for only about 3.5 percent of total exports. In the broader economy, the GDP components of the Mexican economy rest on two sectors: services at 67 percent and industry at 28 percent, of which mining (i.e., petroleum) and manufacturing account for 24 percent. In 2005, some 75 percent of the population of over 110 million lived in urban areas and thus were driven by a bulging consumer economy. Affected in part by drought and depleted land, each year a growing number of farmers migrate from the countryside and are faced with three options: move to the city, move to the border and northern states in search of jobs, or cross the Rio Bravo—legally or illegally—into the United States.[2]

What is most ironic is that over the past two decades—and without being fully resolved within either the World Trade Organization or North American Free Trade Agreement—Mexico and the United States expended tremendous effort and political capital in agricultural discourse over such worldly pursuits as regulating avocado imports, sugar quotas, and fights over the measurement of sanitary standards for milk, pork, and poultry. The political rhetoric of nationalists in Mexico has caused the government to follow a seventy-year-old status quo policy, in spite of clear evidence of persistent shortfalls in agricultural production. While the historic relationship between the United States and Mexico regarding agricultural imports/exports and policy is important, the fact remains that overwhelming demand for food in Mexico (as well as the unilaterally lowered trade restraints in Mexico in the 1980s) has dramatic implications for both nations. U.S. agricultural exports to Mexico have more than doubled from 1994 to 2004, rising to $8.5 billion. Three product categories dominate these exports and account for three-fourths of U.S. exports to Mexico: grains and feeds, animals and processed products, and oilseeds and their byproducts. Correspondingly, three-quarters of Mexican agricultural exports to the United States are comprised of vegetables, cattle/beef, fruits, and beverages (primarily beer). Thus, the current dynamics of growth pose a tremendous problem for the future with regard to how to feed the Mexican population, while at the same time managing Mexican concerns regarding the impact of increased American agricultural imports.[3]

All the hype of the 1990s over strawberry, avocados, and melon imports does not erase the fact that Mexico is now, and will long be, a net importer of foodstuffs. The combination of the growing population and the yearly trends to a less productive agriculture sector leave Mexico with few choices. The unproductive nature of Mexican agriculture is rooted in the aftermath of the Revolution of 1910 when good faith efforts were made to distribute expropriated lands by reducing the concentration of the large haciendas into the *ejido* system. As Herman von Bertrab, a key private sector envoy and coordinator of the Washington office of the Mexican negotiating team during the NAFTA talks, noted, the formation of the postrevolutionary government structure "was authoritarian in character and tended to stifle democratic opposition outside its ranks—and sometimes within them. By controlling the

Billion U.S. dollars

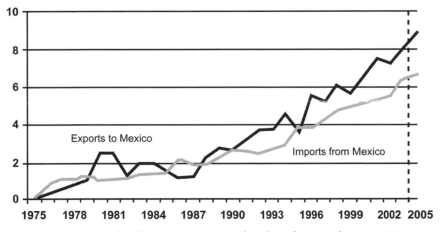

Figure 1-1 Growth of U.S.–Mexico Agricultural Trade since the Late 1970s
Source: USDA, Foreign Agricultural Trade of the U.S. database.

most important levers of power, the system achieved an extraordinary cohesion and hold over social and economic fabric of society. The private and communal ejido properties of the agricultural sector provide an example."[4] The ejidos' holdings by one estimation in the 1980s accounted for 205 million acres, with an average size of 79 acres. Between 1980 and 2000 the agricultural share of GDP dropped from 8.2 to 5.5 percent, accounting for about 20 percent of employment.[5]

The diverse Mexican agricultural sector has three types of landholdings: the ejidos, private, and public. The southern more tropical region of the country produces rice, sugarcane, coffee, and bananas, as well as some cattle. Farmers in the central portions of the country, in the region from Mexico City to El Bajío, produce oilseeds, grains, fruits, and vegetables, as well as some pork and poultry. A large number of small rain-fed farms in Central Mexico grow staples such as corn and beans. The northern and Gulf states produce a wide variety of crops that include corn, wheat, oilseeds, cotton, sorghum, sugarcane, and forage crops. Larger irrigated farms are found in the north as well as extensive range-fed cattle operations producing export stocker/feeder cattle of European crossbreeds for eventual shipment to the United States for fattening. Modern poultry and pork producers have also expanded operations in the north near commercial crop areas and growing urban consumer centers such as Monterrey, Hermosillo, and Torreón. While Canada, Japan, Central and South America and the European Union nations all trade with Mexico, the United States is overwhelmingly the prime trading partner in agricultural products, supplying over 75 percent of Mexico's imports and taking 85 percent of its agricultural exports.[6] In spite of the current scale of agricultural production in Mexico, the historical context of the ejido–land reform policies are important to a fuller understanding of the dynamics of the Mexican economy and politics.

LAND REFORM: RISE OF THE EJIDO

Mexico, with a population of 14.3 million in 1920, faced a decade of recovery after nearly ten years of revolution, distribution and capital flight. One key result was a major shift in land policy. Defined literally *ejido* means "exit" or "way out," with the root of the word dating from the Aztec word referring to the communal land held on the outskirts of villages. These parcels of small acreage given to a vast number of small farmers generally have only been able to produce enough for the family that occupies the plot of land. Much debate and research has been conducted on the impact of the 1917 land reform championed by revolutionary Emiliano Zapata in the November 25, 1911 "Ayala Plan" associated with the battle cry *tierra y libertad*, "land and liberty." Zapata's plan called for the redistribution of land to Mexico's indigenous farm population. Yet by the 1960s, in spite of numerous modifications and massive government subsidies, it was apparent the crop production capacity of the traditional ejido system could not economically meet the demands of the growing nation: "Crop yield was found to be lower in the land reform sector than in the private sector.... [B]oth average and marginal returns to expenditure on farm inputs were found to be considerably higher in the former than in the latter. Since output per farm worker was considerably lower in the land reform sector, it may be inferred that there remained a considerable discrepancy in the standards of living of the inhabitants of the rural areas. Hence, while giving land to the poor farmers, land reform by itself is seen to have produced little favourable effect on rural income distribution."[7] Despite ample evidence that the *ejido* system was vastly less productive than private farming (due to obsolete cultivation techniques, which lead to low yields per hectare), President Luis Echeverría (1970–76) increased redistribution of land and touted a new policy of heavy government investment in the economy toward what was termed "shared development"—politically popular but functionally unproductive.[8]

In principle, the ejido is the property of the nation granted by fiat to a community of peasants or *ejidatarios*, yet it is not a form of communal property.[9] Treated as small private property, or *minifundio*, it was a means to please the ejidatario and as John Bailey concluded, though less productive in most cases than private farms, "[t]he *ejidos* enjoy a sacred status even more exalted than does social security in the United States."[10] The majority of these plots of land are on the average no larger than a few acres (by one estimate 400,000 farmers farm less than twelve acres or five hectares) and, while popular at the time of creation, the nationwide agrarian reform did little to improve the production or plight of rural Mexico. Thus, the revolutionary tenet that the

"Mexican nation" retained all rights and ownership of land formed the cornerstone of the Mexican Revolution. "The *ejido* farmer," according to von Bertrab, "was more subject to political influence, however, because almost all financing and crop insurance came from the government; he could also be deprived of the land he harvested because in principle it was not his."[11]

The ejidatario was granted a limited "use title" that in theory could be passed to an heir, but in fact the small landowner had no right to sell, lease, rent, or mortgage his assigned allotment. This of course was not adhered to as land has been both rented and sold. PRI authorities were unwilling to enforce laws that would create any unrest. Thus, while the redistribution of land under the ejido system granted by Article 27 of the Constitution of 1917, Mexico struggled for nearly four decades after 1920 to return to a prerevolution level of production. Furthermore, in a related matter in Article 27, the near total embrace of the ejido scheme of land usage (not ownership) over time helped fuel both a rise in nationalism and a turn toward an antiforeign mindset that helped underpin popular political sentiment for the nationalization of the oil sector. In the name of concerns over "foreign" intervention, a concept of fear fueled by those bent on maintaining power, conversations between the United States and Mexico were stalled over latent, mostly theoretical and ideological issues that did little or nothing to increase domestic food production. As one part of the PRI government in the 1980s and early 1990s bashed foreign agricultural imports, the highly controlled government agency for grain purchases, CONASUPO (National Company of Popular Subsistence), worked overtime to buy domestic crops as well as arrange importation of adequate foodstuffs. Set up to purchase a dozen different crops during the 1980s at government guaranteed prices, the activities of the agency were limited to only beans and corn by the mid-1990s, and such purchasing ceased altogether in 1998.[12]

An alphabet soup of Mexican agencies and programs was developed in hopes of stabilizing prices and offsetting any impact of NAFTA. Programs ranged from price supports to import protections such as PROCAMPO (Program of Direct Support for the Countryside) and PROGRESA (Program for Rural Education, Health, and Nutrition). The 1991 agricultural marketing program, ASERCA (Support Services for Agricultural Marketing) was primarily a substitute for CONASUPO in 1995. The "Alliance for the Countryside" was established to encourage increased agricultural productivity and efficiency through crop rotation. Available credit for farmers continues to be a major impediment to expanded production, with the government reducing subsidies in hopes the private credit market will be more active in rural lending. However, rural credit has declined over the past decade. One further critical impact on the rural Mexican economy is the continued out-migration during the 1990s and early 2000s to large cities and north to the United States.[13]

The critical nature of Mexican agricultural production will remain acute given regular droughts in the region compounded by a lack of water (i.e., groundwater depletion) and water planning, and the scarcity of arable land (well over 70 percent of Mexico is jagged mountains). Due to a lack of a coordinated land-use policy, today only about 10 percent of the total area of the nation is suitable for sustainable agricultural production (only some 57 million acres as compared to 464 million acres in the United States). Furthermore, widespread erosion, overgrazing, deforestation, lack of adequate fertilizers, lack of access to groundwater, and poor crop rotation methods have leached much of the soil so that it is beyond economic use.[14] The drop of the water level in the underground aquifer is a precarious problem given the fact the lower it falls the saltier the water; over one million acres of formerly prime farmland has been damaged without recovery due to unchecked salinization. Today a majority of Mexico's cultivated land requires regular irrigation with much of the remaining land left fallow. While some 20 percent of Mexico's arable land is irrigated (most of which is the result of surface storage from rain runoff), water and water use will most likely be the most important long-term factor is determining potential crop yields. The OECD recently concluded that "water use in Mexico is on an unsustainable path." Recent concerns about the allocation of irrigation water from the Rio Grande are a case in point.[15]

Thus, efficiencies inherent to scales of economy of the large landholdings of the Porfirio Díaz era from 1876 to 1910 were sacrificed in the name of populist land reform that was a primary plank of the PRI for seven decades, until it was dethroned by the PAN party and Vicente Fox. Yet, not even Fox, who ran as a man of the people and an outsider to the normal PRI governmental channels, could put the kingdom back together nor was he likely to try sweeping reforms that would alienate the farmers. For example, attempts to acquire critical ejido land for a new international airport 15 miles from the capital near Texcoco failed due to violent protest from the farmers—ejidatarios and their supporters in the finest tradition of the Revolution held government authorities at bay and near powerless to proceed without a bloody confrontation. The landlocked and very congested urban Benito Juárez Airport in Mexico City is unlikely to be moved before 2030.[16]

THE SINKING CITY

In the next twenty years Mexico will face a dramatic challenge to feed and clothe its people. At issue is how Mexico will reclaim fallow areas and make maximum productive use of the small percentage of land available for crops. By the year 2020, the national population will exceed 123 million (up from 30 million inhabitants in 1950 and 50 million in 1970), with two dramatic trends that set the framework for the future of Mexico: first, the declining population that lives in rural areas is less productive yearly and second, they are totally noncontributors to the enhancement of agriculture at any level. In fact a case could be made that supports environmental claims that the urbanization and the "sprawl" created by migration to the overcrowded cities only accelerates the inability of the nation to be self-sufficient. During the upcoming decade, five major centers of population concentration will evolve in Mexico to have a stranglehold on the political and economic future of the country: Mexico City, Monterrey, Guadalajara, Aguascalientes, and Ciudad Juarez on the U.S.–Mexico border across from El Paso. The combined population of these five metro-centers in 2005 exceeded 43 million. By 2020, estimates for the five super-metro Mexican urban areas could exceed 70 million.[17]

The most telling urban impact however will be that of the metro area of Mexico City, the second largest metropolitan center in the world after Tokyo, which in fact is or will soon include most of the vast state of México and will grow from over 25 million in population in 2004 to the 37–40 million range by 2020. How will ample fresh food and water be made available to meet the needs of the capital? The underground aquifer accounts for about 70 percent of the city's water and is being depleted at a rapid rate. Visible evidence that Mexico City is sinking is obvious with a visit to the Zócalo in the city center—the capital is 34 feet lower than the day Cortés arrived in 1519.[18]

The growth of Mexico City is rivaled only by that of Bombay, Tokyo, and Rio de Janeiro—all of which have only an elementary notion of how to handle their growth. Few limits on growth have ever been considered, except minimal efforts to bring air pollution under control by encouraging large-scale manufacturers not to locate in the Mexican capital and limiting automobile usage based on the number on the license tag. And daily smog, crime, and congestion due to inadequate infrastructure limit the capital's options. Thus, without an immediate urban plan the future for Mexico City will prove difficult. A number of straight-line projections actually predict the population of the ancient capital of the Aztecs will number closer to 45 million in 2020. Notwithstanding a recent OECD report that touted the need for a new metropolitan "vision" for the capital, I do not see managed growth as a possibility due to the fact the city does not have the capacity to provide the basic needed services—ample electrical power, potable water, housing, transportation, garbage removal, and sewage—to sustain such mammoth explosive urbanization.[19]

Mexico City is and will long be an urban planner's darkest nightmare. The capital covers over 1,000 square miles at the beginning of the twenty-first century and could sprawl to 1,500 square miles over the next two decades. Debates over growth such as those over the expansion of the intracity highway system and the location of the new international airport will overshadow the efficiencies needed to manage the city. The outlying cities of Querétaro, Puebla, and Toluca have increasingly begun to feel the impact of urban flight from the capital. As Jonathan Kandell has noted in La Capital this "megalopolis" could become the greatest urban concentration in history.[20] Efforts to control or manage Mexico's growth, as well as such negative factors as choking traffic, the pollution and smog that accompanies automobiles and trucks, the need for more water, and the challenge of basic daily waste disposal, will outstrip the resources available in Mexico to secure the viability of the capital.[21]

The second alarming factor is that the population of the Mexican nation is and will remain very young, with some 50 percent in 2005 under the age of twenty-one years. Only about 4 percent of the population is over sixty-five. The paradox of Mexico in terms of demographics is that while the broader economy has clearly emerged during the latter part of the 1990s and early 2000s as a dynamic industrial platform, with ties and markets worldwide, the population stratification resembles that of a small agrarian nonindustrialized emerging nation. Birthrates began to fall from 6.5 children in 1970 to 3.7 children by the mid-1990s. The current fertility rate in 2004 was 3.0, with some estimates projecting a drop to 2.0 by 2020.[22] Education levels have only gradually increased. Clearly the overall national economy and demographic patterns in no way resemble the industrial power Mexico aspires to be. Given the impact of the aging patterns of Japan and the European nations, there are those that would argue that it is better to have a young and hungry workforce versus one that is aging, nonproductive, and a drag on the wealth of the nation due to yearly higher demand for social services, medical care, and basic subsistence. In terms of current and future impact on the United States, the outlet, both legal and illegal, for such population growth in Mexico will be northward across the Rio Grande. And unlike Japan or Europe, the Mexican border region could be one of the major generators of future jobs as the American workforce ages and America's national identity changes over the next three decades.[23]

At three times the geographic size of Texas, Mexico is the world's twelfth largest nation in terms of land mass. Of this land area over two-thirds is arid or semi-arid. The overall share of agricultural output has declined each decade since World War II. Attempts at improved efficiencies and direct investment in the agricultural sector have made little impact except in localized/seasonal

Table 1-1 Mexican Agriculture Imports to the United States

Product	1999	2003
Fresh Vegetables	1,912,945	2,271,469
Live Animals	961,884	1,241,433
Wine and Beer	782,073	1,196,340
Other Fresh Fruit	1,128,418	1,056,466
Processed Fruit/Vegetable	486,329	475,674
Snack Foods	143,346	286,469
Other Consumer	130,714	178,917
Sugar/Sweeter/Bases	140,495	138,792
Nursery Products	109,925	122,308
Panel/Plywood Products	181,771	94,128

Source: Department of Commerce, U.S. Census Bureau, Foreign Trade Statistics

products. The fact that an acre of land in Mexico produces one-fourth as much corn as an acre in the United States accounts for why 82 percent of agricultural products are imported from the United States (75 percent) and Canada (7 percent). Mexico has been a net importer of grain since the 1970s. It is not that Mexico does not have the will or capacity—some 20 percent of the labor force or about 8 million people are engaged in agriculture—instead the growth of the population has exceeded the ability to grow, process, package, distribute, and feed one of the youngest nations in the hemisphere. In terms of future development, foreign direct investment has not gone into the agricultural sector, but rather to industry, infrastructure, and the retail sectors. Furthermore, the government for over five decades has let the political rhetoric of the 1910 Revolution overshadow the reality of the changing and growing nation. The PRI base of support drew tremendous strength from the ejido sector only in terms of a rallying cry. While in power, the PRI did little to improve the efficiency and capacity of the ag sector, other than maintain a status quo that would have succeeded absent growth. Thus, the amendment of land ownership caveats embedded in Article 27 of the Constitution of 1917 was modified by the Salinas administration on February 27, 1992. For the first time in over seventy years mandatory government land "redistribution" came to an end. Other pivotal changes included a change in property rights, enforcement and jurisdiction of agrarian laws that were selectively transferred from the federal to state authorities, and mercantile associations. The loose equivalent of co-ops in the American agricultural sector, these associations can now own "pieces of land" as well as pool resources and labor in order to improve production efficiency. Addressing the free market and promoting

Table 1-2 U.S. Agriculture Exports to Mexico

Product	1999	2003
Coarse Grains	9,214,850	8,437,767
Soybeans	3,287,211	4,179,645
Live Animals	4,895,538	3,188,117
Other Intermediate°	567,319	2,831,117
Wheat	1,823,970	2,599,836
Soybean Meal	299,305	674,736
Feeds & Fodders	427,578	556,485
Panel/Plywood Products	388,096	533,842
Red Meats	345,870	526,348
Animal Fats	316,790	434,398
Soft/Treated Lumber	317,974	258,355

Source: Department of Commerce, U.S. Census Bureau, Foreign Trade Statistics

°Other Intermediate = Goods and services that are used as inputs or components in the production of other goods.

investment in crop production was central to the success of the constitutional modifications of 1992.[24]

Out of fear, long before NAFTA or the WTO came into play, concerns were raised that the domestic Mexican market would be overrun by U.S. agricultural products as the Mexican farm sector was gradually liberalized. As tariffs under GATT were lowered to below 10 percent, pre-1990 Mexico was already heavily dependent on the United States for food and feed grains, as is evidenced by the fact that Mexico has been a net importer of grain products since the 1970s. Government controls and pricing of grain imports (and not technology or land reform) were able to forcefully keep control of supplies as well as keep prices stable. The daily price of tortillas for the masses was of much more real concern than oil cost, infrastructure needs, or even a growing cash cow like tourism. Furthermore, the agricultural technology gap yearly widened as the United States expanded production efforts via research, development, and enhancement of extension services. Mexico gave little attention to these critical developmental concerns on a broad national basis. Simply put, Mexico had no Hatch Act. When the Mexican agricultural sector could not meet demand, the United States, through extensive marketing programs and excellent transportation modes, stepped forward to sell and export food and grain to Mexico.[25]

In spite of public and private concern and farm subsidies, the overall farm sector has had little or no boost in production. Productivity is further hampered by a near total lack of affordable loans and farm credit for seeds, equipment, irrigation, infrastructure, and fertilizers. And when able to produce crops, the larger domestic market, in spite of government oversight, does not have a modern, functioning, farm-to-market system. An attempt was made in the mid-1990s under a program known as Procampo (Program of Direct Support Payments to the Countryside) to allow direct payments to farmers for corn (maize), wheat, beans, and other grains.[26] Stratifying small and large growers, this system progressively faded away. Thus, the small ejido's production is either consumed by the grower or sold in a narrow localized community market. Concern over the deteriorating conditions in rural Mexico is well founded, yet to date these conditions have demonstrated little prospect for substantial recovery. And these structural problems in Mexican agriculture predated guidelines for cross-border trade developers in Chapter 7 of NAFTA.[27]

From the inception of trade talks with Mexico in the 1980s on cross-border free trade under NAFTA, it was clearly understood if for no other reason than the agriculture concerns aired by Canada in the U.S.-Canadian FTA, market access by American growers and agriculture policy would be the prime issues for Mexico. Politically the Salinas administration knew the country needed free trade and better market access. To balance the introduction of free trade—and thus closer ties with the United States—while at the same time maintaining the "spirit" of the outdated nationalistic rhetoric was a constant balancing act.

IMPACT OF NAFTA ON MEXICAN AGRICULTURE

While there have been news-making stories on Mexican exports of avocados and strawberries along with import news on U.S. boxed beef and chicken or Cuban sugar (embargoed from the United States yet oftentimes transshipped to Mexico), no media event will compare with Mexico's reaction to corn or maize. Indigenous to its ancestral home of Mexico, corn has been cultivated south of the border for over six thousand years. As the basic staple food of the daily Mexican diet, the nation boasts more varieties of maize (over sixty) than any other country and some 15 million Mexican dryland farmers depend in part on a yearly corn crop. Mexico, second only to tiny subtropical Malawi with a population of 10 million, has the world's highest annual per capita corn consumption. Corn availability and pricing are central to the Mexican economy, with corn as the centerpiece of the Mexican diet—tamales, tacos, tortillas, and *atole*. Over a million ejido small plots annually produce about half of the 21–23 million ton demand for corn, with another quarter produced commercially, and the last quarter dependent on imports. And a number of the Mexican Indian tribes with ancient roots "believe that the maize plant is sacred and represents the origin of life itself."[28]

Long before NAFTA, Mexican agricultural imports began to dramatically increase in the late 1970s. The leading import was and has continued to be corn. Thus, as Midwest U.S. corn growers edged up production of both white and yellow (feed) corn to Mexico, concerns were voiced over both pricing and limits on exports to the Mexican market. U.S. exports of corn to Mexico comprised 13 percent of all U.S. corn exports worldwide in 2003. Mexico is the world's second highest annual per capita corn consumer with 68 percent of corn directly used as food for human consumption. Thus, efforts were launched to increase Mexico's corn production, which resulted in an abrupt elimination in 1996 of the fifteen-year transition period to only three years and the introduction of genetically modified organisms or GMO corn (also referred to as "transgenic Maize or Bt corn").[29] The GMO maize took root in exports to Mexico in the mid-1980s (before NAFTA), but in 1998 the Mexican government instituted a moratorium on future planting and research—quite possibly influenced more by a moratorium imposed by the European Union than the reality of local demand. While GMO crops and products are produced in over a dozen countries, an estimated 95 percent of the GMO crops are grown in four countries: the United States, Canada, Argentina, and China. As one author noted, "The entry of transgenic corn [no different in taste and appearance from regular corn] into Mexico was never authorized but neither was it expressly prohibited."[30]

However, limits on GMO maize did not include imports due in large part to the daily growing domestic demand, which in 2004 was over 6 million metric tons annually—a full 25 percent of all consumption. Given the inefficient farming, a wave of droughts, and a rising population, Mexico to some is a prime candidate to advance production with GMO crops. Purists argue the GMO maize will in time alter the true nature of naturally grown Mexican corn. A battle between environmentalists and advocates of GMO corn has been addressed by the Agriculture Secretariat and the Mexican Congress without a resolution. Yet the major source of protest on the grounds that GMO corn is a health risk and an attack on the cultural integrity of Mexican maize producers has come from the Joint Policy Advisory Committee (JPAC) efforts before a NAFTA mandated panel known as the Commission for Environmental Cooperation (CEC). The views expressed and resulting report on maize and biodiversity from a March 2004 symposium in Oaxaca have received mixed reviews.[31]

Without a clear resolution of the GMO status in Mexico, urban demand and gradually less productive agricultural methods loom as the beginning of the end to food self-sufficiency in Mexico. The dynamics of this change over the next two decades strike at the heart of the country's social and economic stability. In an extensive review of Mexican development, David Barkin noted, "The obstacles to modernization of small-scale agriculture are substantial. The theory of comparative advantage predicts that such farmers will convert their resources to the production of more profitable crops or use more productive technologies to produce traditional foods," and thus, "the modernization of agriculture through improved technology and through the application of the theory of comparative advantage has done little to resolve the problems of rural development or to eliminate hunger."[32]

While Mexico has long been a leader in corn research, the last decade of only meager research has allowed the United States to fully capture the field, notwithstanding a fall 2004 World Bank report that noted: "The total volume of Mexican maize production was actually higher after 1994 than in the previous fifteen years. It is therefore difficult to support the claim that NAFTA caused an implosion of maize production in Mexico."[33] Historically, the United States has been the world's largest corn producer, accounting for 40 percent of world production and over 60 percent of world exports. The resolution of the issue of GMO corn becomes even more urgent given the fact that the final quotas under NAFTA are scheduled to be lifted in January 2008, shortly after a new Mexican president takes office. If Mexico does not regain a stake in domestic corn production—with or without GMO maize—the Mexican corn market will be forever altered with plentiful cheap U.S.-subsidized GMO corn. Given the consumer demands and growing population, the debate over corn and corn imports will be second only to the energy demands of the growing urban areas of the nation that in turn depend on corn. Given Mexico's low corn yields, commercial viability is a question, especially when compared to other higher valued alternatives, such as fresh produce, alfalfa, peanuts, and pecans.[34]

AGRI-FOOD SECTOR

While corn issues dominate agricultural issues between the United States and Mexico, other products such as grains, cotton, oilseeds, beef, pork, sugar, and beer are also at the heart of the Mexican food chain. To feed a growing urban economy has required an ongoing investment in domestic food processing capacity backed by the growing imports of both unfinished food products and consumer-ready products. In no area of a more integrated regional North American trade regime over the past decade have consumer food products flourished. Scarce water, arable land, and outdated technology all affect Mexico's domestic productivity capacity. Mexico's agri-food sector is one of the most polarized domestic industries, due in part to the fact that local producer/manufacturers can not satisfy the demand. Hampered by lagging technology and capital shortage, a number of trends have emerged which will reshape the domestic markets in Mexico as well as long-term implications for an ever growing demand for U.S. foodstuffs.

With the possible exceptions of tequila, beer, and avocados, Mexico has little or no comparative advantage in terms of cross-border food products with the United States. In those agricultural/food products areas in which Mexico cannot compete head-to-head, in spite of open market caveats in both NAFTA and the WTO, nontariff barriers usually at the local and regional level are designed to slow the spread and market acceptance of American products. However, such barriers have had little impact since 63 percent of U.S. agricultural exports to Mexico are consumer-ready and intermediate goods. As in most nations such actions are not necessarily unusual and are viewed (while irritating to outsiders) as prudent to Mexico's self-interest. Mexico's frustration with such items as its internal markets, distribution networks, lack of trade financing, and governmental red tape can also be a source of blockage for foreigners striving to enter the Mexican market. A brief look at two sample products—beef and sugar—allows a partial understanding of the dynamics of cross-border business, markets, and nontariff barriers that impede trade.[35]

Linkage of the cattle industry in Mexico with the Southwest United States has its roots over two centuries ago. Cross-border trade in hides, tallow, bone meal, and breeding stock was one of the prime foundations of early trade on the Rio Grande frontier.[36] As the economies of both nations have grown so too has the demand for beef. Mexico is the second-largest importer of U.S. beef after Japan. The Mexican beef industry produces primarily for their domestic market. With per capita consumption at 45 kg, up 21 percent since 1997, Mexico today can supply only 80 percent of a annual growing demand for beef products. Historically, a majority of Mexico's herd moves north to U.S. feed lots. Mexican ranches, generally viable on a much larger scale than localized ejido farmers, are faced by falling market prices (and thus low profit margins), rising production costs, and a nagging shortage of borrowing capacity and credits. However, in 2004 record high U.S. prices for feeder calves resulted in near record import of some 1.4 million head. There are few Mexican feedlots due to cost of feed, capital, and inadequate water in many regions, and thus a majority of the domestic cattle are grass-fed. Nevertheless, Mexico exports on average about 800,000 head to the United States annually, and imports about the same dollar equivalent in "variety" meats (tripe, rumen, kidneys, etc.) which have little or no market in the United States. Dave Price in *Beef* magazine noted, "This increases the 'drop' value of U.S. slaughter cattle, which translates into higher live-weight prices."[37] The cross-border trade in cattle and beef products functioned smoothly, for the most part, until late 2003.

The announcement of bovine spongiform encephalopathy (BSE)—mad cow disease—on December 23, 2003 in Washington State upset U.S. beef product exports worldwide, but especially to Mexico. This disruption was further exacerbated, given the fact that Canada has taken efforts to use BSE as a wedge with Mexican buyers and the government to create an atmosphere of a nontariff barrier directed toward American beef. Mexican ranchers, while unable to meet domestic market demand, pressured SAGARPA to declare BSE a major health hazard in order to keep U.S. beef out of their market. Given the fact that beef exports to Mexico have grown from 80,000 metric tons in 1993 to over 350,000 mt in 2003 (valued at some $855 million) to balance the negative impact, the U.S. Meat Export Federation, with offices in both Mexico City and Monterrey, has worked to limit negative publicity and reopen the Mexican consumer market. These activities along with consumer demand for quality U.S. meats opened the Mexican market to boneless beef products from animals less than 30 months of age. Mexico's domestic cattle market is vital to the economy; however, production will be difficult due to low profitability, meager credit, and adverse climate conditions. In spite of the BSE incident, the overall North American cattle and beef markets are increasingly more integrated; however, without substantive investment and herd improvement, the Mexican domestic beef production sector is expected to continue a gradual decline over the next decade.[38]

Sugar, like corn, beef, and cotton, is a worldwide commodity produced by over one hundred nations. Over 70 percent of sugar is grown and consumed by local domestic markets. The major sugar exporters include Brazil, Thailand, the European Union, and Cuba, while the leading importers are the former Soviet Union, the United States, Indonesia, Japan, Korea, and Canada. In terms of production, Mexico ranks sixth, and due to a high level of domestic consumption (ranked seventh) has only a small amount of excess sugar for export. Annual per capita consumption in Mexico is 47 kg. The Mexican sugar industry has been fragmented and greatly affected by government regulations. A number of failed attempts to privatize the sector as well as inadequate capital investment to upgrade facilities and technology have resulted in less than optimum production. The sugar sector has subsidized exports as well as domestic subsidies for raw sugar storage. Much like PEMEX, the Mexican

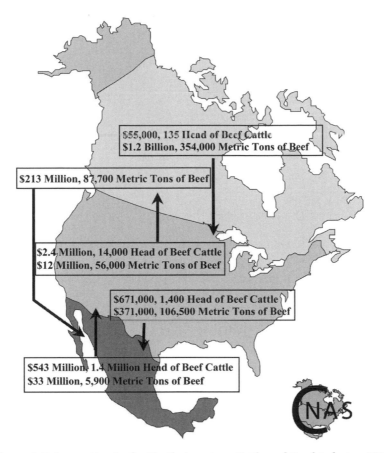

$55,000, 135 Head of Beef Cattle
$1.2 Billion, 354,000 Metric Tons of Beef

$213 Million, 87,700 Metric Tons of Beef

$2.4 Million, 14,000 Head of Beef Cattle
$12 Million, 56,000 Metric Tons of Beef

$671,000, 1,400 Head of Beef Cattle
$371,000, 106,500 Metric Tons of Beef

$543 Million, 1.4 Million Head of Beef Cattle
$33 Million, 5,900 Metric Tons of Beef

Figure 1-2 Integration in the North American Cattle and Beef Industry, 2004
Source: Center for North American Studies, 2124 TAMU, Dept. of Agricultural
Economics, Texas A&M University, College Station, TX 77843-2124.

sugar industry has a bloated workforce of over 300,000 scattered nationwide,
working in over sixty sugar mills. These large employment numbers are due to
the fact that there are 158,000 cane growers averaging about 4 hectares (9
acres) per grower producing a total yield of some 300 tons of cane. Production
is expected to increase by 17 percent from 5.1 million metric tons in 2003 to
6.0 million mt by 2013.[39]

Under the 1994 NAFTA provisions duties on sugar are scheduled to phase
out over fifteen years and decline annually to zero by 2008. The sugar portion
of NAFTA was hotly contested by U.S. producers mainly in Louisiana and
Florida who feared Mexico would dump excess amounts of domestic sugar in
the United States due to the provisions that allowed increased U.S. exports to
Mexico of high fructose corn syrup (HFCS). In time it was believed that the

Table 1-3 World Sugar Supply and Utilization, 1999–2003
(average 1,000 metric tons, unless noted otherwise)

Country	Crop°	Production	Consumption	Net exports	Per capita use/kg
Brazil	C	20,752	9,484	11,450	53
India	C	20,015	19,430	931	17
EU	B/C	18,060	14,381	3,748	40
China	B/C	8,340	8,898	−458	7
USA	B/C	6,969	8,680	−1,358	33
Mexico	C	5,026	4,877	244	47

Source: USDA, Koo and Taylor, 2004.
°B = sugarbeets C = sugarcane

HFCS, used largely in the soft drink industry, would result in a substitution or replacement for sugar. Thus, excessive Mexican exports of sugar could affect the price and production of sugar in the United States, as one observer notes: "the United Sates has a program that supports artificially high prices for the benefit of its domestic producers and granting an outsider unlimited access to this market could backfire."[40] In order to modify the accord and to cool concerns, as well as secure U.S. Congressional approval of Mexican sugar the two governments exchanged a "side letter" that altered the original provisions. The agreement stipulated that projected Mexican sugar production would have to exceed Mexico's consumption of both sugar and HFCS for Mexico to be considered a "net surplus" producer. Mexican envoy von Bertrab recalls, "The final redefinition would be painful to Mexico but not grievous, because the conversion of soft-drinks sweeteners to fructose would require heavy investment and take time. Besides, the taste of a sugar-cane-sweetened soft drink is certainly preferred by most Mexican consumers."[41] Shortly after these comments, Mexico rejected the side letter agreement and claimed that it should be entitled to export its total net surplus sugar production to the United States on a duty-free basis.

With production of sugar rising slightly after NAFTA was inked, Mexico realized it would rather sell its surplus to the United States, where prices were as much as three times those of the world market. Thus, following a surge of HFCS exports to Mexico, the Mexican sugar industry initiated an antidumping investigation. The Mexican government concluded the growing fructose imports were unfair and imposed an antidumping tariff of up $175 per ton on HFCS. The United States contested the duties, and a review by the WTO agreed with the United States. Mexico was unmoved by the WTO finding and decided to retain the duties. Any major gains in Mexican exports are diminished by two factors: first, sugar production in Mexico does not anticipate

Table 1-4 Chronology of CFTA and NAFTA, 1989–2008

January 1, 1989	Implementation of Canada Free Trade Agreement
January 1, 1994	Implementation of North America Free Trade Agreement
	Mexico eliminates tariffs for United States on sorghum, certain citrus fruits, and fresh strawberries.
	United States eliminates tariffs for Mexico on corn, sorghum, barley, soymeal, apples, pears, peaches, fresh strawberries, beef, pork, oranges, and poultry.
January 1, 1998	Canada and United States complete 9-year transition period associated with CFTA
	Remaining Canada-U.S. tariffs are eliminated
	Mexico and United States complete 4-year transition period under NAFTA
	Mexico eliminates tariffs for United States on pears, plums, and apricots
	United States eliminates tariffs for Mexico on non-durum wheat, soy oil, and cotton
January 1, 2003	Mexico and United States complete 9-year transition period under NAFTA
	Mexico eliminates tariffs for United States on wheat, barley, rice, dairy, soybean meal and soy oil, poultry, peaches, apples, frozen strawberries, hogs, pork, cotton, and tobacco
	United States eliminates tariffs for Mexico on durum wheat, rice, limes, winter vegetables, dairy products, and frozen strawberries
October 1, 2007	Mexico and U.S. to eliminate tariffs on U.S.–Mexico sugar trade
January 1, 2008	Mexico and U.S. to complete 14-year transition period under NAFTA
	Mexico to eliminate tariffs for U.S. on corn, dried beans, and milk powder
	United States to eliminate tariffs for Mexico on frozen concentrated orange juice, winter vegetables, and peanuts.

Source: Economic Research Service, USDA

extensive growth, and second, it is further offset by a growing annual domestic demand. Unlike Mexico, which produces sugar almost exclusively from cane, U.S. sugar is produced both from cane and sugar beets.[42]

CONCLUSION

Much like the pent-up demand for adequate energy, the dynamics of agriculture will, in the near term, strain both the domestic internal markets of

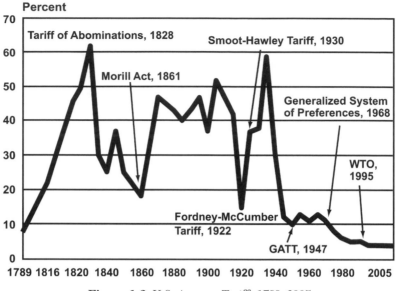

Figure 1-3 U.S. Average Tariff, 1789–2005

Mexico and the U.S.–Mexico relationship. Market pressure due to demand and international prices that affect local prices have resulted in the modification of government policy as global market determinants reshape the Mexican economic system as it pertains to agriculture. Some have argued that the de facto relationship between the high-producing market in the U.S. agricultural sector and the less-productive high-consumer-demand markets in Mexico will continue into the future. The function of Mexico's comparative advantage will be in a narrow range of export products. The bulk of processed food products made by firms in Mexico, both domestic and multinational, will stay in the Mexican market to meet local demand. Mexico's top four largest food processing sections are: the tortilla industry, nonalcoholic beverages, beer, and dairy products—none of which is a threat to U.S. markets.

The U.S. has had and will expand a comparative advantage in grains, animal products, and oilseed while Mexico will remain a leader in vegetables, fruits, and some beverages. The gains by each country—for example, the export of U.S. corn to Mexico and the U.S. importation of avocados and tomatoes—are not a zero-sum game. At issue, and of concern to Mexico, is whether or not the U.S. producers will either dominate and/or impede via tariff, pricing, or sanitation reasons those products for which Mexico still has a slim advantage. Given the tremendous investment of U.S. multinationals in all sectors of the agribusiness economy in Mexico, there will be increased interdependence of both

Table 1-5 U.S. Agribusiness and Food Processing Industry in Mexico

U.S. Company	Mexican Affiliate or JV	Products
American Cyanamid	Asociación Americana de Soya	Pesticides and agrochemicals
American Soy Bean Association	Amex Casing SA de CV	Soy products
Amex Casing Company	Grupo Modelo	Tripe processing and sausage casing
Anheuser Busch	Arbor Acres de México	Beer
Arbor Acres Farm	Dulces Arbor SA de CV	Breeder poultry
Arbor Confections	Grupo Maseca SA de CV,	Candies
Archer Daniels Midland	Gruma, ALMEX	Flour mill, wet corn milling and soybean products
Asgrow Seed	Asgrow-Mexicana SA	Vegetable, seeds
BASF K&F		Flavoring extracts, chemicals
Basic American Food	Productos Vegetales de México	Dehydrated vegetables
Basic Vegetable Products	Vegetales de México	Vegetables
Borden's	Borden's	Milk and dairy foods
Campbell Soup	Campbell's de México	Canned fruits, vegetables, preserves
Cargill	Carmex SA	Food products, animal feeds
Chef Solutions	Orval Kent de Linares	Frozen fruit
Chevron	Chevron Phillips Chemical International	Pesticides, agrochemicals
Claude Laval	Separados Lakos	Farm machinery and equipment
Coca-Cola	Corporación del Fuerte	Flavoring extracts and syrups
	Embotelladora de Cuauntla	
Con-Agra	Universa SA de CV	Grains, foodstuffs, pork, poultry
Conagra Grocery Products	Conagra Food Mexico	Food (Del Monte, Hunts)
Continental Grain	Continental Grain	Grains, field beans
Corona Cookies	Industrias de Córdoba	Cookies and crackers
CPC International	Productos de Maíz	Consumer food products, corn
Deere and Co.	Industrias John Deere	Farm machinery and equipment

(continued)

Table 1-5 *Continued*

U.S. Company	Mexican Affiliate or JV	Products
DeKalb Plant Genetics	Semillas Hibridas	Hybrid corn, sorghum, sunflowers
DeKalb-Pfizer Genetics	Alimentos Mexicanos Selectos	Seeds
Del Monte	Dewied Internacional	Pasta
Dewied International Inc.		Natural casing for saugages
Dexter Midland		Sausages, prepared meat products
Diversified Avocado Products	Empacadora de Aguacalientes San Lorenzo	Frozen fruit
Farmland Food, Inc.	Farmland Food de Mexico	Wheat, corn, soybeans, processed meat
Fermenta ACS		Pesticides and agrochemicals
Frito Lay Inc.	Sabritas	Snacks (Lay's, Ruffles, Doritos, Cheetos)
General Foods	Birdseye de México	Frozen vegetables
General Mills Inc.	Gigante Verde y Cia.	Green Giant frozen vegetables
Germain Seed	ABT of Mexico	Seeds
G.M. Trading Company	Procesos G.M. de México	Animal hide processing
H. E. Butt Grocery Company	H.E.B.	Retail groceries
H. J. Heinz	Holdmex	Food products
Harris Moran Seed		Farm supplies
Hector Garcia	Frutindustrias Mexicali SA de CV	Fruit and juice concentrates
Hershey International	Hershey de México	Chocolate products
Hicks, Muse, Tate & Furst	Products del Monte	Investments
Hormel Foods	Hormel Alimentos SA de CV	Food products
Hunt-Wesson	Productos Industrializados del Fuerte	Tomato products
Imexico Enterprises	Molinera del Valles	Flour mills
International Minerals and Chemical Company	Frier and Frier Internacional de México SA de CV	Flavorings
International Multifoods	La Hacienda	Prepared feeds, feed ingredients
International Flavors & Fragrances	Internacional Flavors & Fragrances Mexico	Flavoring extracts and syrups
Itek Corporation	Frutito SA de CV	Fruit concentrate and frozen fruit

36

Company	Mexican operation	Products
J. M. Smucker Company	J. M. Smucker de México	Jams
J. R. Norton		Horticultural processing
Kellogg	Kellogg de México	Breakfast food products
King Seed Company		Seeds
Kraft Foods	Kraft SA de CV, Productos de Alimentación de Salud de México SA de CV	Frozen foods and dairy products
Lance	B. I. Gonzalez	Consumer food products
Lopez Brothers La Bodega	Kanshoku de México SA de CV	Vegetable oils
L.T. Endo		Frozen chicken meat and cube steaks
Lyntec	Lyntec de México SA de CV	Agricultural products
McCormick & Co.	Grupo Herdez, Grupo Pesa	Seasons, flavorings, specialty foods
Monsanto	Nutra Sweet	Pesticides and agrochemicals
Monterey Mushroom	Grupo San Miguel	Food
Munoz, Inc.	Indabil SA de CV	Bakery products
Oscar Mayer	Sigma Alimentos	Processed meats
Patterson Foods	Estrella	Frozen foods
Peavey/Conagra Trading		Flour, feeds, and seeds
Pepsico Foods	Sabritas, Gamesa, Geupec, Gatorade de México	Beverages, food products, services
Pepsi-Cola	Pepsicola Mexicana SA	Beverages and food products
Pet, Inc.	Almacenes Refrigerantes	Specialty foods
Petoseed	Petoseed de Baja California	Seeds
Pfizer Inc.	Cadbury Adams Mexico	Soft drinks
Philip Morris [Kraft Foods, General Foods, Birds Eye, Oscar Mayer]	Cigarros La Tabacalera, Sigma Alimentos	Soft drinks, cigarettes, dairy, soups, canned fruits and vegetables, dehydrated fruits, vegetables
Pilgrim Foods	Oranjugos SA de CV	Frozen orange juice
Pilgrim's Pride	Unión de Queretaro	Poultry hatcheries
Pillsbury Co.	Pacific Star	Frozen foods, juices and vegetables
Pioneer Hi-Bred International	Hibridos Pioneer de Mexico SA de CV	Farm products and corn seed
Procter & Gamble	Procter & Gamble	Food products
Quaker Oats Co.	Fabrica de Chocolates La Azteca	Breakfast cereal, chocolate candy

(continued)

Table 1-5 *Continued*

U.S. Company	Mexican Affiliate or JV	Products
Quality Baker of America Bread	Bimbo	
Ralston Purina	Purina SA de CV	Animal feed, cereals, food products
RJR Nabisco	Grupo Gamesa SA, Marcas Alimenticias	Food products
SAF Products	Safmex	Food preparation
San Diego Seafoods	Heriberto Jara	Shrimp processing
Sara Lee	Kir Alimentos, Grupo Bimbo	Processed meats and baked goods
Seagram	Grupo Gemex	Beverages
Simplot	Marbran, Congeladora y Empacadora Nacional, S.A.	Frozen foods and guacamole
Sonora Produce Corporation	Jugo Fresco y Nacional Fruit Juice Extracting	Fruit juices
Stokeley Company	Stokeley Mexicana SA de CV	Food processing
Sun World	Agrícola BAS SA de CV	Vegetable packing
Tanimara & Antle	Tecnica Exportadora del Valle	Vegetable packing
Tate and Lyle	Tate and Lyle de México	Sugar
Tootsie Roll	Tri de Latinoamerica	Candy and confectionary products
Trans-Agra Holiday Corp.	Procesadora Internacional de Frutas, SA	Fruit processing
Tyson Foods	Procesadora Industrial Citra SA de CV, Trasgo SA de CV	Chicken products
U.S. Meat Export Federation	U.S. Meat Export Federation	Promotion of U.S. meats
United Brands	Numar	Palm oil, food products
United Catalysts, Inc.	Quimica Somex SA de CV	Catalysts for food industry
Universal Flavors	Universal Flavors de México	Flavoring extracts and syrups
Universal Foods	Universal Foods/Ambesco de México	Food products and flavoring
Wal-Mart	Walmex and Bodega Aurrerá	Retail groceries
Warner Lambert	Chicle Adams	Candy products
World Wen, Inc.	Tecnica Mexicana de Alimentación	Coffee and candy

Source: Mexico City, *Bancomex Trade Directory of Mexico,* 2004; American Chamber of Commerce of Mexico, *Directory of American Companies in Mexico,* 2004–2005.

nations well into the future. Thus, according to Michael Porter, the "opportunity to prosper" will remain a factor in long-term competitive success:

> National economic prosperity is not a zero-sum game in which one nation's gain is at the expense of others. A healthy process of economic upgrading can allow all nations to enjoy a rising standard of living. The choices required to act on the prerequisites for economic success, or not to act, will ultimately fall to each nation.[43]

2

—◻━◄▽►━◻—

LA FRONTERA: THE BORDER AND IMMIGRATION

We have to keep our borders open for trade, open for investment, open for well-intended migrants, open for the people that are at the border that live and contribute to both economies, but closed for terrorism, closed for organized crime, and closed for smugglers.

Having a secure, dignified, humane migration flow between the United States and Mexico is essential for both our countries. The biggest pending issue between both countries is the shared responsibility we have to regulate the migration flow. . . . To have a migration agreement with the United States, the United States has to reform its migration laws.
> —Carlos de Icaza González, Ambassador of Mexico,
> December 10, 2004

America's immigration system is also outdated—unsuited to the needs of our economy and to the values of our country. We should not be content with laws that punish hardworking people who want only to provide for their families, and deny businesses willing workers, and invite chaos at our border. It is time for an immigration policy that permits temporary guest workers to fill jobs Americans will not take, that rejects amnesty, that tells us who is entering and leaving our country, and that closes the border to drug dealers and terrorists.
> —George W. Bush, State of the Union, February 2, 2005

THE UNITED STATES–MEXICO border is one of the most dynamic border zones in the world. Once viewed as merely a buffer area far from the mainstream of either nation, this border has been in the spotlight of attention and the focal point as both countries assess a number of defining issues, including cross-border trade, immigration, drugs, security, explosive urban growth, and water rights. Annually setting records in urban growth and commercial trade, the border area, which runs 1,951 miles from south of San Diego on the Pacific to

Boca Chica at the mouth of the Rio Grande on the Gulf of Mexico, is a blend of two nations. The final location of the border was largely the result of the Manifest Destiny doctrine of the United States as the eager nation expanded westward. The arbitrary and irregular boundary "line," marked by bulky Spanish missions and lightly defended presidios, was first contested by the French and British in the late 1700s and early 1800s in the colonial era to unseat the claims of New Spain. The Spanish attempted numerous efforts to move north and occupy the vast region in advance of eager American settlers (mostly from the southern states) who moved to the Southwest. Following the 1803 Louisiana Purchase, Thomas Jefferson asserted the Rio Grande—known as the Rio Bravo del Norte in Mexico—was the southwestern boundary of the young American nation, but could do little to defend his claim.

With Mexico's independence from Spain in 1821, the new Republic of Mexico struggled to occupy and develop the vast northern territory. These efforts were hampered both by the gradual migration of Americans into the harsh region as well as the political instability and inability in Mexico City to integrate the northern frontier into the nation's economic system. During this pivotal period, the flamboyant military chieftain General Antonio López de Santa Anna reigned as president eleven different times between 1833 and 1855. By the end of his many exploits, Mexico had ceded about half of its territory to the United States, hallmarked by the declaration of independence and succession of the Republic of Texas in 1836. With Texas's accession to statehood in 1845 and the conclusion of the Mexican-American War of 1846–48 (known in Mexico as the "War of the North American Invasion"), the boundary was firmly established and delineated along the Rio Grande by the 1848 Treaty of Guadalupe Hidalgo. This boundary line down the middle of the Rio Grande from the Gulf of Mexico to El Paso accounts for over 1,250 miles of the border, and the overland portion from El Paso to the Pacific of 698 miles was settled by the purchase of a strip of land in 1853 along what is now southern New Mexico and Arizona and thus set today's modern border. In sum, the newly acquired land north of the Rio Grande extending to the Pacific over time became all or part of eight U.S. states. As one noted author has observed, "All international borders are at once fascinating and disconcerting. The [U.S.–Mexico] dividing line is stark and unmistakable. But it is not impermeable."[1]

Deep-seated historical tensions and conflict have defined the economy and society of the borderlands as twin border cities gradually emerged; yet notwithstanding, such cross-border neighboring communities tended over time to become more interdependent. Since 1800, the border has been not only an urban and rural growth area as communities were established to lay claim to the region but also a key commercial and trading zone. The primary regional trade of this early period included the movement of freight and passengers overland by wagon and mule. The shipment of products such as buffalo hides, tallow, *piloncillo* (brown-sugar cones), mescal, tobacco products, and salt was both very slow and expensive. Trade, under the close watch of government officials, was critical to supply the missions and forts that dotted the southwest border region. While Mexico was the leading producer of silver coinage for world commerce for over two centuries, on the northern frontier there was little or no banking and a short supply of specie, thus most trades were by barter. Further complicating settlement were rebel factions in northern Mexico on both sides of the Rio Grande, numerous separatist movements, and Indian (*indios bárbaros*) incursions, along with a vast smuggling network. By 1850, cross-border trade expanded to cattle shipments, consumer merchandise from New Orleans, and farm equipment through the Ports of Matamoros and Laredo. There was a tremendous surge in Rio Grande trade during the Civil War to export Confederate cotton in exchange for finished goods and munitions. In the years after 1865 the northern state of Tamuliapas, without the initial approval of the central government in Mexico City, endeavored to establish a duty free *zona libre* to parallel the border in order to attract distribution facilities and trade services to the towns south of the Rio Grande. Competition was fierce on both sides of the river as each town wanted to become designated as the primary trade route into Mexico.[2]

The defining moment for border commerce and urban development along the frontier came in the early 1880s when New York railroad and financial tycoons gained cross-border trackage rights and looked southward for the most strategic border locations across the Rio Grande. First selected were Laredo (1881) and El Paso (1884). Rail bridges across the Rio Grande in Texas, and later overland rail via California, linked Mexico with U.S. markets. While additional rail lines and bridges crossed at a number of locations, the primary corridor by 1890 would be Jay Gould's International and Great Northern Railroad (I&GN), years later to become what is today the Union Pacific Railroad, crossing at Laredo. In time, the connection from the Midwest hub of St. Louis via Dallas and on to Laredo through Monterrey to Mexico City would delineate the primary regional trade corridor and future flow of overland north-south commerce. The railroad captivated the imagination of border merchants, cattlemen, and politicians along the Rio Grande frontier. The railroad connected the region with the rest of the world—reducing overland travel time from Laredo to San Antonio from five days to five hours; and the travel time from Mexico City to New York City from eight weeks to one week. The railroad linkage paved the way for the introduction of new technology, better market access, economic development and the dynamic border urban growth that followed and remains to this day the most significant economic event in the chronicle of the borderlands history.[3]

By 1900, north-south trade corridors were well established through Matamoros-Brownsville, Laredo–Nuevo Laredo, El Paso–Ciudad Juarez, Nogales-Nogales, and San Diego–Tijuana. These corridors are today augmented by a dozen developing border crossings such as Pharr, Del Rio, Eagle Pass, Mexicali, Otey Mesa, and San Isidro. Growth along the early border region with the addition of the railroad was primarily limited to light trade shipments, supplies—such as furniture, clothing, and dry goods—raw materials for construction, mining equipment, and agricultural products. Trade—not immigration—dominated border activity. Some 300,000 persons of Mexican ancestry were counted in the 1900 U.S. Census with most living in the border region. Going southbound, the early industrialization of Monterrey's steel business and the expansion of mining in northern Mexico attracted a tremendous amount of investment and infrastructure improvements that were greatly damaged or abandoned during the Mexican Revolution from 1910 to 1919, which might be better categorized as a civil war. U.S.–Mexico relations were under constant assessment during the disruption south of the border. In the classic history of the revolution, *The Wind that Swept Mexico*, Anita Brenner candidly assessed neighboring relationships, "To the degree that Mexico–United States relations grow warmly cordial, most Mexicans become uneasiest. They often quote what some one of them said long ago: 'God preserve us from the friendship of the United States!'" Notwithstanding, the disruption caused by the revolution created an extensive northward migration and capital flight to the United States, much of which never returned to Mexico. The World War I period created further stimulus to the border economy as farm workers were allowed in for temporary stays. As soon as the war was over American labor unions in the 1920s protested such temporary farm worker visits and the federal government limited the number of Mexican workers.[4]

Officially, the first extensive temporary farm worker program was curtailed with the passage of the Immigration and Nationality Act of 1924 due to new enforcement procedures that primarily consisted of a ten-dollar head tax for applicants to obtain an entry visa. However, this did not stop routine crossings and seasonal agricultural workers. The creation of the U.S. Border Patrol in 1924 was a reaction to additional pressure on Congress to take action, yet the new border agency was grossly underfunded and understaffed. The Border Patrol was authorized to assign no more than 450 men to watch both the Mexican and Canadian borders. This equated to one agent per 10 miles of the nearly 2,000-mile southern border. Crossing over a Rio Grande bridge or western land port was a formal process that most entrants avoided in order to cross at a number of other unofficial sites. The Great Depression dampened migration during the 1930s, with annual legal immigration from Mexico numbering about only 1,700 per year. During the same period the apprehensions of illegal immigrants averaged 9,000 per year between 1931 and 1941. War soon changed this trend, as the demand for agricultural workers in the United States again appeared during World War II and caused the creation of the Bracero Program (1942), in force until it was discontinued in 1963, again due to U.S. labor union complaints. After a short time, a new catalyst to Mexican immigration appeared in a side note to the 1952 Immigration and Nationality Act known as the "Texas Proviso," which gave nearly a

Table 2-1 U.S. Border Demographic Characteristics (SMSAs)

	Laredo	El Paso	Imperial	San Diego
Spanish spoken at home	91.3%	71.2%	65.3%	21.9%
English spoken at home	8.0%	26.7%	32.2%	67.0%
Hispanic or Latino	94.3%	65.8%	72.2%	26.7%
Population	210,000	688,039	145,744	2,862,819

Source: U.S. Census Bureau, 2000

blanket approval to hiring undocumented workers and prohibited the prosecution of U.S. companies or farmers that hired such undocumented aliens.[5]

The root of today's immigration policies and concerns dates from the mid-1960s, first due to the uneven economic conditions in Mexico and second, the gradual attraction to jobs on the border as a result of the Border Industrialization Program, which is better known as the maquiladora or twin plant manufacturing sector.[6] These factors coupled with the fact that the Mexican government did very little to enhance job creation or major improvements in the educational system. The maquiladora program was one of the few stable sectors in the Mexican economy as a series of peso devaluations from 1972 to 1994 caused economic turmoil that in turn triggered recession and additional immigrant flight to the border and across.[7] These demographic changes and a shift from rural to urban growth became increasingly noticeable on the border. In many regards the border is a microcosm of the future of U.S.–Mexico relations. Cross-border interaction brings numerous challenges and opportunities often overlooked in the broader scheme of binational priorities. With an annual economic growth rate of 8 percent over the past decade, if the border were a country it would rank ahead of Poland and just behind Thailand. As one of the fastest growing regions in the world, the border region's projected urban growth by 2006 will exceed over 14 million people. The population of the U.S.–Mexico border could double by 2025.[8]

FRONTERIZOS

In northern Mexico, six border states in *el norte* or *la frontera* span the region: Tamaulipas, Nuevo Leon, Coahuila, Chihuahua, Sonora, and Baja California. Since Mexico does not have counties, the border region is governed by thirty-five *municipios* or municipalities with strong oversight from the governor of each state. The *frontera norte* and its inhabitants, *los fronterizos*, have long been viewed in Mexico City as an apprehensive, distant, and sometimes foreboding part of Mexico. The border states on the U.S. side of Texas, New Mexico, Arizona, and California (today with a combined four-state population of 72 million, fully 25 percent of the total U.S. population in 2005) contain many border communities scattered in twenty-five adjacent border counties.

Crossings at the border increase yearly. Dating from the first congressional immigration laws passed on August 3, 1882, the geographical zone of the border, or the distance a visitor can travel without going into the interior, on each side has been defined differently as from 12 miles (26 km) to 62.5 miles (100 km). Day visitors to the United States may by law travel inland up to 25 miles (40 km). Beyond this point undocumented persons will need to complete a U.S. Homeland Security–Immigration tracking form, the I-94–Arrival and Departure Record. U.S.–Mexico border alien arrivals and departure records are on file since May 1903.[9]

For the most part, cross-border cooperation between the twin cities has been cordial, in spite of the vast differences in services, governance, and local regulations. In addition to local community officials and police forces, there is an added layer of state and federal oversight. Issues and concerns on a broad number of topics such as border retail commerce, safety and security, bridge operations, cross-border fire response protocols, and drug interdiction have been routinely handled on a day-to-day basis. One prime example of local cooperation is the Border Liaison Mechanism (BLM) created in 1993 and cochaired by the U.S. and Mexican consuls in border "sister cities." This activity was mandated to bring together representatives of local, state, and federal agencies, along with representatives of the business community, to review a variety of cross-border issues ranging from port security to health care. Until September 11, 2001, most of this oversight and enforcement was directed toward drug interdiction, immigration, and truck safety on the U.S. side and in Mexico a close watch over illegal arms movement, smuggled merchandise, and cash. U.S.–Mexico trade during the decade of the 1990s saw explosive growth, increasing over 300 percent. While the first response was to close both the Mexican and Canadian borders after 9/11 (a near impossibility given the combined distance of some 5,000 miles), all were aware that the nation was entering a new and uncharted era. After 9/11 security concerns with Weapons of Mass Destruction (WMDs) and potential terrorists crossing into the United States changed the entire border focus among law enforcement agencies. Furthermore, there was a marked increase in federal activity on the southern border as additional manpower and equipment were added following the creation of the Department of Homeland Security in November 2002.[10] The heightened concern with the southern border only augments the U.S.–Mexico relationship, which has been marked by over 150 years of agreements and treaties focused primarily on boundary security, immigration, commerce, water rights, and the environment.[11]

The primary impact and concern of border community leaders, given the historical shortfall of federal funding for border needs, is the growing list of unfunded federal government mandates to provide services and facilities for which there is little or no local funding. Ever mindful of the need for safety and security, for decades border communities have been apprehensive of directives from either Washington, D.C. or Mexico City since both capitals

Table 2-2 U.S.–Mexico Border Treaties, Agreements, and Operations, 1848–2005

Year	Agreement	Purpose
1848	Treaty of Guadalupe Hidalgo	Boundary
1853	Gadsden Purchase	Boundary
1882	Chinese Exclusion Act	Immigration
1884	Meandering Rivers Agreement	Boundary
1889	International Boundary Commission	Boundary
1906	U.S.–Mexico Water Treaty	Water
1917	Immigration and Nationality Law	Immigration
1921	Quota Act	Immigration
1924	Immigration Act of 1924	Immigration
1924	Creation of the U.S. Border Patrol	Security
1933	Rio Grande / Rio Bravo Rectification Project	Boundary
1936	Good Neighbor Policy (Latin America)	Good will
1936	Rio Grande Compact Commission	Water
1942	Emergency Farm Labor Program "Bracero" Program (ended in 1964)	Guest workers
1944	Treaty of 1944: Utilization of waters of the Colorado and Tijuana Rivers and of the Rio Grande °International Boundary and Water Commission (IBWC)	Water
1952	MacCarron-Walter Act PL No. 414 Immigration and Naturality Act & "Texas Proviso"	Farm labor
1954	Operation Wetback-U.S. INS	Immigration
1963	Chamizal Convention (El Paso)	Boundary
1965	Simpson-Mazzoli Bill: Immigration Act of 1965	Immigration
1965	Border Industrialization Program (BIP)	Maquiladoras
1983	U.S.–Mexico Border Environmental Agreement °known as the La Paz Accord	Environment
1986	Immigration Reform and Control Act	Immigration
1986 (Aug.)	General Agreement on Tariffs and Trade °accession of Mexico	Commercial
1987	Bilateral Trade and Investment Framework Agreement	Commercial
1990	Immigration Act of 1990 ("IMMACT 90")	Immigration
1993	North American Free Trade Agreement °North American Development Bank (NADBank) °Border Environment Cooperation Commission (BECC)	Commerce
1993	Border Liaison Mechanism (BLM)	Sister city forum
1993	North American Agreement on Environmental Cooperation (NAAEC)	Environment

(continued)

Table 2-2 *Continued*

Year	Agreement	Purpose
1996	Illegal Immigration Reform and Immigration Responsibility Act (IIRIRA)	Immigration
1996	Border XXI	Environment
2001 (Oct.)	USA Patriot Act	Security and borders
2001	Partnership for Prosperity	Immigration
2002	Border 2012 Program	Environment
2002	U.S. Immigration and Naturalization Service °Operation Hold-the-Line, Texas °Operation Gatekeeper, California °Operation Rio Grande, Texas °Operation Safeguard, Arizona	Immigration
2002 (Mar.)	U.S.–Mexico Border Partnership Agreement	Security
2002 (Nov.)	Homeland Security Act	Security and borders
2004	U.S.–Mexico Transboundary Aquifer Assessment Act (S. 1957 pending)	Water
2004 (Jan.)	Temporary Worker Program (proposed)	Immigration
2004 (Dec.)	Intelligence Reform and Terrorism Prevention Act	Security and borders

Note: The above highlights the key agreements between 1848 and 2004, but not all events such as special commissions findings, treaty side agreements, IBWC actions, etc.

have persistently demonstrated a limited understanding of the dynamics and needs of the border region. This in spite of the fact that the duties and fees collected along the border represent substantial revenue for the treasuries of both countries. Nevertheless, trade and commercial activities along the border continue to expand. A significant trend toward more diversification of the border communities away from purely retail, finance, and transportation-logistical-distribution services to a broader cross-section of new business and services followed with the passage of NAFTA.[12]

In the 1970s and 1980s, unemployment rates in the U.S. border towns were never less than 10 percent. After Mexico entered GATT in mid-1986, trade and commerce on both sides of the border began a wave of expansion that continued with the passage of NAFTA in 1994. Such growth brought new companies, technology, attention to urban growth needs, and employment. A young and growing economy taxed the ability to keep pace as education, health care, housing, transportation infrastructure, and social services struggled to meet demand. The border communities in Mexico fared no better. Environmental agencies and municipality programs on both sides of the border have endeavored to cooperate to assess and mitigate the concerns with rapid urbanization, waste disposal (urban and industrial hazardous), and air

Figure 2-1 Rio Grande Watershed
Source: TNRCC.

quality to address the economic growth in the region. Compounding these concerns is the lack of infrastructure in unincorporated areas, in what is known as the *colonias*. Binational agreements in 1906 and 1944 apportioned the waters and "water usage" of the Rio Grande and resulted in the creation of the International Boundary and Water Commission (IBWC).[13]

The U.S. side, however, continues to contend with elevated high school dropout rates in the range of 40 percent. Low educational attainment is highly

Table 2-3 Border SMSA Population, 1970–2010 (thousands)

	1970	1980	1990	2000	2010°
San Diego	1,357	1,861	2,498	2,814	3,215
Tijuana	277	542	747	1,125	1,512
Calexico			17	23	
Mexicali	267	495	602	764	914
El Paso	359	480	592	680	754
Ciudad Juarez	407	680	789	1,217	1,615
Laredo	73	99	133	193	263
Nuevo Laredo	149	272	300	612	745
McAllen	182	283	384	569	743
Reynosa	137	240	283	419	605
Brownsville	40	210	260	335	412
Matamoros	138	258	303	416	523

Source: U.S. Census; INGEI.

Note: U.S. population can be as much as 10% undercounted, while "official" census numbers for Mexico border cities are generally as much as 30% underreported.

°projected.

damaging to the local economies in a time when unemployment along the border in 2005–06 is dropping, and there is a demand for more skilled labor. In spite of the fact that the job market on the U.S. side of the border is constantly expanding, many of the young first and second generation workers from seventeen to twenty-three years of age leave the border for jobs in larger metropolitan areas. And most do not return. This mobility is further augmented by the dramatic inflow of migrants from Mexico, most of whom move inland to larger metro-areas. Bill Emmott, editor-in-chief of the *Economist* in a review of global trends noted, "The United States, far from having the jobs sucked away from it [as Ross Perot claimed in the early 1990s], has enjoyed falling unemployment and, if anything, has sucked Mexican labor northwards across the Rio Grande, through legal and illegal immigration."[14]

IMMIGRATION

Immigration and the resolution of the legal status of aliens entering or already in the United States will become one of the most volatile local and national political issues in the years to come. The longer the delay in developing a consensus on how to resolve and manage this immigration issue, the greater the impact on the relationship between the two nations. Demographically, America is a vastly changing nation. The "Hispanic-Latinos" population, as classified by to the U.S. Census Bureau, comprised only 2.6 percent of the U.S. population in 1950, and in the course of five decades has increased over 10 percent and is expected to reach 15 percent by 2010.[15] Given the fact that Hispanics are

Table 2-4 Hispanic Immigrant Population Remittances Sent Home

State	Remittances Sent to Latin America	Number of Immigrant Adults	Percent that Send Remittances	Times per Year	Amount Sent per Remittance
CA	$9,610,000,000	5,378,555	64	12	$235
TX	$3,180,000,000	2,547,203	47	13	$225
AZ	$606,000,000	535,119	42	11	$240
NM	$103,000,000	132,784	38	9	$230
NY	$3,562,000,000	1,428,614	81	14	$225
FL	$2,450,000,000	1,796,959	47	13	$230
IL	$1,528,000,000	830,020	66	12	$225
NJ	$1,371,000,000	606,479	68	14	$235
GA	$947,000,000	345,253	81	13	$255
NC	$833,000,000	290,877	42	14	$240
U.S.	$30,140,000,000	16,701,130	61	13	$240

Source: Inter-American Development Bank, 2005.

increasing in numbers five times faster than Anglos, when compared with the total U.S. population in mid-2005 of 300 million people, this equates to over 50 million individuals with ties to south of the border. In the 2000 census, over 60 percent of all Mexican immigrants were in Texas (22 percent) and California (46 percent), and they are joined each year by as many as 400,000 fellow countrymen. The four states with the largest Mexican immigrant population are California, Texas, Arizona, and Illinois. As the immigrants began to move nationwide away from the border (in search of jobs), the percent of Mexican immigrants living in the four states dropped from 89 percent in 1990 to 72 percent in 2002—yet the number residing in these states went up 87 percent from 3.8 million to 7.1 million. In the latter part of the 1990s, Mexico had one of the highest out-migration rates of its citizens in the world. Large population concentrations of Mexican immigrants are now found in New Mexico, Maryland, New York, Pennsylvania, Florida, New Jersey, Georgia, Colorado, and Illinois. This demographic shift has been dramatically easy to track—"follow the money"—given the level of annual dollar remittances.[16]

The flow of money earned by workers in the United States and the remittance abroad has been a factor for over a century, but did not reach an active level until the Bracero Farm Worker Program during and after World War II. By the 1950s, the flow of millions of dollars back to Mexico began to reach significant levels. Ranking as the third leading hard dollar generator to Mexico in 1956, behind only tourism and agricultural exports, total remittances were estimated to be $120 million annually.[17] As the methods for sending money improved, they went from informal couriers known as *viajeros* to postal money orders and cash, and eventually, over 80 percent of funds are now wired for a fee (ranging from $12 to 25) by Western Union. The number and dollar amount of remittance transfers has increased yearly. While a large number of countries receive remittances globally, remittances by Mexican nationals from the United States far exceed those from India, Pakistan, Egypt, and Morocco. And in Latin America, Mexico receives more than the combined annual total of Brazil, El Salvador, the Dominican Republic, and Colombia in dollar terms.[18] Five states in the central highlands are the leading recipients in Mexico to receive funds: Michoacán, Zacatecas, Guanajuato, San Luis Potosi, and Jalisco. By 2004, over one-half of the annual remittance total, or about $16 billion, of the estimated $30 billion sent abroad went directly to Mexico. This dollar inflow today ranks third behind foreign exchange generated by tourism and the Mexican export oil revenues. Furthermore, this inflow amounts to an estimated 2 to 4 percent of Mexican GDP and as Daniel Griswold notes, "Unlike government-to-government foreign aid, remittances bypass the political process and go directly to individual families and communities."[19]

The ability to send money home is one of the primary motivating factors to emigrate to the United States—legally or illegally. To provide identification for immigrants the Mexican government issues a *matricular consular*, a program first started in 1871, to provide proof of identity, which is critical to access banking services, obtain a drivers' license, or deal with government entities. Such identification is critical to sending money back home. The multiplier effect and the macro impact on the purchasing power of the remitted dollars on the domestic Mexican economy is tremendous, stimulating home construction, new business start-ups, transportation, and consumer purchases, as well as augmenting the daily living needs for relatives left back home. The annual growth of remittances abroad is in the 15 percent range; not surprisingly the growth shows a close correlation to the number of new immigrants entering the U.S. economy.[20]

At the heart of the current immigration issue is the never-ending flow of some 7–9,000 new illegal immigrants per day crossing over the southern border from not only Mexico but also from throughout Central and South America as well as the Caribbean. If this trend continues, those of Mexican origin will be the fastest growing "majority minority" in the U.S. borderlands and across the nation by 2030. Thus, any policy decisions, in spite of the origins of aliens termed OTMs (or other than Mexican), will primarily be debated and couched in terms of immigration from Mexico. The U.S. Census Bureau noted that Mexico accounted for nearly 69 percent of the total unauthorized resident population in January 2000. And Mexican nationals in 2004—who, once across, tend to stay longer in the United States, many never to return home—account for about one-third of all new immigrants, legal and illegal.[21]

Response to the immigration issue in the United States is split basically between two factions: either for or against managed immigration.[22] The two opposing views tend to be intolerant to compromise and thus daily farther grow apart. The pro-immigration proponents point to a nation that was built on the tradition and backs of immigrants, noting that the fresh flow of new immigrant workers is pivotal to economic development and growth. For example, during the turn of the twentieth century thousands from Mexico (along with Chinese immigrants) were recruited to work on the railroads, large-scale farm operations (cotton, fruit, vegetables, and sugar beets) and in Southwestern copper mines. As Tom Barry notes, "Moreover, the percentage of U.S. residents who are foreign born [in 2003]—about 6 percent—is far below the 14 percent of the high point of immigration [primarily European] in the 1900 1920 period."[23] However, unlike the migration of Italians, Creoles, Japanese, Germans, Chinese, and Poles, who entered en masse in the early twentieth century and then stopped abruptly, "Mexican immigration, at least since 1970, has proven to be a steady surf rather than a single tidal wave."[24]

Those against uncontrolled immigration point to the "floods" of illegal immigrants that are a "silent invasion"—prone to engaging in crime, using unwarranted social services, and swamping the public schools, thus increasing the cost of education to taxpayers. Resentment of undocumented workers includes repeated claims that by working for lower wages they take jobs away from legal citizens. From 1942 to 1964, the Bracero Program did provide for limited documentation of aliens, but failed overwhelmingly to stem the flow of undocumented immigrants. INS operations to halt and apprehend illegal entrants included Operation Wetback (1954), the model that would be repeated numerous times in various sections of the border to attempt to check the crossings. By the mid-1960s a number of demographic and economic factors in both the United States and Mexico contributed to the illegal immigrant situation that mushroomed out of control by the early 1980s. Table 2-5 provides a snapshot of events and factors that are the basis for the policies and immigration problems faced today. Government policy makers, due largely to political sensitivity and pressures from vocal special interest groups, have avoided dealing with the illegal immigrant situation, which has only enhanced and magnified an already untenable situation. Regardless of the number of border guards and special operations to apprehend illegal immigrants, the cross-border inflow of immigrants yearly is spinning out of control.[25] Taking action at the local level along the border, civilian border watches known as "Minutemen" in early 2005 launched an active program to attempt to report illegal crossings.

A new approach to immigration was needed, and after over two decades of legislative stalemate Congress acted. The result was the most significant attempt to manage illegal immigration (itself now two decades old) with the passage of the Immigration Reform and Control Act of 1986 (IRCA) which placed emphasis on permanent immigrants and not temporary entry to curtail migration of *indocumentados*. Temporary entry (usually undocumented) continued as thousands daily crossed to shop and work. Two key parts of this legislation were the legalization of over 2.4 million Mexicans already in the United States and second, IRCA attempted to place employer sanctions and fines on those U.S. companies that did not follow INS guidelines on

Table 2-5 Factors Accounting for Illegal Immigration Surge since Mid-1960s

°postwar surge in births in Mexico, thus ballooning available workforce after 1965

°economic stagnation of the populous rural sector and resulting flight to big cities and the border

°lack of productive lands and capital, which discouraged farmers who sought jobs elsewhere

°spread of education and mass media coverage, which raised expectations and awareness of U.S. market and opportunities

°the beginning of growing Mexican-American communities away from the border, which created a network to assist new immigrants

°a period of relatively low unemployment in the United States (1965–74), which created a gradual need for entry-level labor while high unemployment (and underemployment) remained in Mexico

°"Texas Proviso" from the 1952 Immigration Act, which was extended to allow the "legal" employment by U.S. farm interests of "illegal" aliens

°inadequate INS, Border Patrol, and Customs staffing in the border region; no employer penalties; poor technology to track repeat offenders

°LBJ's well-publicized Great Society War on Poverty made the United States look attractive for both legal and illegal aliens to access cross-border social services

°the Mexican government's "official" stance after 1965 to encourage out-migration to the north since it said it could not deny its citizens the "right" to leave the country

°the U.S. Immigration Act of 1965, which redefined and eliminated the preferential treatment for European immigrants, allowing Latin Americans, Asians, and Africans greater access to a limited number of immigrant visas

Source: David Simcox, quoted in Grayson, *Prospects for Mexico,* 205–17.

undocumented aliens. In retrospect these actions only fueled the inflow of immigrants. The INS (except for some limited enforcement of large high-profile companies, banks, and governmental entities) did not have the personnel, technology, and funding to bird-dog small and medium-sized companies who day-to-day hire (on a cash basis) over 85 percent of undocumented aliens. The expanding American economy depended on (and in some industry sectors demanded) a steady flow of entry-level workers. By the 1990s, 50 percent of the new jobs created were filled by newcomer immigrants—legal and illegal—to the United States. According to *Barron's,* "the U.S. underground economy is growing apace, mainly because of off-the-books work." Such unchecked growth has its deep roots in Mexico. In the case of Mexican authorities—who have repeatedly stated they have no formal "immigration policy" as such vis-à-vis Mexico–U.S. migration flows—and thus have long maintained a policy of "deliberate nonengagement," a lax approach of benign neglect seemed appropriate to address the immigration policy, seen in Mexico as a safety valve to offset the chronic inability of the Mexican economy to create jobs for the expanding working age population.[26]

In the most provocative borderlands book of the new century, *Mexifornia*, Victor D. Hanson is candid in his pointed assessment of the "immigration mess":

> The Mexican government [with] its passive-aggressive attitude toward the United States is intellectually dishonest [with] the immigration problem. Simply put, Mexican elites rely on immigration northward as a means of avoiding domestic reform. Such is the case with Mexico, which both deliberately exports its unwanted and, once they safely reach American soil, suddenly becomes their champion and absent parent, as much out of resentment toward the United States as in real concern for people whom they apparently are so gladly free of.[27]

Indications of Mexico's professed non-engagement are not fully justified due to Mexico's near "unofficial"-official endorsement of a number of immigration-oriented programs and semi-official actions lending support to its citizens moving north (and south back to visit Mexico) to the United States. These actions are not without cause given the increasing amounts of the dollar remittances flowing back to Mexico. Quize-supported governmental activities include the establishment of the "Paisano Program" in 1993 to facilitate seasonal returns, primarily during *Semana Santa* (Easter Week) and during the Christmas–New Year's period, to visit their native homes. President Fox during 2003 and 2004 made special trips to the U.S.–Mexico border to ceremoniously welcome those returning. Second, a "Mexican Communities Abroad Program" (much like a sister-city concept) was created to maintain contact with migrants. Third, an extensive monetary matching program was established in Zacatecas in 1993: "dos por uno" (two for one), in which the state government added or matched two additional dollars for every remittance dollar reinvested in the local community by immigrants. In 1996, the matching was increased to "tres por uno" (three for one), and the federal government is considering using this grassroots community investment program nationwide. To support these efforts in hometown development the Mexican government is attempting to reduce the bureaucratic hurdles to import equipment, and the banking community is working to lower the cost of sending money transfers. And lastly, a measure was approved to allow dual citizenship, with "no loss of Mexican nationality," for those who become U.S. citizens—with the implicit right to be able to vote in *both* U.S. and Mexican elections, regardless of residence. By 2006, it is conceivable (if the measure clears the Mexican Congress) that some 5 million Mexican-Americans could vote both in the next Mexican presidential election in July 2006 and then vote in the fall U.S. midterm congressional and local elections.[28]

Correspondingly, Washington policy makers have not been willing to address immigration. Except for two brief enhanced border apprehension efforts, "Operation Gatekeeper" at San Diego and "Operation Hold the Line" in the El Paso sector, the Clinton administration clearly determined to stay "as far away as possible from the thorny issue of immigration reform." President Clinton had already had an indirect brush with an immigration issue when, as governor of Arkansas, the Cuban Mariel Boatlift detainees rioted in his state, and "he never forgot the lesson that immigration and successful politics rarely mix well." Former U.S. Ambassador to Mexico Jeffrey Davidow defined the pre-2000 attitude toward addressing immigration:

> This was unfortunate, because the policies regarding the admission of foreigners into the United States are so sensitive that they are best discussed when the country is at peace and prosperous. But perhaps President Clinton understood that there was something strange about America's prosperity in the 1990s. The statistics and the stock market said we were getting richer. Our enemies were defeated, and our power was unchallenged in the world.
>
> While race-baiting and violent anti-immigrant sentiment had largely disappeared from the American political vernacular, there was a nagging anxiety about the growing number of foreigners in the United States. Americans were asking, "Where did all these people come from?"[29]

In September 1996, Congress again acted passing the Illegal Immigration Reform and Immigrant Responsibility Act (IIRIRA) which further attempted to manage immigration, to include a measure many viewed as harsh that after 1997 allowed the INS authorization to bar reentry to the United States if an alien overstayed his/her visa deadline for departure. The spirit and framework of both the 1986 and 1996 immigration laws failed to address the grassroots flow of illegal aliens at the source—the official government attitude and immigration policy avoidance by Mexico. In spite of the fact that from 1994 to 2001 (pre-9/11) the annual U.S. border enforcement budget of the INS and Border Patrol nearly tripled to over $2.5 billion, the immigrant flow continued nearly unchecked.[30] While the federal agencies have operated within their resources, they are clearly overwhelmed by the volume of crossings facilitated by little or no Mexican intervention in smuggling operations. The smugglers, known as *coyotes* or *polleros*, maintain an extensive and well-organized operation targeting crossings at sparsely populated locations along a vast and harsh border. This rush to push people northward across the border by coyotes, regardless of desert conditions, has resulted in abuse and an increase in death—of Mexicans as a result of Mexican coyotes—in the border desert areas of New Mexico and Arizona. The inflow of Mexicans and OTMs resulted in an increasing local backlash along the border that has become part of the debate on how to limit and/or manage immigration.[31]

Anti-immigration rhetoric hit a new high in November 2004 as a result of an Arizona state law, Proposition 200, passed by 56 percent approval, which requires positive proof of U.S. citizenship before immigrants have access to public services, including healthcare, child care, drivers' licenses, or a public library card. Penalties for those who hire or assist undocumented aliens could result in criminal charges. As was the case with a similar measure in California,

Table 2-6 Border Arrests by Sector, FY 2002–03 (in thousands)

	San Diego	El Centro	Yuma	Tucson	El Paso	Marfa	Del Rio	Laredo	McAllen
2003	112	92	57	347	89	10	50	71	81
2004	139	75	98	491	104	11	54	75	97

Source: U.S. Border Patrol

Proposition 187, which passed in 1994 and was struck down by the courts, there will be a vigorous challenge in the courts of the new Arizona law. The impact at the state level is reflected in the annual cost of illegal immigrants in California: $7.7 billion for education, $1.4 billion for healthcare, and $1.4 billion for illegal aliens held in prison.[32]

The Arizona anti-immigrant law of 2004 is the first tangible action that will fuel the upcoming debate in the Bush administration and Congress to act on immigration. The issue is further clouded given the fact that immigration from Mexico shows no sign of dropping. Following September 11, 2001, Mexican officials were first informed to expect few if any changes in the U.S. immigration policies. In the weeks before the 9/11 attacks, President Bush had begun limited talks with President Fox on the idea of a limited guest worker plan. In the new post-9/11 era, there is little doubt that U.S. immigration policy will be inextricably linked with terrorism and border security. The implementation of the "United States Visitor Immigration Status Indicator Technology" program, or US-VISIT, an enhanced border screening and entry program, in the fall of 2004 is a case in point. Unlike the 1984 Reagan-Mondale presidential debates in which immigration and the Simpson-Mazzoli Bill (source of the 1986 IRCA) were closely reviewed; any talk of another blanket amnesty, highly supported by the Mexican government, was played down in advance of the 2004 U.S. presidential campaign and did not receive much coverage during the months prior to the November election. As the former governor of Texas, President Bush was well aware that nearly one of every four voters in his home state is Hispanic; to wit, Bush increased his Hispanic share of the presidential vote from 43 percent in 2000 to 59 percent in 2004.[33]

The magnitude of the immigration issue has expanded due to continued dispersal of aliens throughout the United States and the overwhelming challenge to enforce laws as well as a continued high demand for entry-level workers in such U.S. industries as construction, agriculture (including poultry processing and meat packing), and service sectors (including hotels, outdoor maintenance, and restaurants). Some 36 million people of Latin American descent in 2004 comprised 13 percent of the U.S. population; by 2050 the U.S. Census Bureau estimates the number to reach 24 percent or 103 million. One study on the magnitude of unchecked immigration has concluded:

The United States can anticipate the entry of another 14 million immigrants between 2000 and 2010 with net migration of at least 400,000 Mexicans per year. Under these assumptions, the foreign-born population would increase from 31 million in 2000 to about 40 million in 2010, to represent 13 percent of the total population. The Mexican-born population would grow from about nine million in 2000 to almost 13 million in 2010; at that point, more than ten percent of the Mexican-born population would be in the United States with less than 90 percent in Mexico.[34]

While the engine of the U.S. economy continues to run at a fast pace there will be little organized call for overall reform, except for those affected in either irritated border locations or a specific industry where workers believe they are being financially hurt—due to loss of job opportunities—by immigrants. Since the mid-1990s, even with the 1999–2000 mini-recession, U.S. unemployment has remained in the 5 to 6 percent range (some would argue this is near full employment factoring in those who actually want to work). In the construction industry, home and commercial, low interest rates have caused nearly a decade of tremendous expansion, thus a demand for entry-level labor to fill jobs not being filled by the domestic U.S. workforce. Travel and tourism, hotels and restaurants, agriculture operations, and a broad spectrum of service industries continue to fuel a steady demand for the off-the-books worker. The challenge of the second Bush term is to forge a temporary-worker program that does not allow blanket amnesty. In late December 2004 and again during his January 2005 State of the Union Address, President Bush was candid in his view on the efforts needed to reform immigration by proposing a program of registration of temporary guest workers that addresses the needs of both workers and employers: "It's a compassionate way to treat people who come to our country. It recognizes the reality of the world in which we live. There are some people—there are some jobs in America that Americans won't do and others are willing to do."[35]

Reaching an agreement in Congress over the next couple of years will be controversial and could be tied to pending trade accords, such as the Central America Free Trade Agreement (CAFTA) or delayed until after the midterm congressional elections in late 2006—thus reducing legislators' exposure to criticism in their home districts. Reform should be structured to provide adequate border control, while at the same time ameliorate the situation of those that are outside the current immigration laws, record immigration entry into the United States, and carefully create a guest worker program that allows any new immigrant a clear path toward legal status as a taxpaying citizen. Blanket amnesty is not acceptable and does not work. Amnesty only fuels the flow of illegal entrants; furthermore, it will not pass in Congress. Balance is needed to insure we do not lose the competitive advantage of our workforce while at the same time providing prudent national security.[36]

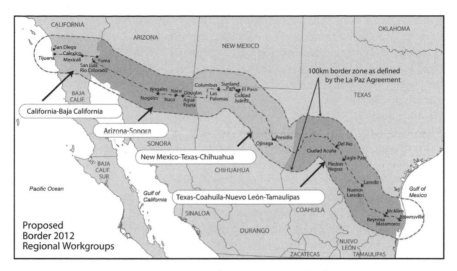

Figure 2-2 United States–Mexico Border
Source: Border 2012: U.S.–Mexico Environmental Program.

CONCLUSION

The implied relationship between immigration, border security, and the threat of terrorism is indeed a fact of the post-9/11 era and was inked into law with the passage of the Intelligence Reform and Terrorism Prevention Act in December 2004. While there is apprehension on the final structure of immigration reforms, few view Mexican workers as a direct threat to national security. The concern that terrorists might enter the United States via Mexico is based on the possibility that al Qaeda–sponsored terrorists could cross via the southern border and is linked with this sweeping legislation that mandates a number of immediate changes.[37] The concern is a direct result of the changing nature of attacks against the "homeland" of America after 9/11. We live in an era in which there are no fronts or conventional weapons; the terrain of the fight—termed "asymmetric warfare"—has forever been altered in all future conflicts. Thus, not only our southern and northern borders, but also our seaports and airspace are, for the first time since the British burned the White House nearly two hundred years ago, vulnerable to compromise and outside threats.[38] Falling short of placing the military on the border, surveillance will be increased with the extensive use of remotely piloted aircraft and the increase of manpower along the border. The Border Patrol is to add two thousand new full-time active-duty agents (if funded by Congress) by 2010 in addition to an increase of eight hundred immigration and customs officers over the same time frame. Further measures include stronger enforcement of visa requirements, added restrictions on the issuance of social security cards, a federal standard for state-issued driver licenses, and a more extensive attempt to detect fraudulent documents. Methods to enhance biometric data collection will be expanded beyond the initial protocols of the US-VISIT program begun in the fall of 2004. Entry and exit data will be collected regardless of the port of entry and all U.S. citizens will be required to have a valid passport for travel outside the United States by 2007. In order to enhance processing of aliens, additional expanded detention facilities with an additional capacity of over thirty thousand "beds" are to be provided by the end of the decade.[39]

The Mexican economy cannot provide the capacity to generate quality jobs, and there are serious cross-border wage differences that exist as the new migrants continue to enter in ever-larger numbers. Further compounding security concerns, by early 2005 Mexican drug cartels were active in all the Mexican border towns in a violent struggle for territorial control. Enhanced security measures on the Southern border have deflected the immigrant flow from one sector to the other, yet fall short of needed personnel to fully patrol the border. Few measures will stem the tide. Thus, it is critical to develop policies and procedures to insure safety and security as well as to identify, document, and certify this immigrant inflow. A fully articulated immigration policy from Washington will be avoided until the issue approaches a crisis level. The views on immigration are mixed but overall reflect a concern for better accountability, enforcement, and a clearly defined path to legalization:

> Since there is no way to let in "good" illegal aliens but keep out "bad" ones, countering asymmetric threats to our people and territory requires sustained, across-the-board immigration law enforcement. Anything less exposes us to grave dangers. Whatever the arguments for the president's amnesty and guest worker plan, no such proposal can plausibly be entertained until we have a robust, functioning immigration-control system. And we are nowhere close to that day.[40]

3

=0=◄▽►=0=

BLACK GOLD: ENERGY
DYNAMICS OF MEXICO

*In the Nation is vested direct dominion of all the minerals or substances
which in veins, layers, masses or beds constitute deposits whose nature
may be distinct from the constituents of the lands, such as minerals from
which there may be extracted metals . . . petroleum and all hydrocarbons,
solid, liquid or gaseous . . .*

—Article 27, Constitution of 1917

AT THE BEGINNING of the twenty-first century, Mexico was the world's seventh
largest oil producer, drawing on what is routinely termed a tremendous pool of
proven oil and gas reserves—an estimated hydrocarbon reserve to last for the
next two decades. This abundance of petroleum and natural gas, while
impressive, has in recent years been underutilized due to the dynamic national
growth that daily has caused domestic energy demands to outpace Mexico's
ability to extract, refine, and distribute adequate supplies. In spite of the fact
that Mexico is a net energy exporter, for nearly a decade there has been
abundant evidence to highlight both the lagging exploration infrastructure and
the overall inefficiency of the Mexican energy sector to refine and distribute
petroleum products. As Mexico expands its industrial base as well as copes
yearly with a more urban nation, there will be extensive pressure for the
generation of economical electrical power in addition to oil and gas supplies.
The roots and mathematical dynamics of the energy markets and demand in
Mexico predate the current situation by over a century.[1]

Outcroppings of bubbling springs of oil—"black gold"—in Mexico were
reported as early as the 1500s, and were long a part of Indian lore for ages prior
to the arrival of Europeans. The development of the Mexican energy industry
began in earnest in the mid-1870s and was highlighted by massive foreign
investment in railroads, mining, telephone systems, and oil exploration during
the Porfirio Díaz era from 1876 until 1910. Notwithstanding Díaz's political
antics to maintain power, overall economic development was impressive—for

example, rail track mileage increased from 750 miles in 1870 to over 12,000 miles by 1900. However, the rush of foreign investment in exploration of Mexico to capitalize on the oil business intensified in May 1901 when Mexican Petroleum Company, a private concern, hit a tremendous gusher at El Ébano, southwest of Tampico. By 1905, American and British investors held in excess of 90 percent of the capital in the mining and oil industry. Eagerness to develop the domestic economy during the Díaz reign and its impact created a backdrop for the revolutionary unrest that followed for nearly a decade after 1910.[2]

The result was the rise of nationalistic fervor that rejected foreign intrigue and, in the case of the energy sector, precluded outside foreign influence. The legal grounds to limit foreign influence were embodied in Article 27 of the Mexican Constitution of 1917, and were based on a long-standing principle in Spanish law that declared that all subsurface resources belonged to the state and not to the owner of the surface rights. Thus, one of the prime objectives of the revolution—to gain national ownership over resources—was achieved. In *The Prize*, Daniel Yergin noted of the bittersweet achievement: "Mexico had captured the oil but could not develop or market it without foreign capital, while investors had little desire to bear the risk and expense of development without secure contracts and the prospect of profits."[3] And the eventual embodiment of Article 27 was the creation on June 7, 1938 of the government-owned Petróleos Mexicanos (PEMEX), which in 2005 ranked as the world's sixth largest oil company. The Mexican nation, not PEMEX, owns the petroleum and hydrocarbon reserves of Mexico. PEMEX retains the exclusive rights to oil exploration and production in Mexico; revenues from operations account for over one-third of the national budget.[4]

At the time of the drafting of the 1917 Constitution Mexico was, as a result of U.S. and British investment and exploration, the world's second largest oil exporter after the United States. Actions by Mexico to mandate sovereign control over natural resources would have a lasting impact on not only U.S. and British relationships with Mexico, but also on how other oil-rich nations addressed domestic extraction, refining, distribution, and export of petroleum, as well as repatriation of profits. U.S. and British exploration firms had assumed that since they had purchased the surface rights for exploration they would be exempt, or "grandfathered," from the spirit and intent of Article 27 of the new constitution. Infuriated at the passage of the article, the foreign oil companies declined an offer from the Mexican government that would require an exchange of surface titles for a fifty-year concession to continue domestic operations. The foreign oil companies operating in Mexico did not want to set a precedent that would affect future explanation in other countries. In spite of the turmoil, by 1920, Mexico supplied 20 percent of domestic American oil, and by 1921, Mexico was the second largest oil producer in the world.[5]

A lengthy legal and political battle followed between the Mexican government and the foreign oil companies. A final move to exert the sovereign intent of Mexico climaxed with the nationalization of the oil industry by President

Lázaro Cárdenas (1934–40) on March 18, 1938.[6] Many demanded that President Franklin D. Roosevelt intervene, yet cooler heads prevailed and in the spirit of FDR's "Good Neighbor" policy for Latin America, the United States decided against any overt invasion of Mexico. Nevertheless, the extensive legal fight was pursued to no avail. Mexico, however, was very cooperative with the United States during World War II by allowing nearly unlimited access to extracted supplies of minerals and petroleum. The European war during the late 1930s and the British blockade of the Atlantic cut off Mexican exports. As Mexican exports to Europe abruptly declined, exports to the United States rose from 67 percent of their total output in 1938 to an astonishing 84 percent by January 1940.[7] John Mason Hart noted in *Empire and Revolution*, "the war needs of the United States in the 1940's dictated that they [Mexico] overlook the hard feedings that came from the struggle to control [oil] fields, mines, and ports.... [T]he Mexican government used the crisis of World War II to re-establish American business operators in the country and at the same time expand exports to the North."[8] And by 1949, concern over Mexico's ability to meet petroleum demand resulted in a select few foreign oil and gas firms being granted limited concessions that allowed for reimbursement of exploration costs and limited participation based on the amount of foreign direct investment; these were further backed by favorable tax treatment.[9]

The battle over the role of foreign involvement has thus been a long struggle with Mexican traditionalists who view any outside investment or assistance as suspicious. One result was the Petroleum Act of 1958, which further defined the scope and intent of Article 27. However, by the late 1980s both the domestic Mexican economy and the implementation of policies in the Carlos Salinas de Gortari administration (1988–94) greatly fueled the domestic demand for PEMEX energy production to keep pace. One element of this new economic era, as well as a manifestation of the rise of globalism, was the membership of Mexico in the General Agreement on Tariffs and Trade (GATT) in July 1986. GATT, more so than NAFTA in 1994, was the most significant event to improve, diversify, and open the country's economy.[10] In restructuring the economy, the Salinas administration sold some 1,155 state-owned companies. Within a few years, annual inflation was reduced from over 150 percent to the 12 percent range. Nevertheless, the oil and gas industry remained firmly closed and in the hands of PEMEX. Foreign direct investment in the broader industrial sector from 1989 to 1993 exceeded $35 billion, fully 40 percent higher than expected. Investors flooded Mexico with FDI in new production facilities, infrastructure, and the Mexican Bolsa. Thus, many touted what seemed to be never-ending growth during the period as the "Mexican Miracle." However, as the economy cooled, capital flight ensued but the demand for petroleum continued.[11]

To address the ongoing demand for petroleum products and electricity requires Mexico to depend on three domestic sources: crude oil and oil by-products, natural gas, and hydro-generation. Historically, the crude oil sector has commanded most of the attention. Mexico produces three grades of crude oil: heavy Maya-22, which is high in sulfur and accounts for over half of total production; light low-sulfur Isthmus-34, which represents 28 percent of production; and extra-light Olmeca-39, which represents about 20 percent of output. With the third largest proven crude oil reserves, behind only the United States and Venezuela in the Western Hemisphere (ninth worldwide) in 2004, Mexico had an estimated "proven, probable and possible" 48 billion barrels of oil reserves. Officially, 18.9 billion barrels comprise actual "proven" reserves.[12]

To date, production in the southern part of Mexico exceeds that in the northern area. Proven reserves in southern Mexico are in a band spreading from the Chicontepec region, in the state of Veracruz, southeastward into the Campeche Bay of the Gulf of Mexico. By 2004, three-quarters of Mexico's oil was produced from shallow water offshore sites in the Campeche Bay. For example, the Cantarell field in the bay produced about 2.3 million barrels per day (bbl/d) of the total Mexican crude production. Due in large part to nitrogen injection, which is intended to increase production by raising reservoir pressure, the Cantarell field witnessed an output increase of over 60 percent from 1994 to 2002. Cantarell accounts for an estimated 70 percent of PEMEX's 3.4 million bbl/d output production of heavy crude and over 35 percent of natural gas. In total, Mexican production is estimated at 3.8 million barrels per day—2.02 million bbl/d of oil is consumed in Mexico and approximately 1.78 million bbl/d in net oil exports.[13]

To maximize production at Cantarell during the past five years, wells are injected with nitrogen from a $1 billion plant owned by a BOC Gases–led consortium. However, the long productive life of this cornerstone of the Mexican petroleum sector is projected to show rapid decline by 2006–07. Repercussions of this decline on the broader Mexican economy could produce a ripple effect in both the Mexican and U.S. economies. While there have been scattered reports of new deepwater discoveries in the Gulf of Mexico, no proof has yet come forth to determine if such a new field would be commercially viable. In the meantime, George Baker, Houston oil consultant, noted that the decline of the Cantarell field, without an immediate new domestic source of oil, is ample concern for caution, "On that one fact lies PEMEX's credit rating, as well as Mexico's sovereign rating, and the whole multiplier effect of the [Mexican] oil industry."[14]

Nevertheless, other major fields such as the Abkatum field in northeastern Tamaulipas along the coastal areas have been largely underdeveloped. While production in proven fields has been consistent, the opposite is evident with regard to refining capacity and the development of new fields. The irony of the Mexican energy sector is that due to limited refinery capacity, Mexico must import one-quarter of its gasoline and diesel, while at the same time Mexico is a leading supplier of crude—about 1.6 million barrels per day or 16 percent of total U.S. crude imports—to the United States. Saudi Arabia has been the

Table 3-1 Mexico's Petroleum Refineries

Refinery	Location (Estado)	Capacity (thousands of b/d)		
		Distillation	Catalytic Cracking	Catalytic Reforming
Salina Cruz	Oaxaca	330	80	50
Tula	Hidalgo	320	80	65
Salamanca	Guanajuato	245	00	25
Cadereyta	Queretero	275	65	20
Minatitlán	Veracruz	200	40	31
Ciudad Madero	Tamaulipas	195	43	35
Total		1,565	368	226

Source: EID/DOE; Pennwell and North America Energy Working Group
Note: Pemex controls 50% of a refinery in Deer Park, Texas.

number one provider of crude to the United States, followed by Venezuela then Mexico, over the past two decades. Thus, one prime question is the level at which refinery operations in Mexico, along with imports, can keep pace with urban and industrial growth. Scattered blackouts experienced between 1998 and 2004 were a manifestation of further problems that can be expected over the next decade due to the shortfall of not only refining but also infrastructure requirements for additional pipelines, transmission lines, and power plants. An example of the critical nature of the situation is accentuated by the fact that while rich in natural gas reserves in southern Mexico, inadequate infrastructure prevents supplying the central population centers of the country—Mexico City, Toluca, Zacatecas, Guadalajara—as well as the four highly industrialized and urban centers in the four states in the north, primarily located in the cities of Hermosillo, Chihuahua, Torreón and the region around Monterrey. Hence, Mexico is a net importer of natural gas from the United States and will be so well beyond 2015.[15]

Refinery capacity is hampered by outdated facilities. In 2004, six refineries had a distillation capacity of 1.73 million bbl/d. PEMEX has indicated an extensive need to modernize to increase capacity; however, even an increase of 15 percent in production between 2003 and 2008 will not keep pace with demand. Mexico imports over 120,000 bbl/d of high-octane fuels and blending components, and still supplies remain inadequate to address the long-term needs of the economy. In addition to an estimated $20 billion to improve existing refineries, the Mexican Energy Ministry has noted the need for two or three new plants by 2010. Either new refineries will need to be added, at a lag time of three to five years per facility, or Mexico will need to drastically increase imports of refined crude products and natural gas.[16] One key to meeting the shortfall is the decision by PEMEX to dramatically increase the amount of Maya crude. Maya is "heavy" crude with a very high sulfur content,

Table 3-2 Western Hemisphere Oil Capacity

	Oil Reserves billions/b	Net Oil Exports barrels/day	Type of Crude	Exports to U.S. barrels/day	Oil's Share of Export Revenue
Mexico	18.9	1.78 million	Maya and Isthmus	1,569,000	10%
Venezuela	77.8	2.25 million	Tiajuana Light	1,183,000	80%
Equador	4.6	293,000	Oriente	139,000	44%
Colombia	1.8	299,206	Caño Limón	166,000	26%
Argentina	2.9	326,000	—	54,000	8%
Brazil	8.5	°net importer of 240,000 barrels/day	—	50,000	N/A

Source: Energy Information Administration, 2003/2004 data

which requires the addition of coking units as well as expanding the capacity for fluidized catalytic cracking—the results of these upgrades to increase the production of high-octane gasoline and light cycle oil. The United States in 2003 was a net importer of oil from Latin America to include 1,569,000 barrels per day of crude from Mexico, second only to Saudi Arabia at 1,726,000 bbl/ per day. Mexico's revenue from oil exports accounts for about a third of the federal budget. The formidable task of increasing low-sulfur fuel has long-range environmental ramifications. Major trade-offs will affect the speed and quality of domestic fuel production. For example, coker diesel is high in sulfur and low in cetane, thus upgrading refineries will incur substantial capital expenditures. Furthermore, Mexico is working to reduce the amount of natural gas that is lost due to flaring, while at the same time planning to drill over eighty new producing wells by 2011.[17]

Aware of the need to provide an ever-increasing demand for infrastructure to augment Mexico's industrial expansion and urban growth, the Mexican Congress in 1992 amended the constitution to attract direct foreign investment and allow limited private generation of electric power.[18] Providing adequate electrical power to sustain even current levels of growth is problematic. During the 1990s alone, electricity consumption increased an incredible 60 percent. Nationally, Mexico's average electricity demand is projected to grow 6 to 8 percent annually through 2010, and in some areas in northern Mexico, such as the regions around industry-intense Monterrey, Torreón, and Saltillo, annual demand rate growth could exceed 15 percent. Thus, the intent of the 1992 constitutional modification was to encourage private independent power producers to build generation facilities. However, there was one major limitation: all power produced must be sold by the Federal Electricity Commission (CFE) and regulated by the CRE or Energy Regulation Commission, both state-owned power agencies, at a fixed

Table 3-3 Global Oil Production Forecast (Mn b/d)

	2000	2005	2010	2015	2020
OECD:					
United States	9.03	8.72	8.87	9.71	9.95
Canada	2.74	3.01	3.20	3.37	3.55
Mexico	3.54	4.08	4.24	4.39	4.44
OECD Europe	7.06	7.33	7.20	6.92	6.65
Other OECD	0.98	0.93	0.92	0.90	0.88
Developing Countries					
South and Central America	3.78	4.19	4.82	5.58	6.48
Pacific Rim	2.31	2.62	2.63	2.59	2.55
OPEC	30.93	35.15	40.78	48.32	57.46
Other Developing Countries	4.96	5.38	6.25	7.23	8.38
Eurasia					
Former Soviet Union	7.83	9.67	12.02	13.72	14.89
Eastern Europe	0.24	0.28	0.30	0.33	0.36
China	3.26	3.09	3.07	3.05	3.02
Total Non-OPEC	45.73	49.30	53.52	57.80	61.12
Total Production	*76.66*	*84.46*	*94.31*	*106.12*	*118.58*

Source: EIA/USDOE

price. Private operators were prohibited from selling directly to end-users. Thus, Mexico is far removed from any U.S.-style deregulation scheme. Among the first large-scale generation of the private electrical plants were contracts awarded by the Mexican government to Canada's TransAlta to build and operate a 259 MWE gas-fired plant in Chihuahua and a contract with Iberdrola of Spain to build a 1,036 MWE power plant near the port of Altamira in Tamaulipas. While the first decade of private production generated only 5,000 megawatts of capacity, it is expected that over twenty-five such plants will be needed to meet the minimum electrical needs by 2010.[19]

The issue is how much and how fast the Mexican government will open the energy section to private foreign investment. An initial step to harness the near-absolute control of PEMEX was the partial divestiture in 1992 of the state con-glomerate into four independent operating divisions: exploration and production, natural gas and basic petrochemical, refining, and secondary petrochemicals. Following passage of the revised foreign investment law in December 1993 the wave of privatization during the Salinas administration expanded the inter-pretation of competitiveness and further defined rules for foreign direct invest-ment. Additional legislation in 1995, outlined in the Reglamento de Gas Natural, created the CRE to regulate the privatization process in electricity and natural gas, as well as open private sector investment in the storage, transportation and distribution of natural gas. In terms of the laws' impact on government-owned

Table 3-4 Natural Gas Production and Net Imports

Indigenous Production (MTOE)	1995	2000	2010	2020
OECD North America (including Mexico)	592	674	799	478
OECD Europe	199	222	276	238
OECD Pacific	31	54	87	68
Transition Economies	585	631	882	1316
China	17	30	57	78
Rest of world (excluding Mexico)	396	486	795	1630
World total	1819	2098	2895	3807
Net Imports (MTOE)				
OECD North America (including Mexico)	−2	−2	61	526
OECD Europe	104	153	232	386
OECD Pacific	42	42	42	74
Transition economies	−74	−108	−173	−363
China	0	0	0	0
Rest of world (excluding Mexico)	−76	−91	−168	−629
World total	−6	−6	−6	−6

Source: IEA

PEMEX, the national energy agency maintains a state monopoly over the gas upstream sector under the new law, with midstream and downstream segments now completely open to the private sector, as long as the private sector firms are not engaged in more than one function. These actions, which include thirty-year licenses determined by competitive bid, have resulted in the natural gas sector being the least regulated energy subsector in Mexico. It is hoped that these changes do not prove to be too little, too late. Thus, to many analysts, natural gas—with proven reserves of 15 trillion cubic feet (Tcf)—is of even greater concern given the fact that the current production is about 4.8 billion cubic feet per day (Bcfd), and demand by 2006–07 is expected to reach over 7 Bcfd.[20]

A great deal is at stake to ensure the economic viability of Mexico as well as stable relations with the United States. The gradual deregulation of the natural gas industry since 1995 will prove to be the most significant event in the evolution of the modern Mexican energy sector. Both urban growth and industrial expansion have resulted in predictions of rolling blackouts and a crippling power crisis as early as 2006, if improvements are not made.[21] A shortage of pipelines running from the gas-rich south to the central and northern population centers has forced Mexico to flare gas. An estimated $2 billion worth of natural gas was burned off oil wells between 1995 and 2000. A secondary concern is the need for additional transmission lines. The impact of the shortage of natural gas became acute by 1999–2000 as Mexico doubled imports of natural gas from the United States. The demand for natural gas is not limited to Mexico, as is evident by the fact that world demand for natural gas is growing faster than the demand for oil. And worldwide natural gas output is not expected to peek until beyond 2020.[22]

Increasingly cross-border movement of natural gas along the Texas-Mexico section of the border will rise to record levels during the next two decades. In spite of the fact that only a few pipelines and transmission lines span the U.S.–Mexico border, efforts will grow to integrate energy supplies between Mexico, the United States, and Canada. Greater integration between the United States and Mexico will primarily benefit Mexico. Such economic cooperation has received a mixed response from U.S. states bordering Mexico, and an interconnected north-south power grid has been opposed for years in California.[23] In contrast, the Texas Railroad Commission, the key state agency regulating all matters concerning the oil and gas industries, has endeavored to cut red tape in order to expand gas line capacity to Mexico. Three Texas border counties—Webb, Zapata, and Hidalgo—have averaged over 900 million cubic feet of annual natural gas production. Texas has the largest concentration of gas reserves in the United States, estimated to be in excess of 42 trillion cubic feet.

The first significant export of natural gas from the United States to Mexico began in 1997 through the Texas-to-Monterrey pipeline. By 2003, PEMEX connected with fifteen cross-border gas transfer stations to include Tijuana, Mexicali, Naco, Ciudad Juarez, Samalayuca (south of Juarez), Piedras Negras, Arguelles (Coral and P & F), and two lines (Tennessee and Tetco) in Reynosa.[24] In mid-2002, capacity of these cross-border lines more than doubled to 140 billion cubic feet from 1990 exports. The locations of Naco, Samalayuca, Tetco, and Tennessee are being enlarged for a combined total of 275 mmpcd. And to address expected import demand by 2006, three new pipelines are in the planning stage to add 1,170 mmpcd of capacity—nearly doubling cross-border exports.[25]

Table 3-5 U.S.–Mexico Border Electrical Power Interconnections

Location	KV	MV
Miguel–Tijuana	230	204
Imperial Valley–La Rosita	230	204
El Paso–Juarez (2 locations)	230	200
Eagle Pass–Piedras Negras	138	36
Laredo–Nuevo Laredo	138	100
Falcon–Falcon	138	80
Brownsville–Matamoros	138	120

Source: NAE Working Group

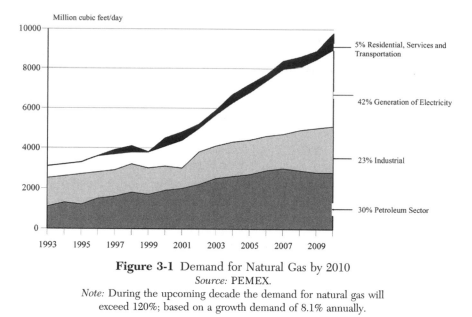

Million cubic feet/day

5% Residential, Services and Transportation

42% Generation of Electricity

23% Industrial

30% Petroleum Sector

Figure 3-1 Demand for Natural Gas by 2010
Source: PEMEX.
Note: During the upcoming decade the demand for natural gas will
exceed 120%; based on a growth demand of 8.1% annually.

The U.S. Department of Energy has expressed concern with the projected rapid demand and has concluded production plans in Mexico are failing to keep pace: "Even with an ambitious development program and the expectation that gas production will increase by an average of about 9 percent annually through 2010, Mexico will still only be able to supply about 80 percent of its growing domestic needs by 2010."[26] For example, the electrical sector consumption of natural gas in Mexico is expected to double from 1,358 million cubic feet per day (mmcf/d)—or about 29 percent of total natural gas consumption—to 2,791 mmcf/d in 2006, an estimated 36–40 percent of consumption. Thus, in spite of large oil and gas reserves, Mexico is projected to be a net gas importer well past 2020.

What are the alternatives for the generation of additional domestic energy? Currently, Mexico has about 1.3 billion short tons of recoverable coal reserves and generates 4 percent of total energy needs from coal. Coal resources are generally low in quality due to high ash content as well as less economical to mine yearly. It is estimated that 70 percent of the Mexican coal is anthracite and bituminous, and 30 percent is lignite and sub-bituminous. A majority of the coal is in the northern state of Coahuila south of the U.S.–Mexico border. Coal is used in both industrial coke ovens and to a limited degree to generate electricity. Furthermore, Mexico imports coal from the United States, Canada, and Colombia. Total yearly consumption of coal, both domestic and imported, has averaged 13 million short tons.

A second alternative is hydroelectric power. While there are no major river systems within Mexico, a network of some thirty-five small and mostly outdated hydroelectric plants operated by CFE produce 10,000 megawatts, or about 20–25 percent (depending on drought conditions) of total electricity in the country. CFE has estimated hydro potential at over 40,000 mega watts electric (MWE). Arid conditions, budget shortfalls, requirements to retrofit old hydro plants, and environmental concerns are unlikely to add adequate new hydro capacity except in far southern states of Chiapas, Veracruz and Oaxaca—miles from consumers. And Mexico has a lone saltwater-cooled nuclear power plant at Alto Lucero in the state of Veracruz rated at 674 MWE. Electricity is directly linked to the well-being of the Mexican economy. The demand could quickly outstrip production given the projection that over the next decade, net operating capacity would have to increase by over 50 percent to satisfy demand. The OECD is very candid in its assessment of the critical resource: "without an in-depth reform of the electrical sector, power shortages are likely to occur in the coming years and hamper economic growth."[27]

The challenge for Mexico in the area of energy will be the degree to which a six-decade-old dinosaur like PEMEX—in fact the embodiment of Article 27— can be modified to first appease the traditional left, who invoke nationalism as a response to any foreign investment efforts in the oil and gas sector, while second, allowing the development of a framework to insure adequate energy for a growing nation. Salinas began the initial efforts in the early 1990s to privatize the broader Mexican economy, yet other than a partition of PEMEX, little change followed. Privatization of the electrical energy sector was the only measurable change to the energy sector that was passed on to the Ernesto Zedillo administration (1994–2000). Strapped with the 1995–96 recovery following the radical devaluation of the peso in December 1994, Zedillo held the line on privatization, yet provoked little change at PEMEX. In 2000, the optimism of the Fox administration's ability to address the energy sector was voiced in the pre-inaugural weeks to the business sectors in Mexico, Canada, and the United States and followed with the appointment of Raul Munoz Leos, formerly president of Dupont de México, to head PEMEX.[28] Taking over the helm of the 100,000-plus-employee icon of Mexican nationalism, Munoz outlined an estimated $19 billion strategy to address the role of PEMEX in the upcoming decade as well as the critical need to enhance the development of the Mexican energy sector. Munoz noted the success and ultimate impact would depend on three main goals:

- enhance, expand, and strengthen PEMEX's operations to maximize extraction of current-proven reserves, to include primary emphasis on light crude and natural gas; exploration to date has been insufficient and underdeveloped;
- in order to continue to be a recognized player in the global energy arena, the highest international standards need to be adopted to insure cost effective efficiency—to include enhancement and development of the best technology, improved management practices, and the upgrade

of all facilities; without increased production in existing operations the nation will fall further behind in the efforts to keep pace with demand;
- reform the existing regulatory framework to allow for more operating flexibility, increased investment, and capacity—"change" will be needed at a faster pace to maintain transparency and competitiveness—transparency and controls to address a legacy of corruption and embezzlement of funds, contract kickbacks, and bogus supplier contracts.[29]

While change within PEMEX is at best incremental, a prime test for both the oil giant and the Fox administration will be how to address the timely strategy outlined by Munoz. Time will only tell if the plan outlined by Munoz will bring change and results, given the fact he was asked to resign in early November 2004 and replaced by Luis Ramirez Corzo. A barometer of change and transparency with both the "spirit" of Article 27 and the pending urgency for energy sustainability depend on how a new scheme known as *contratos de servicios multiples*, "multiple service contracts" (MSC), will be developed to attract foreign direct investment in the energy sector while providing a comfort level for the outside firms to return to Mexico. Concern with future production is paramount as Ramirez soon learned the scope of the problems at PEMEX and has called on lawmakers to open the energy sector to private investment. While a broad base of service contracts has been performed by foreign companies, the MSC is intended to attract a cutting-edge technology that was allowed in Article 6 of Mexico's Oil Law of 1958, the use of "contractors" for the purpose of enhancing operational efficiency, as long as the contractors acquire no interest in the production and are *not* paid in kind.[30]

The primary test of MSC contracting falls in three key areas of the Mexican energy sector: enhancement of existing fields, expansion of refining and distribution (pipelines) capacity, and the specific development of one of the largest national gas fields in the hemisphere—Cuenca de Burgos. Located in the northeast portion of the state of Tamaulipas and bordered on the north by the Rio Grande and the Gulf of Mexico to the east, Burgos is estimated due to the likelihood of having a very high drilling success and an

Table 3-6 Services Permitted Under MSCs

1. Drilling	8. Production Engineering
2. Logging	9. Reservoir Engineering
3. Stimulation	10. Geological Engineering
4. Cone Analysis	11. Facilities Design and Construction
5. Seismic Processing	12. Environmental Studies
6. Permit Administration	13. Facilities and Wells Maintenance
7. Nuceli Analysis	14. Geologic Modeling

Source: PEMEX.

initial production yield of 1 trillion cubic feet of natural gas to be completed by 2006. To attract both the investment and technology needed to maximize the development of the field, it is anticipated that the extension area will be divided into eight to twelve "blocks" or sectors, each of approximately 30–50 square kilometers. Mexico spends some $14 billion yearly on imported gasoline, natural gas, and petrochemicals due to shortfalls in domestic production.

CONCLUSION

The spirit of the Mexican Revolution of 1910 included many dynamics, of which national control over land and minerals was a focal point—hence, the notion that hydrocarbon belongs to the state. The backlash to the excessive foreign investment activities in Mexico during the Díaz administration was addressed in the 1917 Constitution. The intent of articles to control Mexico's natural resources was well founded a century ago but does not reflect the reality and dynamics of the energy sector that has emerged in the early twenty-first century. Mexico has changed. A once very rural nation, Mexico is yearly more urban and more industrial. No longer an insular economy, Mexico has developed into a leading export-import platform. Demand for electricity produced by natural gas and the location and extraction of crude oil will be the prime focus of Mexico's efforts to sustain growth and urban tranquility. These efforts will daily become more complicated and competitive with the energy demands worldwide, particularly those of China.[31]

Exploration of, as well as sovereignty over, the natural resources of Mexico is not the question—it is an established fact. The challenge is how to modify the letter of Article 27, as well as portions of Article 28 concerning "strategic areas," while maintaining the spirit of the law in order to effectively develop the needed energy resources over the next two decades and beyond. Timing and effective implementation of a resource development plan for Mexico is of the essence. To not act is not a solution. The nationalist left, industrialists, urban centers, and PEMEX will need to develop prudent collaboration to avoid massive disruptions in the basic fiber of the Mexican economy—of which energy resources have become the pivotal component. However, to date the Fox administration's efforts at energy reform have been shouted down and ignored in the fractious Mexican Congress. The *Economist* summed up the problem, "Unable or unwilling to free the oil industry, Mexico's politicians are flogging their cash cow into the ground."[32]

Oil-rich Mexico monthly falls further behind in taking adequate measures to maximize efficiency in the energy sector. Current production capacity, even if increased, would be ill prepared to meet demand due to a significant shortage in refining and pipeline capacity. This, coupled with a tremendous demand for natural gas has major consequences for both Mexico's stability as well as U.S.–Mexico relations. The impact of oil should never be underestimated:

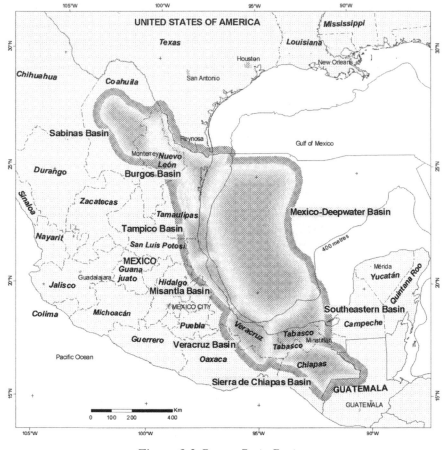

Figure 3-2 Burgos Basin Region
Source: Wood Mackenzie.

Whenever petroleum and PEMEX become foreign policy issues...Mexicans
manifest extreme sensitivity to questions of sovereignty, economic independence,
and national dignity. This does not mean that Mexican nationalists are inherently
"irrational" and that they long so idealistically for sovereignty and independence
as to disregard practical economics and shun pragmatic choices. Quite the contrary. Economists within Mexico's government have conducted detailed analyses
of the effects of Mexico's petroleum development and revenue earning on very
practical issues, such as the inflation rate, excess liquidity, the balance of payments, and the overall "absorptive capacity" of Mexico's economy. There has
been widespread concern to promote economic development and social progress
throughout Mexico. But these practical issues are ultimately conditioned by the
fateful triad of nationalist ideals.[33]

To expect increased construction of pipelines and transmission lines as well as the importation of gasoline products and liquefied natural gas to answer the shortfall is a major fallacy. The legacy of the change ushered in by the Fox administration (and the PAN party) is based largely on the new political dynamics in Mexico that has been affected by the rise of "more" democratic governance. A divided national legislature following decades of control by the PRI has resulted in fragmented small parties and factions within the Senate and House of Deputies struggling to forge a solution to modify Articles 27 and 28. Fox was unable to open up the state-owned energy conglomerates, and it is expected that his successor in 2006—regardless of party—will be unable to crack a deadlocked congress. A continued strict interpretation of and adherence to Article 27 (and any other legal trappings that prevent development of the domestic energy resources) could leave Mexico in the dark. Timely solutions to increase production of oil, natural gas, and electricity in the next five-to-ten years will avert drastic reactionary measures in the future. One old sage mused, How dark does it need to be in Mexico before the lights come on?

Benchmarks and Trends

- Mexico's demand for domestic energy will outpace produced supply (not reserves) both in the short- and long-term. The population in Mexico is expected to grow at a pace of approximately one million per year. With a population of 100 million in 2000, by 2020 the population will range from 118 to 122 million. The growing population, given the fact that some 50 percent of the population in 2000 was under twenty-one years of age, will result in increased strain on the urban centers nationwide as well as the growing border towns.[34]

    Impact: Without extensive efforts to expand all aspects of the energy extraction, transportation and generation of electricity could cause extensive government fiscal shortfall and social unrest. The viability of the Mexican energy sector and utility infrastructure is critical to the economic future of the county. Any prolonged shortfall of unrest would result in the flight of investment capital, as well as expanded illegal immigration, to the United States.

- A power shortage in Mexico will affect the United States most specifically the cross-border twin communities in the four border states of California, Arizona, New Mexico, and Texas. The two thousand miles of border is expected to be one of the fastest growing regions in the hemisphere and can ill handle increased urbanization pressures. Furthermore, the Southwest United States and most of northern Mexico are arid areas, so the issue of water along the border, and more specifically the impact on the Rio Grande, is expected to be critical to the sustainability of the region's growth.

Impact: Mexico, more so than any other oil-producing nation, could have a tremendous impact on the available level of the U.S. Strategic Petroleum Reserve.[35] Nevertheless, one irony is that as the demand for oil becomes greater, so too will the demand for water. And the time could come when a gallon of potable water will cost more than a gallon of gasoline.

- The impact of oil to U.S. security cannot be underestimated. Mexico's petroleum resources, as well as the policies that are developed over the next decade are vital to the interest of the United States. And as time passes—given the on-and-off-again dialogue over issues such as water, immigration, trade, drugs, and oil—U.S.–Mexico relations (while always important) will tend to be both more parochial and more complex.

Impact: Mexico is not just another oil-producing nation. U.S.–Mexico relations, in addition to becoming more complex, could also be strained as both nations endeavor to address the energy dynamics of the next two decades. And in sum, it is well known that sensitive issues between neighbors must be balanced against security and the sustainability of the region.

4

≈□≺▽≻□≈

MEXICO VERSUS CHINA

China is sucking away Mexico's jobs. Globalization is entering a fateful new stage, in which the competitive perils intensify for low-wage developing countries much like the continuing pressures on high-wage manufacturing workers in the United States and other advanced economies. In the "race to the bottom," China is defining the new bottom.
                                                                —William Greider

The next century will belong to China, and it will become the first ancient culture to rise, fall and rise again.
                                                                —J. Yify Lin

THE GLOBAL TRADE landscape changes daily. The globalization of products, services and markets is having a profound impact on all sectors of the world economy.[1] One driving force of this trend is the relationship between Mexico and China and its influence on the U.S. economy. In every community across America some 40 percent of all finished products (retail as well as industrial), sourced components, and assembly plant parts have a direct or indirect link with Mexico and/or China. For economic development and public policy leaders, it is critical to appreciate the dynamics of the Mexico-China relationship in order to understand and gauge the shifting realities that could affect the competitiveness of the U.S. domestic economy. No more sweeping change occurred than that of the accession of China to the World Trade Organization (WTO) on September 17, 2001. And in the process, it is most ironic that Mexico, the nation with the greatest number of bi- and multi-lateral trade agreements, was up until the last moment vastly opposed to China's membership in the worldwide trade body. In fact, it was because of Mexico's emergence as a major manufacturing platform, as well as its external trade expertise through the 1990s and into the turn of the century, that it clearly perceived China as a long term threat. The Mexicans' arguments and objections were not without merit.[2]

The darling of investors during the early 1990s, the "Mexico Miracle" had been touted as the model for the emerging markets and economies of the so-called "newly industrialized" nations. The model of Mexico, with its 2,000-mile border with the United States and thus quick access to the vast North American market, has an advantage the rest of the emerging world does not have. Mexico inked the North American Free Trade Agreement (NAFTA), survived a radical peso devaluation in late 1994, made its political leap into a broader acceptance of democracy—witnessed by the election of Vicente Fox in 2000—and by the turn of the century began gradually to reap the benefits of its transition to a more open economy, undergirded by a steady inflow of foreign direct investment that averaged $12 billion plus per year (not including annual remittances of over $14 billion) from 1996 to 2004. NAFTA, for all its preapproval hype, proved a major success for Mexico—however, not exactly in the terms that anti-NAFTA opponents in the early 1990s anticipated and feared.[3]

By the mid-1990s, Mexico, in spite of the late-1994 devaluation and the stagnation that followed during the first half of 1995, was on track to becoming a more open economy as well as more diversified at its grass roots.[4] According to the Dallas Federal Reserve, the crisis of confidence caused by the devaluation lasted only eight months before a positive economic trend returned—a pleasant surprise given the fact that in previous peso devaluations recovery of the Mexican economy was marked by three-to-five-years of post-devaluation stagnation. On the other hand, the rapid rebound by early 1996 was not without cause. Three decades of foreign investment (including the lost decade of the 1980s and periods of currency fluctuation), annual increases in offshore manufacturing in the maquiladora sector, the benefits of NAFTA, and the ability for domestic Mexican firms to go to foreign capital markets in the United States, Asia, and Europe were all critical to Mexico's stabilization and growth. However, such real world success was a double-edged sword.

Though historically the two nations have had a love-hate relationship, the ties and trade connections between the United States and Mexico have increased dramatically. The fears of the old-line Partido Revolucionario Institucional (PRI) nationalists—in power for over seventy years—that the "giant to the north" was to be dealt with, when possible, on Mexican terms began to dissolve in the wake of trade and commercial interaction which more than doubled from 1995 to 2003. An example of Mexico's concern for its national identity was its relationship with Cuba. For decades, Mexico's often vocal support of Fidel Castro and Cuba, while seemingly more symbolic than substantial, consistently resulted in votes in the Organization of American States (OAS) and United Nations for Cuba and against the United States.[5] This nationalist posturing was clearly intended to send a signal that Mexico could and would act independently of the United States. Strong sentiments in Mexico were gradually replaced during the Salinas administration (1988–94) with near-total abandonment of an insular foreign policy, in favor of a strategy that, while still supportive of Cuba, seeks global interaction via various trade agreements and an aggressive program to attract foreign direct investment. The Zedillo administration (1994–2000) continued a measured pro-Cuba stance, not so much to snub the United States but in fact to explore ways to modify the long-standing courtship. As former U.S. Ambassador Jeffrey Davidow noted in his post-Mexico tenure in Mexico City, the Fox administration's Cuba policy vacillated to the point of confusion.[6]

As a sitting member of the UN Security Council in 2002, President Fox and his then- minister, Jorge Castañeda, looked to reshape the scope of external relations in order to give Mexico an even stronger role globally. A strong peso, which according to some reached "a sustainable edge" during the early years of the Fox administration, resulted in a perception by some that Mexico would reach a level of "convergence" with the U.S. economy.[7] Closer economic ties were extolled as Mexico became the second leading trading partner of the United States—with two-way cross-border trade exceeding $240 billion in 2002—behind the economically stagnant Canada and ahead of trade with recession-prone Japan. However, not all political factions in Mexico were in agreement. Opposition parties led by the PRI and the Partido de la Revolucion Democratica (PRD) were not so quick to tout a closer U.S.–Mexico relationship. An inaugural forecast by Fox that the Mexican economy was expected to grow at a 7 percent rate proved optimistic as the U.S. economy cooled in the wake of the dot-com meltdown. The political opposition remained highly skeptical due to their dislike of the Fox administration's "appearing" to get too close to the United States. A critical low point in the U.S.–Mexico relationship was reached when Mexico's representative on the UN Security Council, Aguilar Zinser, voted against support of U.S. efforts in 2003 to enter Iraq and bring down the tyrant Saddam Hussein. Notwithstanding the critical juxtaposition between the two countries, a broad mutual cooperation, rather than antagonism, will define the relationship for decades to come.[8]

In essence, the young Turks and technocrats of the Salinas-Zedillo era endeavored to control—as best they could—foreign interaction on their terms and make it as favorable to Mexico as possible. Thus Mexico, even with more open markets and the shift to a more active multiparty system that will prevail in the next two decades, should never be taken lightly in terms of its nationalist sentiment. Closer commercial ties do not always match the domestic Mexican political agenda that will drive the PRI and its allies to be even more vocal in the approaching 2006 presidential elections. And there should not be excessive expectations about the links between open markets and the fostering of more "democratic" institutions. The roots of this transition began in earnest shortly after Mexico's July 1986 entry into the General Agreement on Tariffs and Trade (GATT)—the precursor to the World Trade Organization (WTO)—with membership a result of strongly recommended industrial political changes following a number of disruptive peso devaluations. What followed economically for Mexico was a new era of spectacular inflows of FDI and growth. In terms of global commercial interaction in the 1990s, Mexico used an aggressive trade regime approach that in most cases had it on the offensive. For the most part, the trade linkages during the late 1980s and 1990s did not involve Asia in general or China in particular, yet did result in Mexico's concluding trade agreements with over two dozen nations.[9]

MEXICO GOES GLOBAL

The first significant roots of Mexican global outreach can be traced to the death of the Bracero Program, a binational agricultural workers' arrangement between Mexico and the United States. Initiated by the Roosevelt administration during World War II as a means to increase the labor supply during the planting and harvest seasons in the United States, this program proved critical to America's demand for higher wartime production. The cross-border agricultural worker program continued basically unchallenged until abruptly halted by the Kennedy administration in 1963. U.S. labor unions added pressure on the grounds that the Mexican workers, who at the peak of the program in the early 1960s numbered about 450,000 (some seven times higher than the wartime peak), infringed upon U.S. jobs. This pressure occurred even though organized U.S. labor, except in the meat-packing and poultry industries, had little to do with day-to-day agriculture. The result was that both American growers, who depended on the workers, and consumers were penalized, as well as the Mexican laborers. And given the increasingly more complex concerns with U.S.–Mexico immigration issues, the era of the Bracero Program now seems all but lost.[10]

Mexico, it was felt, had to develop a means to provide a substitute program to absorb the lost jobs. In fact, on the heels of what we now know was the first wave of Mexican globalization, Mexico City hosted the 1968 Olympics, the Mexican administration of President Gustavo Díaz Ordaz (1964–70) sent teams of government officials and businessmen to Asia to investigate various offshore manufacturing methods and means to enhance and attract both new manufacturing and global FDI that were emerging in South Korea, Japan, Taiwan, and New Zealand. The efforts to expand global production resulted in the creation by Mexico of the Border Industrialization Plan (BIP) in 1965. Very narrow in scope due to existing concerns at the time with both "foreign intrigue" in the affairs of the nation and the role of the United States, the original offshore, or twin-plant, program was very limited in execution, but not in its eventual broader intent. The underlying goals of the BIP were basically threefold: determine a means to create jobs, attract direct foreign investment (to include a means to obtain much-needed foreign exchange), and absorb any and all technological expertise that was possible to expand the country's domestic industrial base.

Under the BIP, foreign-owned plants were allowed immunity from most Mexican import duties. Correspondingly, this program was further enhanced by U.S. tariff schedules (TSUS) under the reimport chapter known as "806.30/ 807.00," thus allowing offshore firms to avoid having to pay import duties on the value added to their products due to valuation additions created by "offshore" assembly of parts and/or raw materials and labor. Furthermore, production sites and plants of the initial BIP firms were limited to a narrow band along the U.S.–Mexico border and foreign land ownership was very restricted. By the end of the 1960s, maquiladoras were principally located in Reynosa, Nuevo Laredo, Ciudad Juarez, and Tijuana. The government man dated limit of 49 percent foreign property ownership remained in force. During the early years from 1965 to 1975, no one could have envisioned the success of what became known as the maquiladora program.[11]

Since the early 1970s, there have been over a dozen changes in the Mexican offshore investment laws as well as a new layer of international accords such as GATT-WTO and NAFTA that have modified the maquiladora sector. Restricting the maquila laws was primarily to define taxation laws on intercompany transfers and expansion of operations into the interior of Mexico. In its sum total, by the late 1990s, the maquila industry was the number one hard currency generator in Mexico, surpassing revenues generated by both oil exports and tourism. Mexico's maquila experience was vital to its gradual steps toward globalization and abandonment of bankrupt policies such as the import substitution industrialization (ISI) regime of the 1950s and 1960s.[12]

In concept and in fact, the maquila industry envisioned in the late 1960s was one of labor-intense low-paying jobs. While this effort was intended (at least in spirit) to make up for the demise of the Bracero program, it was in fact, in terms of jobs created for the displaced Mexican farmworkers, a poor substitute. Up until the mid-1990s, a majority of the maquila jobs were filled by women and very few, if any, by former farmworkers from the Bracero era. Taking advantage of tariff laws as well as abundant and inexpensive labor, foreign companies were able to do piecework and/or assemble and reexport the component parts back to the parent company in the United States for final assembly and packaging. Driven by the global cost of doing business and the increasing need to lower costs and increase profit margins, Mexico gradually became a tremendous complement and/or option for companies looking for economical and cost-effective high-volume offshore production. Herein lies the paradox as noted by James Gerber, "If the maquiladora sector indeed represents purely comparative advantage-based development, then it is simple to predict the evolution of the industry. As Mexico workers gain skills, incomes are likely to rise, and unskilled assembly production will move to a lower cost environment."[13]

As the years passed, the Mexican workforce proved to be both highly trainable and cost-effective for high-volume repetitive production operations. As the cross-border infrastructure into Mexico by road and rail improved and more attractive investment laws were added, foreign firms flocked south of the border. The number of offshore foreign plants along the border in Mexico

Table 4-1 Top Ten Mexican Multinational Firms

1. Cemex (cement)	6. Imsa (diversified)
2. America Moil (telecom)	7. Fcmsa (food and industrial)
3. Maseca (food)	8. Alfa (diversified)
4. Bimbo (food)	9. Vitro (glass)
5. Grupo México (mining)	10. Iusa (diversified)

Source: Expansion and Mexico Watch

grew from 160 operations with 20,300 employees in 1970, to 1,789 nationwide with 460,283 employees by 1990, and in late-2001 peaked at over 3,700 with an employment of 1.2 million workers. By 2002, the high-water mark of maquila operations, virtually all of the Fortune 1000 (approximately seven hundred companies) had a portion of their operations, production components, or affiliates in Mexico. The proximity to the growing U.S. market has been an overwhelming comparative competitive advantage that the newly industrialized countries (NICs) of Asia could not replicate—without locating operations in Mexico.[14] However, it became apparent that due to a combination of factors—including accession to GATT, NAFTA, changes in the foreign investment and tax laws, the impact of foreign direct investment (FDI), and technology transfer to Mexico—the role and scope of the maquila industry's competitiveness had begun to gradually change. After a slump in the 2002–03 period following the mini-recession in the United States, maquila operators dropped in number to 2,900 with monthly employment averaging about 1 million. Furthermore, tremendous progress had affected the competitive advantage offered via the foreign maquila operations due to the gradual expansion of the domestic Mexican industrial base.[15]

Technology transfer via the maquilas, as well as the growth and development of indigenous Mexican firms, gradually changed the nature of production worker skills and demands on labor as well as new intensive automated technology and processes. Examples of emerging Mexican companies that made major strides via the direct and indirect exposure to foreign technology transfer include Grupo IMSA (steel), Grupo CARSO (industrial), Grupo Alfa (diversified), Cemex (cement), Vitro (glass), and Apasco (cement). Mexican cement manufacturers, for example, own more cement plants worldwide—fifteen of the fifty-one major operations—than their counterparts in any other country and account for 34 percent of the world's cement production.[16] While labor costs remained relatively low in terms of the U.S. and European market rates, the domestic and foreign-owned plants in Mexico were gradually moving toward more skills-intensive value-added jobs. The move was due in large measure to the increased specialization of machinery and production processes as well as new means to compensate workers, such as pay-for-knowledge. In essence, fewer workers were needed, while output increased due to the changing technology, allowing in most cases both high quality and cost effectiveness.[17]

PRODUCTION SHIFTS

The shift to more high-tech manufacturing operations is evident at such multinational firms in Mexico as Modine, Visteon, Emerson, Scientific Atlanta, AT&T, GM, Delphi, Rheem, and Caterpillar. For example, efforts to enhance both production and quality were augmented by pay-for-knowledge programs in place of old-style longevity-seniority models. While longevity is considered for certain benefits and vacations, the stress gradually shifted to knowledge-based quality production. This shift to a values-based management style is a clear indication of ongoing—yet incremental—changes throughout both the foreign-owned maquilas as well as domestic Mexican operations. One key measurement of the pay-for-knowledge programs is that, while production and quality is expected to be high and rejected parts low (the hallmark of such production enhancement systems based on "lean" manufacturing), the average hourly pay is often double the average pay in other old-style plants. Furthermore, this compensation model may be a key element to also reducing employee turnover.[18]

Mexico has known since the early 1990s that as long as investors feel safe and labor remains competitive, it would be attractive to foreign direct investment due in large part to the proximity of the U.S. market and plants in the Midwest. While the FDI remained steady and actually increased over the decade of the 1990s, it became apparent that the low-end labor-intensive jobs were in jeopardy of being lost to other countries. Initially, lower-paying jobs shifted from the U.S.–Mexican border region to southern Mexico. Gradually the exodus of low-wage jobs was global in scope, and not just in Mexico. The transition was primarily in three industry sectors: textiles, electronics, and any low-tech, high-labor assembly jobs (e.g., paper products, packaging material, furniture, toys, or bicycles). While numerous factors are considered in the cost of manufacturing, wages are generally the primary reason for relocating labor-intensive processes. The most volatile and price-sensitive sector has been the textile, low-end electronics, and garment industries. Thus, by the early 1990s, companies began to look for areas of lower wages, minimal industrial restrictions, and adequate infrastructure. In terms of Asia, a production shift occurred as companies flocked to Thailand, Malaysia, and Indonesia. For some labor-intense firms in Mexico, the gradual change was first to the Caribbean Islands, Honduras, and El Salvador, followed by Costa Rica and Nicaragua, and to a lesser extent Guatemala and Panama. By 2003, some 250 offshore operations in Mexico moved to El Salvador. In Honduras, U.S. and Korean firms have established a majority of over two hundred maquilas, with an estimated workforce of one hundred thousand. Thus, much of the shift of low-wage jobs out of Mexico predates both NAFTA and China's WTO membership. Furthermore, as select companies departed Mexico there has been a net positive inflow of new investment to establish new operations as well as expand existing facilities. This is further evidenced by the fact that the number of maquiladoras in Mexico has grown since 1995.[19]

The increase in higher-paying, more technical, jobs was most welcomed in Mexico, yet there was a fear of the impact due to the loss of lower-wage positions. The downturn of the American economy, which appeared in early 2001, signaled a change (in the wake of the 2000–01 dot-com meltdown in the United States) as demand declined for automobiles, textiles, telecom equipment, and electronics. It is important to note that the economic downturn of the United States after the turn of the century and the impact of the sluggish growth in cross-border trade with Mexico predates the September 2001 terrorist attacks on New York and Washington, D.C. Furthermore, Mexico's concern with the entry of China in the WTO also predates these events.[20]

In the eyes of Mexico, China has been the problem primarily of the United States, and (prior to the fall of the Berlin Wall) to a lesser degree, of the old Soviet Union, both in terms of global strategic posturing dating from the Cold War as well as the thawing of commercial relationships with the West. By the 1990s, U.S.-China relationships hinged around the annual review of the "most favored nation" (MFN) status. MFN—fueled primarily by nontrade items such as human rights—dominated discussions that in turn affected and shaped trade policy. The Clinton administration attempted to demystify the MFN concept—which is, despite its name, a nondiscrimination clause—by calling it "permanent normal trade relations." However, China's primary intent, above and beyond MFN, was to be an active member of the WTO. Since the inception of GATT in 1947, China had been shut out of the mainstream of global trade accords. Not until the British transferred Hong Kong back to the Chinese on June 30, 1997 did China launch its final push for WTO membership.[21]

CHINA KNOCKING AT THE DOOR

China has been and will be tremendous competition for both Mexico and the United States. In a book entitled the *Awakening of China*, author W.A.P. Martin boldly proclaimed "China is the theater of the greatest movement now taking place on the face of the globe."[22] Martin's words were penned in 1906, thus predating China's current entry on the world stage. A century would pass before Mexico came face-to-face with China. Mexico's concerns about the impact of China—primarily expressed in its worry that low wages and relatively high productivity could quickly undercut any competitive advantage enjoyed with the U.S. market—were well founded and resulted in efforts to attempt to block WTO membership or at least negotiate for terms that would prevent China from dumping products in Mexico (or the United States) and displacing

Table 4-2 Comparative Economies

	United States		China		Mexico	
GDP	$10,065 bn		$1,159 bn		$618 bn	
Population (million)	300		1,410		110	
Population (percent)						
under 15	21.8%		24.8%		33.8%	
over 60	16.1%		10.1%		6.9%	
Top Three Export	Canada	22.4	United States	20.4	United States	88.7
Destinations (%)	Mexico	13.9	Hong Kong	17.5	Canada	1.9
	Japan	7.9	Japan	16.9	Japan	0.4
Top Three	Canada	19.0	Japan	17.6	United States	67.7
Imports	China	11.5	Taiwan	11.2	Japan	4.8
by Origin	Mexico	11.1	United States	10.8	Canada	2.5

Source: Economist

workers by offering lower wages. A sudden impact on the manufacturing sector and the resulting job loss as well as the potential flight of FDI were and will continue to be very valid concerns.[23]

In less than two decades, China went from essentially no workers in "foreign-owned" domestic manufacturing operations to over 18 million by 2003—more workers than either France or Italy. While most observers in the Western world credit China with both its large land mass and vast population, few realize the potential magnitude of the country's impact not only on trade with the U.S. and Mexico, but also the worldwide implications of a redefined Chinese new millennium version of the "Open Door"—opened and targeted at the world, and hallmarked by an aggressive export-led growth strategy.[24]

For over two centuries, and some argue maybe as many as ten centuries, China has been wrapped in self-imposed isolation. Legends of the "Silk Road" and foreign domination by Mongolian and Manchurian rulers, the numerous waves of Japanese invaders as recently as the early 1940s, and highly resented treaty terms imposed by the Western powers have highly motivated China to assert its goals to become an original equipment manufacturer (OEM) sovereignty today, much like Mexico. China has demonstrated a preference for consolidating power within its own land mass and neglecting favorable trade terms with the rest of the known world. In a strange twist of fate, the first outward contact of Chinese with the Western world was their role in providing labor that built much of the transcontinental railroads in the United States during the 1860s and 1870s, as well as the extensive irrigation systems and railroads in the Valle de Mexicali in northern Mexico from 1890 to 1910.[25] Mexico formally inked diplomatic relations with China in 1889 and reconfirmed relations with the new post–World War II Communist government in 1949.[26]

In the last half-century, China has grudgingly opened itself to the world. Coupled with the forces of Communism and the Cold War through 1989, the fall of the Berlin Wall ended in the collapse of the old Soviet Union in 1991 and unquestionably opened discussions among hard-liners in Beijing and those who saw large commercial possibilities on the future course of interaction with the West. The strategy of China, a nation with a population of over 1.3 billion (China has 160 cities with a population over one million, as compared to ten such metro areas in the U.S.), to reclaim a place on the world stage is marked by contrasting features and dynamics—political, economic, military, and cultural—the world at large has yet to fully grasp.[27]

The very country that will host the 2008 Summer Olympics in Beijing has over 70 million people in abject poverty and another 100 million—equal to the total 2001 population of Mexico—living on less than $1 per day. As the seventh largest economy in the world at the turn of the century, China is currently second only to Japan in Asia. Agriculture still dominates the Chinese domestic economy. One of the many East-West dissimilarities is China's struggle with open market economics and the old line insular Communist planned economy model—so often flaunted, yet so long a domestic failure. The consolidation of political power by sixty-one-year-old Hu Jintao as General Secretary of the Communist Party and President of China on September 19, 2004 at the annual meeting of the Central Communist Party signals the West that commerce and global trade will be key components of China's future. Hu, the former mayor of Shanghai, is keenly aware of the impact of commercial development, FDI, and market access. Boasting over one hundred commercial buildings of over fifty stories and the number two "megaport" in the world behind only Hong Kong (eleven of the top twenty megaports are in Asia, and none are in the Western Hemisphere), the most prominent feature of Shanghai's skyline is the industrial multitude of construction cranes that dot all areas of the city and dock areas.[28]

In retrospect, one of the most pivotal moments for China was the return of Hong Kong and the emergence and creep toward a market economy via the theme, "one country, two systems." Fully aware of the economic, technological, and industrial gains in the West, China could now lay claim and ownership to a true and enduring icon of a free market success. The economic impact and dynamic nature of the few square miles of capitalist Hong Kong was a marvel even the Communist People's Party leadership could not ignore or deny. China wanted entry into the broader global economy via the WTO primarily on its own terms. For example, shortly after the return of Hong Kong, China took its first significant plunge into the world capital markets—which up to that point it had entered on only a very modest scale—by raising

$3.9 billion in offering a mere 10 percent of PetroChina, the world's fourth largest petroleum company. By 2020, China's demand for oil will double to 11 million barrels per day. The irony is that the government-owned firm (PEMEX of Mexico is similarly government-owned) has long been fully overshadowed by China's coal industry (coal that is high in sulfur and thus, prone to pollute), which in 2002 accounted for fully 80 percent of the nation's energy needs.[29]

Fashioned by the aging Dong Xiaoping, architect of China's modern reform era in the wake of the disastrous years under Mao, China in terms of its economy—although not its political structure—turned, albeit gradually, on matters of trade to more western-oriented open market policies.[30] The Four Tigers of Asia were further examples in the area of export-led economic development and growth, attraction of FDI, generation of hard currency, and domestic job creation. During the 1990s, GDP per person rose 5 percent annually in developing countries such as Mexico and South Korea that were opening their economies to international trade and the attraction of FDI. By 2001, the GDP per person in Mexico was over twice the output of China. Thus, China's strategy has been to develop its coastal areas into world-class trade zones called Special Economic Zones (SEZs). Much like the wave of development along the U.S.-Mexican border in the late 1960s and 1970s, to create an investment-friendly region China would foster the new industrialization in an effort to absorb surplus labor migrating from the interior (an ongoing serious problem), encourage technology transfer, and increase FDI. FDI in China increased from a record $52.7 billion in 2002 to over $60 billion in 2004, surpassing the United States as the world's leading recipient of offshore investment. China's export-to-GDP ratio has risen from 2 percent to 25 percent since 1970. In spite of the tremendous FDI, the country has relied on massive government spending on public projects for domestic growth. And in the process, government debt has spiked sharply up.[31]

Table 4-3 Comparative World Economic Rankings

	United States	China	Mexico
Biggest economies	1	2	9
Economic purchasing power	1	2	12
Population ranking	3	1	11
GDP per head	$35,200	$900	$6,150
Largest industrial output	1	3	12
Largest services output	1	7	9
Oil production	2	8	5
Coal production	1	2	n/a
Top consumers of oil	1	3	12

Source: Economist

The model of the Chinese export-processing SEZs is the Pearl River delta region of Guangdong province, including Shenzhen and Guangzhou. Described as the "crown jewel of the Chinese economy," this region has become the fastest growing, largest manufacturing, and most productive region in Asia, accounting for over 40 percent of China's total external trade. During the decade of the 1990s, inflows of FDI increased tenfold as China grew at an average annual rate of 9.7 percent—an average annual rate of over 9 percent over the past twenty-five years. One prime example of China's demand-driven growth is the Chinese tremendous appetite for steel. To meet its needs, China has had an impact on the world's annual 400-million-ton scrap steel market, driving up both demand and prices.[32] David Yergin and Joseph Stanislaw, in their extensive coverage of the impact of globalization in *The Commanding Heights*, note:

> This kind of sustained high-speed growth exceeded anything registered by any of the "Asian miracle" economies. And it was reflected in the changing landscape. Agricultural land was transformed into what seemed an endless boomtown construction site and then into modern high rise cities. Shenzhen itself, once a border post of some thirty thousand, grew to 3 million in less than twenty years. But a border still separates Shenzhen from Hong Kong, one of the original tigers.[33]

The westernization influence on the industrial areas of the Chinese coast has not been without pain and conflict ever since the Treaty Ports of Europe imposed their influence in the 1850s. In spite of the economic activity, hardliners in the Communist Party today routinely express concern about the political impact of expanded foreign contact due to increased FDI. Shanghai and Wenchue, for example, were two enclaves of entrepreneurial communalization long before 1990. With direct access to overseas transport, these two towns in their efforts to develop a broad outward-looking commercial base did not always agree with the central party in Beijing. Not unlike the Mexican nationalists who were concerned about President Fox getting too close to the United States, the old political guard in China were concerned about getting too close to the Western world.[34]

Privatization, or as it is referred to in China, "corporatization" of state-owned companies has been difficult. Many in the Communist Party are concerned about the demise of these inefficient and overstaffed wards of the state due to the potential loss of millions of jobs, as well as the loss of revenue for the central government. Furthermore, the banking system remains underdeveloped and overextended (with an estimated $500 billion in nonperforming loans), corruption persists, reform is needed for the creation of property rights (there is no UCC filing system), and the dismantling of export subsidies will prove controversial in a state-run society. While the Chinese yuan (RMB) is in effect loosely pegged to the U.S. dollar (artificially held at 8.25–8.30 to the dollar), concerns persist with both the dynamics of the world

Table 4-4 Top Ten China Exports, 2003

Rank	Export items	Millions
1	Textile garments	$33,897
2	Automatic data processing machines and units	$20,113
3	Footwear and parts thereof	$11,092
4	Textile yarn, fabrics and make-up articles	$9,056
5	Toys	$5,576
6	Furniture	$5,362
7	Radio telephone sets	$5,289
8	Aquatic products	$2,876
9	Electronic integrated circuits & micro assemblies	$2,651
10	Coal	$2,533

Source: Federal Reserve

markets, in regards to the weakness or strength of the dollar, and the impact on domestic inflation, which has periodically hit China.[35] To maintain stability in the wake of change and foreign influence will be critical as the population has increasing contact with the West and the Internet. The World Wide Web is estimated in 2004 to have less than 10 percent penetration, with usage by some 90 million Chinese. However, while over 50 percent of the population have never used a telephone, China is the largest mobile phone market in the world and growing with over 350 million subscribers.[36] Thus, for all the apparent hype of the "new" China, as the challenge to other nations for manufacturing investment and job creation increases with the sudden surge of growth and euphoria with WTO membership, there will also be risk—a risk that the political dynamics and transition in China will not keep pace with the rush to globalization. A very close observer of China in transition noted: "Policy making in Beijing is like steering a supertanker—it takes a long time before a policy gets approval and becomes a reality, and even then the central government has limited power over a vast country."[37]

THE MEXICAN RESPONSE

Mexico is truly at a crossroads. Official figures indicate employment in the maquila sector down nearly 18 percent by 2004, and trending to further decline in the next decade. The move to high tech jobs and the challenge posed not only by China but a host of other low-wage countries sends a clear signal that there will be a flight of low-tech labor-intensive jobs in the garment, electronics, some automotive components, and footwear industries. The recession of the U.S. economy in 2001–02, coupled with a strong peso value, caused concern in the fundamental direction of the Mexican economy. President Fox noted that Mexico's export-led model, which had been underpinned by decades of investment in offshore assembly plants, "to some degree, is worn out." While Fox urged more homegrown research and design, little mention was made that domestic Mexican companies have seldom invested in either adequate amounts of R&D or capital equipment. What looms as more critical to the health of the Mexican economy is the increased dependence on the North American domestic market. In spite of the fact that Mexico is gradually losing a share of the U.S. market to East Asia and China, intermediate and capital goods account for almost 80 percent of Mexico's exports to the U.S., compared to China, which remains predominantly a consumption goods exporter.[38]

Fox entered office with the promise to maintain the nation's steady growth and declared rather dramatically that the target for his administration was a 7 percent GDP growth. The dynamics of the world markets had already begun to shift low-wage jobs out of Mexico. In spite of the continued positive flow of FDI, the banking sector was unable to provide the level of local financing needed to expand the domestic supply base and industrial sector. While a few Mexican large corporate firms, such as Cemex, Imsa, and Vitro, were able to go to the international financial markets to raise capital for growth, their newfound capital sources were increasingly used outside of Mexico to expand or acquire new markets. The global reach of Cemex is a prime example. The Monterrey industrial cement company has expanded operations since 1992 to over thirty countries, including not only the Philippines, Spain, England, Germany, and South Korea but also the United States (Texas). Thus, the early years of the Fox administration explored a number of programs to address the dynamic demand on the Mexican governmental economic and trade policy to open new markets and create more jobs.[39]

In December 2003, Chinese Premier Win Jiabao visited Fox in Mexico. The cordial visit by the Chinese leader was an effort to "normalize relations" and reduce trade tension between the two nations. The problems are complex, in spite of an official statement by the Mexican president describing China as "an opportunity, not a threat." Fox is well aware of China's growing economic and political clout, especially in terms of trade with Latin America. While China in mid-2004 ran a trade surplus of more than $5 billion with Mexico, the real sting to Mexican pride is that China has replaced Mexico as the second-largest supplier of merchandise to the vast U.S. market. Furthermore, China has demonstrated expanded interest in Latin America by tripling bilateral commerce with Brazil since 2000 by 80 percent to $4.5 billion, and bought increasingly larger amounts of soya from Argentina, copper from Peru and Chile, and steel from Brazil, as well as inking a strategic partnership and joint venture with Cuba to mine and ship nickel to help feed the Asian boom.[40]

Demand for these industrial commodities has skyrocketed due to China's growing appetite, with worldwide stockpiles running low and the price of such items as steel and copper jumping in price over 40 percent. President Hu Jintao's first international visit to South America in November 2004 was to

Table 4-5 Mexico: Peso-Value, 1900–2006

Years	Pesos per dollar	Years	Pesos per dollar	Years	Pesos per dollar	Years	Pesos per dollar
1900	2.06	1927	2.12	1953	8.65	1980	23.25
1901	2.11	1928	2.08	1954	11.34	1981	26.22
1902	2.39	1929	2.15	1955	12.50	1982	96.48
1903	2.38	1930	2.26	1956	12.50	1983	143.93
1904	1.99	1931	2.65	1957	12.50	1984	192.60
1905	2.02	1932	3.16	1958	12.50	1985	371.70
1906	1.99	1933	3.50	1959	12.50	1986	923.50
1907	2.01	1934	3.60	1960	12.50	1987	2,209.70
1908	2.01	1935	3.60	1961	12.50	1988	2,281.00
1909	2.01	1936	3.60	1962	12.50	1989	2,641.00
1910	2.01	1937	3.60	1963	12.50	1990	2,945.40
1911	2.01	1938	4.52	1964	12.50	1991	3,071.00
1912	2.01	1939	5.19	1965	12.50	1992	3,110.00
1913	2.08	1940	5.40	1966	12.50	1993	3.10
1914	3.30	1941	4.85	1967	12.50	1994	3.25
1915	11.15	1942	4.85	1968	12.50	1995	6.42
1916	23.83	1943	4.85	1969	12.50	1996	7.75
1917	1.91	1944	4.85	1970	12.50	1997	8.25
1918	1.81	1945	4.85	1971	12.50	1998	8.50
1919	1.99	1946	4.85	1972	12.50	1999	8.78
1920	2.01	1947	4.85	1973	12.50	2000	8.97
1921	2.04	1948	5.74	1974	12.50	2001	9.35
1922	2.05	1949	8.01	1975	12.50	2002	9.77
1923	2.06	1950	8.65	1976	19.95	2003	10.86
1924	2.07	1951	8.65	1977	22.73	2004	11.25
1925	2.03	1952	8.65	1978	22.72	2005	11.75°
1926	2.07	1953	8.65	1979	22.80	2006	12.50°

°estimate

Brazil and Argentina, where he secured, from both countries, the trade status of "market economy." This semiofficial bilateral agreement somewhat skirts the WTO and has the possibility to reduce scrutiny on domestic pricing policies, thus reducing exposure to claims of unfair trade practices or dumping. In exchange, China pledged future investment of some $20 billion each in both Brazilian and Argentine economies over the next decade. Nevertheless, the 2004 United Nations *Trade and Development Report* noted a silver lining to the Pacific Rim boom: "The benefits of rapid Asian growth have also been felt outside the region. The recovery under way in Latin America can be traced to strong Asian demand, resulting in an increase in primary commodity prices and volumes of exports."[41]

With a foreign reserve war chest of over $900 billion, China is looking to further diversify its exposure and leverage broader market entry in investment-starved commodity-rich areas such as South America to secure much needed food, energy, and raw materials. China's continued bullish entrée into Latin America, to include massive investments in port facilities by Hutchison Whampoa and Cheung Kong Holdings on both ends of the Panama Canal (Balboa and Cristóbal), should be a long-range concern for the United States as well.[42]

One counterbalance to pressure from mainland Asia was the signing, of Mexico's twelfth free trade agreement with Japan on September 18, 2004, which took effect in mid-2005. Unlike the Mexico-EU Free Trade Agreement, which has been lackluster, falling extremely short of expectations, the Japanese agreement is expected to be more active given the growing demand in America for automotive and electronic components. Furthermore, Japan's broad investment in the maquila sector bodes well for increased two-way trade. The full impact on the U.S. market is yet to be determined, but given the expansion of assembly operations by Toyota, Samsung, Sony, Honda, Nissan, and Matsushita in North America, new investment and pressure on pricing in the market should be expected. Closer ties in the hemisphere to offset China have been augmented by regional efforts with Mexico's neighbors to the South.[43]

Fox had a preinaugural meeting with the presidents of Central America (Nicaragua, El Salvador, Honduras, Guatemala, Panama, and Costa Rica), representatives of the Inter-American Development Bank (IDB), the Central American Bank of Economic Development (CABED), and the Economic Commission for Latin America and the Caribbean (ECLAC) on November 30, 2000. This resulted in a bold proposal to create a framework for sustainable region-wide economic development projects and attraction of FDI stretching from central Mexico to Panama. The proposal was named the Plan Puebla-Panama—the PPP.

PPP AND REGIONAL ECONOMIC DEVELOPMENT

Little attention was given to the Plan Puebla-Panama during 2000–01. However, with the recession in the United States and the flight of jobs from Mexico, the Plan received greater attention. By early 2002, the nongovernmental organization (NGO) developmental banks and funds had set aside $42 million for the first phase projects in the region. However, in the words of President Fox, in mid-2002 the Plan moved from an idea to a "reality" with a pledge of a line of credit of $4 billion from a group lead by the Inter-American Development Bank. The multi-year funding package could take as much as a decade to fully implement. Thus, in its initial stage the PPP is divided into eight key areas referred to as the "Meso-American initiatives" which include sustainable development, workforce development and training, prevention and mitigation of natural disasters, promotion of tourism, facilitation of commercial activity to include the attraction of foreign investment, development of the region's infrastructure to "enhance connectivity"—roads, ports, and airports, expansion of electrical services, and enhancements to the telecommunications network. The idea is to link the region's 60 million residents into an extensive economic and commercial zone of the future—not unlike the Special Economic Zones on the coast of China or the framework established for economic integration and transportation in the Trans-European Transport Network of the EU. The goals of the PPP were given new life and emphasis with a meeting of the presidents of the PPP nations hosted by Fox at Tuxtla, Mexico on November 13, 2004. However, without a focused approach to the region and private sector participation, development will lag. Thus, Mexican membership in the OECD has been a pivotal catalyst to encourage a broader government and private sector interaction to enhance regional development:[44]

> The globalization of trade and economic activity is increasingly testing the ability of regional economies to adapt and exploit or maintain their competitive edge. There is a tendency for performance gaps to widen between regions, and the cost of maintaining cohesion is increasing. On the other hand rapid technological change, extended markets and greater use of knowledge are offering new opportunities for local and regional development but demand further investment from enterprises, reorganization of labor and production, skills upgrading and improvements in local environment . . . leading public authorities to rethink their strategies . . . at improving the competitiveness of regions by promoting the valorization and use of endogenous resources.[45]

Given a rising level of opposition by environmental groups, these bold plans have many details that have yet to be determined. At issue are Mexico's efforts to assess the niche needed to address the nation's, as well as Fox's, broader PPP efforts. Mexico and the region will need to develop a comparative advantage in order to leverage a generally unskilled and semiskilled labor pool for intense production demands while at the same time develop the higher skilled industries that have slowly evolved in the northern border states. By one measure, the six Mexico border states employ 29 percent of the active workforce, comprise 77 percent of the maquila sites in Mexico, and produce 23 percent of the nation's GDP. The dynamics of the twin-cities that line the border are key to the U.S.–Mexico relationship. And furthermore, in terms of job expansion, to build on the expansive industrial sector along the border will be pivotal for both nations.[46]

In order to maintain the critical role of the northern production area, Fox swiftly created the Northern Border Region Development Program. In large measure, Fox's border czar, Ernesto Ruffo, noted this program marks the first time "dedicated" federal funds have been earmarked for developing the border, signaling that the region is important to the national economy. However, in recent years it has not been the desire for attention from Mexico City that has characterized the region, but instead a cry for the central government to finally clarify the role and treatment of taxes and duties for the maquila sector. By all appearances, the central government has taxed the maquilas at whatever maximum level it could extract via constantly changing and reissued rules. These efforts have gained gradual momentum, giving existing operations and potential foreign investors the impression that Mexico is squeezing more and more taxes out of the maquilas to cover revenue declines in other areas. The confusion and concern began in January 2001, when the NAFTA duty waiver was eliminated and no clearly defined import tax regime was developed. The government of Mexico can be expected to apply more pressure on the maquila sector in order to insure new tax revenue. The danger in such a policy is that it could cause multinationals to divert investment to alternative locations.[47]

In short, three key areas of taxation affect the competitiveness of the maquila sector: import taxes and the impact of Article 303 in NAFTA; changes in the confusing and inconsistent taxing of income and assets, including avoiding double taxation; and antidumping duties or tariffs on imported goods that are deemed to be a threat to the domestic market because they enter the country below fair market value. Prior to 2001, the maquila sector was exempt from such antidumping duties. Is it possible that the taxing authorities at Hacienda (Office of the Mexican Secretary of Treasury) think there is no end to the number one hard currency–generating sector of the economy? One observer noted, "Despite tax uncertainties and real wage increases over the past five years, maquiladora employment grew at an annual rate of 14.4 percent between January 1995 and October 2000. The pace of growth has been remarkable and contrasts sharply with the notion of a fragile industry teetering on the edge of uncompetitiveness due to higher taxes and rising wages."[48] This growth abruptly halted with the recession of 2001. Notwithstanding, past performance does not in any way portend the future growth of the maquila sector, especially given the lack of transparency in the bureaucratic and taxation regime.

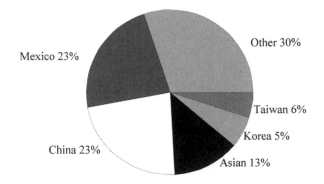

Figure 4-1 U.S. Imports from Nonindustrialized Countries
Source: Federal Reserve.

CONCLUSION

Mexico and the world need to maintain a continuous watch-and-wait attitude because China's rise as a highly competitive low-cost export platform will in fact prove highly disruptive in the next two decades as it attempts to come to grips with a rules-based international system that the nation has long exploited for its singular gain. In the year ended in July 2003, China exported $80.1 billion in goods to the United States, for the first time overtaking Mexico ($78.8 billion) as the second-largest U.S. trading partner after Canada. The very targets and goals of China's global penetration signal a fundamental shift in trading patterns, labor concerns, and environmental dynamics few can predict. However, currency stabilization concerns and capital adequacy, along with banking reform of state-owned banks are key factors to maintain growth in China. Without strong capital attraction of FDI, growth could quickly diminish. Yet by its own measure, China intends to double GDP by 2010, and its share of world trade is expected to triple to 10 percent by 2020, surpassing Japan at 5 percent and standing second only to the United States in the range of 12 percent.[49]

In contrast, Mexico is faced with the possible destabilizing task of dealing with lost jobs, a threat to FDI, and the ongoing issue of cross-border immigration with the United States. Nevertheless, Mexico will continue to be critical to the growth and stability of the region. The dynamics of this regional cross-border relationship will be vital to U.S. commercial interests. The hallmark of Mexico's competitiveness is its location next to the U.S. market and its highly productive workforce. As low-wage jobs leave Mexico, government policy both in letter and spirit must espouse a pro-business posture to attract a steady inflow of foreign direct investment. The proximity of the two countries will have little benefit if a pro-industrial policy does not assure multinationals of the advantages and safety of doing business in Mexico. Such investment in decades to come will be in high value-added production resulting in value-added high-paying jobs. All are factors critical to economic growth and social stability in Mexico.

Thus, the following trends offer a window on issues which need to be monitored.

Trends: Mexico versus China

- China is indeed a potential threat to the stability of the global markets and Mexico with regard to adequate jobs between now and 2020. As China gains an increased market share of the world's manufacturing, low wages and a failure to adhere to WTO covenants will be a significant concern; furthermore, FDI will be channeled away from Mexico. Mexico will in fact forfeit its competitive advantage in low-skilled and low-paying jobs at a time between 2010 and 2020 when it will have one of the largest nineteen- to twenty-six-year-old workforces in the world outside of China. Fears of China's entrance in the WTO are probably somewhat exaggerated due to the fact that low-wage jobs began exiting Mexico prior to 2001; however, in the minds of those who have and will lose their jobs the threat is real and lasting. Additionally, do not expect the 2004 Mexico-Japan FTA to offset, either in the short or long term, the impact of China on the Mexican economy.[50]

Danger and Impact: Increased amounts of funding, both domestic and FDI, will be needed in Mexico both as a social safety net and for the training of value-added jobs in the next generation of manufacturing operations that will demand a higher skilled trainable workforce. It will be critical in the shifting global trends that Mexico remain competitive. Capital investment in both new facilities and expansion and upgrading existing operations will trend toward demand for high-skilled jobs. And thus, the lack of a stable workforce in Mexico could lead to domestic unrest and increased immigration northward.

- The Plan Puebla-Panama, or a similar type of program, will need to be developed for both southern Mexico and Central America in order to provide an additional job outlet for a growing regional labor market. The conclusion of the U.S.–Central American Free Trade Agreement was a positive step toward a hemispheric FTA by 2006. Environmental concerns and impediments need to be resolved as quickly as possible given the lead time needed to develop infrastructure. The advent of any future political unrest coupled with, the absence of multimodal facilities, electrical capacity, improved seaports, and roads will slow the attraction of private investment in the region.

Danger and Impact: Reluctance to act now to encourage smart development of southern Mexico and its Central American neighbors will pose grave and ongoing immigration problems for the United States on the southern border, and thus, strained relations not only with Mexico but also with the Central America region.

- To insure the competitive nature of the existing maquiladora sector, the continued need for value-added jobs, and the lasting attraction of direct foreign investment, legislative measures need to be taken by the Mexican Congress to remedy the lack of coherent decision-making authority at the Hacienda. These measures need to clearly define an understandable and transparent taxation and duties policy (unlike the uncertainty of the Permanent Establishment rules) that reduces the administrative burdens as well as supports and fosters the enhancement of the maquiladora sector.

Danger and Impact: Investors will look elsewhere to establish operations and thus have a tremendous impact on job creation, government revenues as well as diminish the prime source of hard currency exchange. Two factors loom as pivotal: the ability of Mexico to shift from low-wage

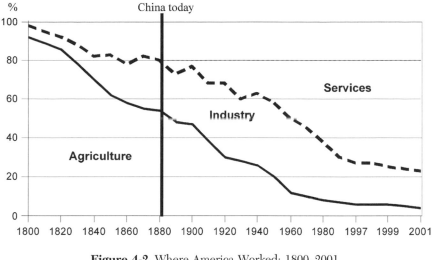

Figure 4-2 Where America Worked: 1800–2001
Source: Federal Reserve.

to high-wage higher-skilled jobs in the more tech-oriented maquila sector and the impact of the short- and long-term stability of China.

- The development and stability of Mexico and China have a daily more direct relationship on the U.S. economy. The globalization of the world has resulted in a very high dependence on foreign products, components, and services resulting in producer countries competing to be the world's low-cost manufacturer. With Mexico and China as our top two trading partners, relationships with them, as well as increased competition, will continue to affect all sectors of the American economy.

Danger and Impact: The shift in the globalization of manufacturing started decades *before* NAFTA. The impact on domestic U.S. production, given the sourcing of offshore components, will continue to diminish manufacturing in the United States. However, as one observer noted, "Short of drastic political reform, China will not overcome its technological dependence on the West."[51] During the upcoming two decades U.S. manufacturing will lead the world in R&D, productivity, and systems design for high-tech high valued-added production in sectors such as medical technology, biotechnology, food processing, aerospace, telecommunications, power generation, computers, and robotics. All of which demand a well educated workforce willing to constantly retrain. Thus, manufacturers, a cornerstone of the American economy, will never fully disappear from the United States.[52] The American workforce, as well as state and local level economic development and public officials, will be faced with a growing shift of the economy from purely production to domestic assembly-based operations. Furthermore, the service sector, in a daily more technical society, will continue to expand to create jobs. Of prime concern for the United States is the training and retraining of displaced workers to insure a growing pool of value-added jobs is filled.

The short-term stability of China in terms of global commerce is first and foremost linked to the value (or overvalue) of the Chinese yuan (RMB). By late 2004, some estimates placed the currency as overvalued by as much as 40 percent. If China does not allow its exchange rate to rise, a sharp devaluation or "crash" could send shockwaves worldwide. However, one buffer is the fact that the central bank of China is one of the leading investors in U.S. Treasury securities; thus, a rapid defalcation of these funds if a crisis did arise could have a significant impact on the U.S. markets and economy.[53] Banking reform is needed in China (to include curbs on lending) along with more regulatory reporting transparency— both key contributing components of the Mexico (1994–95) and Asian (1997) financial and currency crises. In spite of record trade surpluses during the past decade, the value of the yuan has been held in the 8.3 per U.S. dollar range. Options to manage the value of the yuan include widening the band within which it is allowed to trade, and a shift away from pegging it to the dollar to pegging it to a basket of currencies. The long-term objective should be to allow the yuan to become fully convertible.

Contrary to popular belief—China is not too big to fail![54]

5

⸻◦⸻◈⸻◦⸻

MAQUILAS, TECHNOLOGY
TRANSFER, AND TRADE CORRIDORS

The Mexican government goal is to become an economy based on innovation. In the coming years, it expects growth to be dependent on knowledge-based systems and technologies, high value-added goods, and increased sophistication of the business environment through the permanent advancement of local research, design, and development. The strategy is centered on economic, fiscal, and regulatory incentives to thousands of small firms and suppliers in order to consolidate production clusters and achieve a higher growth in productivity. Mexican industries, as well as federal and local governments, are also working hard to support local innovation and R&D through university/business/local governments partnerships. In short, Mexico is moving away from the concept "Made in Mexico" to the concept of "Designed and Created in Mexico."
—Raul Urteaga-Trani, Economic Counselor, Embassy of Mexico

THE GLOBAL DYNAMICS OF MANUFACTURING

GLOBAL SOURCING, increased use of technology, open markets, free flow of capital, and increased productivity have forever changed world commerce.[1] The year 2005 marks the beginning of the fourth decade in an ongoing intensive process to expand manufacturing and enhance productivity to all areas of the globe. The dynamics in the relative changes over the past forty years are marked by technological advances that allow not only multinationals, but also suppliers of all sizes and at multiple locations, to participate in the globalization of trade, logistics, and manufacturing. The rush by suppliers and expediters to meet the requirements of producers and consumers has heightened the arena of competitiveness as well as the demands on manufacturers to produce and deliver on-time, quality, profitable goods and services. A review of the maquila sector in Mexico and the structural changes in manufacturing, tech transfer and logistics is driven daily by increased demand for efficiency, high productivity, and cost savings. Mexico is entering a new era with regard to manufacturing. During this new shift, the next generation of maquila supplier-producers will require an ongoing enhancement of infrastructure and trade corridors from the broader interior areas of Mexico to link with the importer-assembly-distributors network in North America. Security considerations, as well as expansion of truck, rail, sea, air service, and border infrastructure to facilitate multi-model logistics, will shape U.S.–Mexico trade interaction for decades to come.[2]

The demands of offshore manufacturing and global sourcing will remain a tremendous challenge for both producers and suppliers in the near term. Global dynamics will affect the competitive nature of cross-border business during the next decade. Mexico is a vital market given the expansion of the maquila industry and the increased demand on logistical, technical, and professional services; thus, Mexico will remain a pivotal barometer of urban and industrial growth patterns along the U.S.–Mexico border.

MAQUILADORAS

In the case of manufacturing in Mexico, the evolution of offshore production serves as a barometer for trends and challenges in all areas of the world. After an exhaustive evaluation of manufacturing trends on the Pacific Rim by Mexican officials, the Border Industrial Program (BIP) was inaugurated in the mid-1960s. However, sizable offshore foreign investment in manufacturing and assembly operations did not begin until the early 1970s. The BIP, a creation of the Mexican government in the wake of the U.S. cancellation of the Bracero Program (cross-border seasonal farm labor) due to pressure from labor unions, limited the wave of foreign investment in manufacturing to the cities along the northern Mexican border. Touted as a worker program, the maquila program at no time hired displaced farm workers, but instead during the early years preferred trainable young women. The early skills requirements were basically repetitive low-tech piecework. Furthermore, the BIP was established to allow multinational manufacturing to take advantage of favorable offshore reduction in duties. The rise of the maquiladora sector in Mexico preceded both NAFTA and the WTO.[3]

The prime objective for attracting foreign investment and facilities to Mexico was reduced bureaucracy to create jobs and enhance the opportunity for technology transfer that would jump-start both domestic industry and the overall Mexican economy. Overdependence on oil and a series of currency devaluations in the 1970s and early 1980s resulted in modest growth of what became known as the "maquiladora" or so-called "twin-plant" (in-bond) industry. Once established, the maquiladora program encompassed six objectives: 1) provide employment, 2) provide foreign exchange, 3) train workers, 4) develop managerial skills, 5) be a means to enhance technology transfer, and 6) stimulate industrial development and foreign direct investment.[4] Thus, the

Table 5-1 Maquiladora Industry: Top Ten Sectors, 2004

Sector	Number of Plants	Employment
Electronics, machinery, and accessories	622	349,200
Textiles and apparel	577	209,800
Services	296	44,400
Furniture and parts	288	52,300
Automotive equipment and components	269	247,000
Chemicals	123	26,000
Sporting goods and toys	38	9,200
Foodstuffs	35	10,600
Shoes and leather goods	28	5,300
Other manufacturing	473	154,300

Source: INEGI

favorable tariff treatment under U.S. law made offshore manufacturing a viable option to either maintain production and assembly costs or cut costs outright. Originally, the maquiladora plants were allowed to temporarily import duty-free supplies, parts, machinery, and equipment necessary to produce goods and services in Mexico, as long as the output was exported back to the United States. The United States, in turn, taxed (via import duties) only the value-added portion of the manufactured product. The top three maquiladora sectors—transportation equipment, electronics, and textiles and apparel—together compose 75 percent of total maquiladora employment and are well represented in the list of ten leading goods traded between the United States and Mexico.[5]

While numerous foreign manufacturers from Asia and Europe were also attracted to Mexico, very little raw material or components were sourced from Mexico. The automotive industry was among the first to fully realize the significance of cross-border manufacturing and its implications on its competitiveness in the broader North American market. In the case of Asian investment, a majority of the facilities have been in telectronics, textiles, and specialty components. By the mid-1980s, an extensive network of industrial parks emerged in Tijuana, Ciudad Juarez, Nuevo Laredo, Reynosa, and Matamoros. Site location near the U.S. market, expansion of local infrastructure, and ease of border crossing became a high priority. This forward-looking strategy by Mexico to attract investment, new facilities and technology would take an additional decade to be fully realized.[6]

While Mexico did not invent offshore manufacturing, it did realize the prospects of production sharing to produce jobs, access to hard currency, and new technology. Given the proximity to the U.S. market and transportation network, Mexico became a competitive and viable option to locate facilities. For much of the past three-and-one-half decades the maquiladora sector has

Table 5-2 Maquila Industry Economic Indicators, 1999–2009

	1999	2000	2001	2002	2003	2004[2]	2009[2]
Plants[1]	3,297	3,590	3,630	3,003	2,860	2,859	3,300
Employment[1]	1,143.2	1,291.3	1,198.9	1,071.2	1,062.1	1,120.4	1,350.0
Gross Production value[3]	$73.7	$83.0	$80.4	$80.9	$87.5	$97.2	$128.0
Imported raw materials[3]	$60.0	$65.7	$58.8	$59.7	$65.6	$74.2	$101.0
Mexican value-added	$13.6	$17.3	$21.6	$21.2	$21.9	$23.0	$29.0

Source: Global Insight; INEGI
[1]Annual averages
[2]Projection as of September 2004
[3]Billions of U.S. dollars

been dominated by U.S.-based competition, lower prices, and the development of "local" Mexican suppliers. Domestic Mexican component parts, raw materials, and technology services comprised less than 3 percent of the final product prior to 2000. Furthermore, maquiladora operations were allowed, as of October 1972, to locate in the interior of the country. Companies were attracted to the interior on promises of enhanced location incentives and the implied low worker turnover. Patterns of employment and the availability of "skilled" workers have begun to affect the growth of high-tech manufacturing in Mexico. By mid-2000, there were over 3,500 maquiladoras, employing in excess of 1.3 million workers. While these numbers seem large, it is important to note that since the inception of the maquilas in 1965, maquiladora employment has never exceeded 1.5 percent of the available nonagricultural labor force.[7]

The demand for skilled and semiskilled labor will be tight well into the foreseeable future. Manufacturers are scrambling to attract and retain trained workers with technical degrees as well as experienced welders, tool-and-die makers, and machinists. The challenge to staff the expanding manufacturing sector both among the maquilas and domestic Mexican companies hinges on two critical demographic factors. First, the available (employable) labor supply in the 18–28-year-old age bracket is stagnant due in part to the full employment of those who "choose" to work, and second, there is a tremendous void in training new workers due to the understaffed and poorly equipped Mexican educational system. Yearly, multinational firms budget millions for training programs ranging from English classes to the latest in precision chip production techniques. In spite of these challenges, Mexico has a large, growing pool of potential workers to train given the fact that over half of the population is under the age of twenty. To date the government has had only a marginal impact on job training. To insure the availability of employees, a number of private sector companies have cooperated with the Mexican government to establish the equivalent of two-year technical colleges, but the lag time in producing graduates from these centers will continue to produce a shortfall. Correspondingly, while more and more young Mexicans enter the work force daily there will remain a labor shortage of those who are employable, which further increases pressure to train skilled workers.[8]

By the mid 1990s, Mexico had further liberalized foreign investment laws that resulted in a new wave of plants, infrastructure, and investment. It was felt that the liberalization of foreign investment laws under the North American Free Trade Agreement (NAFTA) would encourage more compe-tition, lower prices, and the development of "local" suppliers. Domestic Mexican component parts, raw materials, and technology services comprised less than 3 percent of the final product prior to 2000. Furthermore, maquila operations were gradually allowed to locate in the interior of the country. Patterns of employment and the availability of "skilled" workers have begun to affect the growth of high-tech manufacturing in Mexico. By mid-2000, there were over 3,500 maquiladoras, employing in excess of 1.3 million workers.[9]

Following the completion of NAFTA in 1993, most industrial sectors of the Mexican economy were opened. This resulted in increased foreign direct investment (FDI) as well as the rise of more Mexican-based companies that began to take advantage of both the gains in technology transfer and the advances brought about by the electronic nature of international commerce and manufacturing. FDI in fixed assets for the maquila industry rose from $1.4 billion in 1995 to $3 billion in 1999—nearly one-quarter of the total FDI ($12.7 billion in 1999) placed in Mexico. FDI in Mexico has averaged over $12.5 billion annually from 1997 to 2004. Gains in FDI were realized throughout the hemisphere. For the first time since the mid-1980s foreign direct investment into Latin America (for a brief period) leaped past that in Asia, surging 32 percent to over $97 billion. The three leading beneficiaries have been Argentina, Brazil, and Mexico. Mexico was further set apart from its peers in Latin America in early March 2000 when the Moody's bond rating agency gave the country an investment-grade rating. Moody's cited three key factors in the upgrade: the adoption of a floating exchange-rate system; a doubling of non-oil exports since 1994; and "an unwavering commitment to fiscal discipline" on the part of the government to raise revenues while keeping spending in check. Since the peso crash of 1995 the fiscal discipline (helped by low interest rates and rising oil prices) of the Mexican government and central bank has been evident, maintaining a strong current account balance as well as keeping inflation low. Furthermore, elevating Mexico's credit rating to investment-grade placed the nation in a selective club of emerging countries that includes South Korea, Chile, and Poland.[10]

Production expansion has also been enhanced by the fact that in large measure the open markets in Mexico and increased globalization of the

Mexican economy have allowed for more political stability. Thus, the maquila or production-sharing component to attract hard currency and create jobs is paramount to maintaining a stable Mexico. Merchandise trade between the United States and Mexico has increased over 200 percent since Mexico agreed to join GATT in 1986 and NAFTA was implemented in 1994. For example, the value of cross-border exports and imports passing through the Port of Laredo (due to its strategic location, the primary port on the southern border and the third largest commercial port in the United States, following only Detroit and JFK International Airport) increased 90 percent between 1994 and 1998 to $55.8 billion and then soared to over $80 billion by 2004.[11] In an extensive examination of production-sharing trends and the impact on both the United States and Mexico, the U.S. International Trade Commission highlighted the impact of "liberalization" on cross-border trade as well as the emergence of a vision to create "one market":

> NAFTA accelerated the process of integration even before the agreement came into force. The most important effect was psychological, creating a popular vision that North America is one market. On a more practical level, NAFTA reduced the cost of doing business in Mexico by lowering tariffs on [NAFTA-qualified] imported manufacturing inputs and products destined for the local market. NAFTA also gave the maquiladora industry increased access to the Mexican market, with an amount equivalent to 80 percent of a company's previous year's production level eligible for sale in the domestic market in 1999. NAFTA's rules of origin and the scheduled termination of duty drawback on January 1, 2001, combined to provide an incentive for maquiladora managers to find North American suppliers of components to replace imported input from Europe and Asia, again leading to greater integration of North American manufacturing industries.[12]

Thus, the maquiladora industry has become a significant component of the Mexican economy and vital to the strategic interests of U.S. manufacturing. It

Table 5-3 U.S.–Mexico Trade, 1996–2003 (billions of dollars)

Year	Exports	Imports	Total
1996	96.0	89.5	185.5
1997	110.4	109.8	220.2
1998	117.5	125.4	242.8
1999	136.4	142.0	278.4
2000	166.5	174.5	340.9
2001	158.4	168.4	326.6
2002	160.8	168.7	329.4
2003	165.3	170.9	336.2

Source: U.S. Census Bureau
°estimates

is expected that the maquila and supplier sector will continue a growth of between 8 and 10 percent per year. The linkage between U.S. companies and offshore manufacturing is further enhanced by improvements in the supplier network, demands for cost-effective labor, just-in-time inventories, and a friendly business environment.

In its sum total, the maquila industry has a positive impact in the arena of international competitiveness. However, a downturn in the U.S. economy between late 2000 and early 2002 resulted in a dramatic slowdown in the maquila sector. The industry remained in a slump amid speculation that China was attracting firms away from Mexico. In fact, low-wage jobs began to leave

Table 5-4 2003 U.S. Trade with Mexico (billions of dollars)

	Exports			Imports	
Rank	Product	Amount	Rank	Product	Amount
1	Computer/ electronics	$21.533	1	Transportation equipment	35.458
2	Transportation equipment	12.356	2	Computer/ electronics	29.557
3	Chemicals	9.175	3	Oil and gas	14.439
4	Machinery	8.511	4	Electrical/appliances	10.997
5	Electrical/appliances	6.184	5	Apparel and accessories	7.177
6	Plastics and rubber products	4.826	6	Machinery	5.642
7	Food manufacturing	4.165	7	Fabricated metal products	3.710
8	Fabricated metal products	4.041	8	Misc. manufactured items	3.567
9	Agricultural products	3.586	9	Agricultural products	2.972
10	Primary metal manufacturing	2.854	10	Chemicals	2.370
11	Textiles and fabrics	2.718	11	Primary metal manufacturing	2.342
12	Paper	2.701	12	Beverages and tobacco	1.747
13	Petroleum and coal	2.323	13	Leather and allied products	1.721
14	Misc. manufactured items	2.269	14	Nonmetallic mineral products	1.673
15	Apparel and accessories	1.656	15	Food manufacturing	1.673
	Subtotal:	88.898		Subtotal:	124.766
	All other:	8.559		All other:	13.306
	Grand total:	$97.457		Grand total:	$138.072

Source: U.S. International Trade Commission

Mexico for Central America and East Asian countries in the early 1990s. Export of U.S. supplies and components to Mexican maquiladoras is gradually being affected by global competitors, mainly from Asia. Maquiladora locations and plant expansions in the coming decade will concentrate near the U.S. border. The flight to the interior during the 1990s by multinationals searching for lower wages and reduced turnover has not reaped the expected results. Thus the emphasis can be expected to be on the border in the upcoming years due to shorter logistical turnaround, proximity to the North American market, and ample labor. Furthermore, more high-complexity maquilas emerged along with enhanced cross-border just-in-time processes that unwittingly increased productivity while further streamlining (and many times reducing) the maquila workforce. By late 2003, the flight of maquilas had halted as the U.S. economy expanded. Thus, employment in plants across Mexico began to regain an upward trend.[13]

IMPACT OF GLOBAL TRADE AGREEMENTS

Given the dramatic rise in offshore manufacturing and sourcing, a broad cross-section of multilateral and bilateral trade agreements will have increasingly greater impact on the competitiveness of manufacturing. Embedded in the challenge to meet rising cross-border trade pacts are the efforts to streamline transparency of trade and investment in manufacturing as well as taxing regimes across national boundaries. A pivotal set of trade agreements foretold the internationalization of the Mexican economy with the acceptance of membership in the GATT in 1986 (Mexico had initially rejected membership in the early 1980s), followed by membership in the OECD, APEC, and NAFTA.[14]

This web of international trade agreements and new regulations will progressively impact global trade and offshore manufacturing. In the case of North America, the prime objective of the NAFTA was to allow for two primary items: cross-border trade transparency (the reduction of nontariff barriers) and equal (or as equal as possible) market entry. Under these new guidelines the historical treatment of the maquila sector shifted the accounting treatment of operations from cost centers to profit centers. The applicable U.S. tariff laws have phased out duties and will continue to do so and phase in more market access. While duties continue to be lowered, rising nontariff barriers often negate any advantage created by lower tariffs (due in large part to the fact that the primary source of revenue for most developing countries is customs revenue). Oddly, this comes at a time when both technology and competitive demands require an ongoing evaluation of the cost of doing business in a world of expanding high-tech markets. Nevertheless, world trade continues to expand at a rapid pace. The WTO noted that despite high 2004 oil prices, overall global trade expansion reached a four-year high of 8.5 percent in terms of volume due to diversification of a "more broadly based economic revival" in the growth of world trade.[15]

Furthermore, countries worldwide are exploring methods to be both more attractive to foreign investors while at the same time looking for means to collect more revenue via fees and taxes—to replace revenue streams that have diminished due to the reduction of income from preferential customs duties. "Free trade" and the reduction of duties thus have an impact at the domestic and national level. The International Monetary Fund (IMF) and World Bank argue that any loss in trade revenue taxes can be more than offset by the multiplier effect of foreign direct investment that creates jobs by both expanding the domestic industrial base and facilitating technology transfer. Over the next few years the IMF and the World Bank will define their lending practices to address economic imbalances in emerging markets. To better address the crisis-lending regime, both organizations are exploring reforms that focus on a more proactive role in "crisis prevention," to better predict and prevent such disruptions as the devaluation in late 1994 and financial crisis that continued into 1995. Two key areas to be monitored are reductions in the dangerous mix of swelling short-term offshore debts and imbalances caused by low central bank foreign reserves. Following U.S. Treasury recommendations, in the wake of the 1994–95 Mexican crisis, developing nations have been strongly encouraged to maintain adequate reserves and avoid pegged currency systems, which often result in very tempting targets for currency market speculators.[16]

For nations like Mexico, China, and South Korea, which receive the lion's share of foreign direct investment, such an argument is not unfounded. Investment in these countries has been building for decades. Multinationals tend to like these areas because they have an investment regime (though at times there are changes) that is relatively transparent. Furthermore, there has been a reduced tendency to limit the number of plants in emerging economies such as Romania, El Salvador, or Portugal. These countries have ample labor, yet infrastructure and investment laws are often weak or nonexistent. For example, in the case of Romania, the first full set of foreign investment laws were not developed until 1998–99. Even then enforcement and transparency by local government officials and banks were both lax and inconsistent. Imposing a Western-style cookie-cutter free-market system without the underlying solvency of the host economy and government is a delicate process.[17]

Unrest at the World Trade Organization (WTO) meetings in Seattle (1999) and Cancun (2003) left numerous unanswered questions on the direction of "world" trade policy and the implementation of rules and guidelines that could affect manufacturers globally. Driven first by transparency, talks broke down over market access for agricultural products and standards or rules involving environmental issues. Efforts to solve any disputes were delayed both by the inactivity of the delegates and the small number of fringe protestors who received disproportionately more attention than the WTO meetings. After years of planning and negotiation, resolution of issues for growth and development were lost to a combination of media hype and last minute concerns on the part of a few special interest groups. As a result, there seems to be a trend among small nation members and certain special interest groups to stall deliberations of the WTO in order to advance narrow agendas and specific themes that do not involve the best interest of all nations, but do affect the process established to foster and enhance key elements of global trade. The United States will remain a pivotal world leader as the second Bush administration explores means to conclude the Doha Round of the WTO negotiations (2001) and move on to a continued policy of open foreign markets by means of both bilateral and multilateral regional trade agreements such as the CAFTA. In the meantime, the United States is closely monitoring the trade agreements of its key trading partners.[18]

MEXICO AND THE EUROPEAN UNION

Negotiations have been completed to form a free trade agreement between Mexico and the European Union (EU). The terms of this trade pact became effective on July 1, 2000. Mexico feels there is a tremendous potential to attract additional foreign direct investment with this agreement. From 1994 to 1998 the EU invested nearly $9 billion in manufacturing operations in Mexico. Currently the member nations of the Union account for 25 percent of the total Mexican FDI. The "total suppression" of tariffs among both parties will be phased out over a ten-year period. The agreement contains many of the same items as the NAFTA: market access, safeguards, investments, and rules of origin.[19]

While the EU agreed to lift tariffs on 82 percent of all Mexican trade between July 2000 and December 2003, little substantive impact was noted. The details of the terms of the rules of origin were proposed to open more EU-Mexico trade but in fact were geared to transship products to the broader North American market. In the case of the automotive sector, 45 percent minimum regional content will be required for the first two years, 50 percent in next three years, and 60 percent from 2005 forward. Other key areas covered in the new bilateral trade pact include agricultural products, textiles, and government procurement.[20] The potential of such agreements is tremendous given the fact that the developed and newly developing nations pay 70 percent of their tariffs to each other. Thus new markets' access, not protectionist policies, are the hallmark of expanded global trade. Michael E. Porter in *Competitive Advantages of Nations* noted: "National economic prosperity is not a zero-sum game in which one nation's gain is at the expense of others. A healthy process of economic upgrading can allow all nations to enjoy a rising standard of living. The choices required to act on the prerequisites for economic success, or not to act, will ultimately fall to each nation."[21]

The conclusion of the Mexico-EU pact is a distant second only to Mexico's entry into GATT in 1986 and the conclusion of the NAFTA in 1993. Over the past decade Mexico has attracted a great deal of interest from Europe, especially in the banking and financial services sector. European banking investment in Mexico is the highest and most extensive it has been since the height of the Porfirio Díaz era in the 1890s, with the leading financial groups in 2004 including Citibank, BBVA, HSBC, Santander, Deutsche Bank, Scotiabank, and ING.[22] It is expected that two-way trade between Mexico and the EU will gradually double by 2010 due to the fact that Mexico is an excellent consumer market. Thus, global alliances in a number of manufacturing, financial, and consumer products sectors will target the region for closer market penetration into both the growing North and South American market. For example, the Spanish financial Grupo BBVA has launched an extensive effort to enter the American market with bank purchases in both California (Valley Bank) and Laredo (Laredo National Bank) to capture a piece of the growing Hispanic consumer market—a direct market share challenge to American banking giants Wells Fargo, Citigroup, and Bank of America. Such investment will have a significant impact on Mexico and its neighbors facilitating and augmenting the demands required by increased commercial and consumer activity.[23]

TECH TRANSFER

With the shift of low-wage jobs out of Mexico since the early 1990s, clearly the maquiladora firms (as well as the domestic Mexican industrial sector) will need to emphasize efforts to attract and retain high-tech plants. The geographical proximity of Mexico should never be underestimated and is crucial to the attraction of new FDI to Mexico. Plants of the future will remain very capital-intensive. As John Christman of Global Insight notes, these new operations will be "high complexity plants, tailored to high-end customers, with quick JIT response time for those in volatile markets."[24] Thus, both maquiladora and domestic Mexican operations can be expected to become more vertically integrated with increased R&D and engineering geared toward more value-added production. One Mexican government official noted Mexico was "moving away from the concept of "Made in Mexico" to the concept of "Designed and Created in Mexico.""[25] In order to give better support to OEMs throughout the entire product life cycle, Mexico will have to quickly and efficiently move to the next generation of manufacturing ranging from on-site prototyping, system assembly, build-to-order (BTO) manufacturing, and electronics manufacturing services (EMS), as well as more integrated supply-chain management—all driven by the latest in Lean and Six Sigma manufacturing. And at each step, the process must maintain quality certification within the ISO-9000 (quality) and ISO-14000 (environment) regime.[26]

U.S. manufacturing sectors seeking to leverage the "overnight" advantage or proximity to Mexico in global competitive sourcing include automotive, aerospace, high-tech electronics, software design, medical instruments and supplies, biotechnology, specialized precision machine tooling, and upscale niche market producers demanding near real-time JIT linkage with North American parent firms or end-user customers. Mexico also views these key sectors as the main engine of manufacturing growth and job creation in the next fifteen years. Having attracted more than $50 billion in FDI to the automotive industry since 1966, Mexico is at the mercy of world demand trends and well aware of low cost producers in Brazil, China, and the Czech Republic who "want to beat Mexico at its own game." Thus, one key incentive is to strengthen such areas as the automotive and electronics sectors by way of new investment and enhancement of technical know-how to move up the value-added chain and thus gain larger market share and higher profits. Where Mexico can flourish is in the ongoing productivity of its workforce. In so doing, Mexico aims to become one of the world's top-five car and truck producers within a decade. Expansion of plants owned by Ford, GM, Navistar, DaimlerChrysler, and Volkswagen, along with the entry of Toyota and dozens of automotive suppliers in Mexico, is critical to the country's future. For example, the Volkswagen plant in Puebla—featuring both the new Beetle and new Jetta—will roll out 400,000 vehicles in 2005, an annual 40 percent increase in production, and target an increase to maximum capacity of 500,000 in 2006.[27]

The wave of maquiladora investment in Mexico along with the more open economy raised concerns that foreign multinationals moved to Mexico to avoid rigorous environmental standards in the United States. While the environmental policies created after 1995 have gone through a number of modifications, the final verdict on the impact reveals a mixed picture. In *Free Trade and the Environment*, Kevin P. Gallagher has produced the most concise and insightful examination of Mexico's environmental status. Given the fact that plant pollution is a direct function of the age of the plant and fuel usage, tech transfer in dramatic fashion has resulted in industries like iron and steel, aluminum, and cement that are cleaner and more energy-efficient than their U.S. counterparts. In the case of steel, electric arc furnaces are estimated to use one-third less energy compared to conventional steel making. Nevertheless, Mexico needs a renewed effort to invest more in pollution controls and enforcement of existing environmental laws, as well as in low-tech aging sectors of the economy such as paper and pulp, rubber, and chemicals that need attention. However, Gallagher noted, "Since the trade reforms began in the mid-1980s, Mexican industry has become relatively less pollution intensive. There was no widespread race to the bottom of dirty industry fleeing the United States to Mexico. The cost of abating pollution in the United States will not make firms leave the country; the costs of abating pollution in Mexico will not deter firms from investing in Mexico. Employment in dirty industries in the United States has remained the same, and has actually declined in Mexico."[28]

Pivotal to the emergence of next generation manufacturing in Mexico will be the ongoing need to maintain a trainable work force, expand regulatory reform, enhance infrastructure in all areas, maintain political stability, and secure the availability of cost-efficient and reliable sources of electricity and industrial water. The most critical component to the attraction and enhancement of business is the streamlining of rules and regulations that in recent years have been both inconsistent and a detriment to many investors. Mexico should build on the 1993 competition law and adopt a new competition policy to insure a vigorous domestic economy and inflows of FDI. While the telecommunications, oil, and cement sectors are virtually closed to outside competition, steps should be made to insure impediments to commerce are lifted on local business expansions as well as market-oriented policies to maintain economic growth and job creation. The lifting of nearly all price controls in 1998 (coupled with trade liberalization and privatization) are examples of forward-looking stabilization policies. The OECD lauded such efforts, noting, "Mexico's experience vividly demonstrates how liberalizing trade, enhancing market competition, and reforming administrative processes are mutually supportive."[29] With a measure of transparency and innovation, such changes will complement increasingly more demanding manufacturers and make Mexico competitive with any nation in the world including China.[30]

The competitive challenge of the world economy's requiring companies to reduce costs, improve quality, and improve response time was highlighted in comments by Ralph Watkins of the U.S. International Trade Commission:

> Mexico can compete more effectively with China in the U.S. market in high- to medium-value-added sectors where there is a high ratio of weight to value (major appliances, large screen TVs), where competition is based more on quality than price (medical goods, instruments), where there are frequent design changes or where it is vital to protect intellectual rights. China has gained in low-value-added commoditized sectors, such as apparel, luggage and footwear. Looking at official Mexican statistics from INEGI, from March 2002 through March 2004, the top three winners were transportation equipment (+17,424 jobs), electric and electronics equipment (+9,607) and machinery equipment (+2,447). The top four losers were apparel and textiles (−21,524 jobs), furniture (−3,644), toys (−1,082) and leather goods (−548).[31]

TRADE CORRIDORS AND CROSS-BORDER DYNAMICS

As U.S.–Mexico trade has expanded, so has the growth of the border region. The demands on infrastructure and all forms of services will remain a high priority. The expansion of manufacturing in Mexico will affect all areas of the economy. For example, growth in Texas border communities has outpaced both the state and the national averages in both Mexico and the United States. The Laredo–Nuevo Laredo twin cities for over a decade have been among the fastest growing communities in the nation, and Laredo has been the leading job creator in percentage terms in Texas. During the past decade, a number of key trends have emerged along the border: first, there has been a diversification in all areas of the business sector; second, a tremendous amount of direct capital investment is being added to the U.S. side of the border for transportation, new warehousing, and distribution facilities; and third, the population growth along the border will continue to outpace both state and national averages. The leading reason for this change is the ongoing year-to-year tremendous increase in cross-border trade. Of the $150 billion in merchandise trade between Mexico and the United States for the period July year-to-date 2004 (up 12.7 percent from the previous period), $124 billion or 82.5 percent was processed at the twenty-seven U.S.–Mexico land border ports-of-entry. Laredo, the leading port on the southern border since 1890, referred to by J. Michael Patrick as "the port of choice," processes yearly more merchandise trade than the combined total of the regional ports of El Paso, Hidalgo, Otey Mesa, and Calexico. The long-term multiplier effects of intermodal freight flows (land, rail, and air) on local economic development have been vital to growth and FDI.[32]

The transshipment of raw materials/components, agricultural products, and finished goods will in time tax the capacity of coastal and inland ports to handle the level of trade. Further compounding and taxing cross-border trade is the rising cost of transportation for manufacturers, which has increased over 15 percent in the 2004–05 period. Shortage of drivers and equipment, fuel costs, clogged seaports, and the growing cost of security will be critical competitive factors long into the future. In recent years a new set of foreign investors have entered the Mexican market to enhance seaport facilities in hopes of reducing both supply-chain bottlenecks and rising costs. Over $600 million in foreign investment has been injected by the Hong Kong mega-corporation Hutchison Whampoa, Ltd. in the privatization of the Mexican ports of Manzanillo, Lázaro Cárdenas, Ensenada, and Veracruz as well as long-term commitments by Seattle-based Stevedoring Services of America, Inc., (renamed Carrix, Inc. in 2003) at Acapulco, Progreso, Cozumel, and Veracruz. The U.S. ports on the Gulf of Mexico have gained a renewed interest in "short sea shipping" (the shipment of goods that does not involve more than one continent) with Mexican ports.[33] These efforts have been helpful, yet until extensive improvements are made, full capacity at these ports is over a decade away. The investment, along with new management and equipment, has had a tremendous impact on Mexico's shipping infrastructure. Prior to the port privatization, the ports of Los Angeles and Houston "handled more ocean-borne Mexican cargo than that nation's ports combined." Since 2000, the volume of trade at Mexican ports has grown at an annual rate of 10 percent.[34]

While Mexican seaport volumes have shown some increase, the rail and highway infrastructure to expedite such shipments has not kept pace with the growth in trade. There are many who envision a larger role for Mexico's Pacific ports to handle Asian goods destined for U.S. markets, but to fully realize the gains will require extensive investment that has not been evident. In the 2002 to 2005 time frame, for example, there have been planning efforts at the state level (generally unusual due to the centralized dominance of the federal government in Mexico City) to launch new trade routes to the United States. The first initiative is a program in Nuevo Leon, the last Mexican border state to establish a commercial crossing into the United States at Colombia, Nuevo Leon in 1996, and 14 miles north of Laredo to define a new corridor that would parallel or supercede the Monterrey Laredo Dallas Kansas City route.[35] The Villa XXI Multimodal District, predicated on the theory of open borders, (i.e., direct pass-through to inland terminals), is intended to bypass the traditional cross-border commercial processing in Nuevo Laredo–Laredo. A second Monterrey group has extended this concept to include plans to link the deepwater Port of Manzanillo through Monterrey, Laredo, Dallas, and on to the inland terminal at Oklahoma City or Kansas City. One future long-term link to the primary central corridor will be the eventual role of Kelly USA Logistical Center in San Antonio. The third plan to open new cross-border access is a corridor from Topolobampo on the Pacific coast, up the Copper Canyon, and across the Rio Grande border at Presidio, Texas. All three ideas are grand but fail to take into account a number of variables. First is the tremendous cost of the overland infrastructure either by road or rail: new rail alone would cost over $1 million per mile to construct. Second, U.S. carriers and their risk managers (i.e., commercial insurance companies) are hesitant to allow their equipment into Mexico, and third, and most importantly, north-south trade has to cross the border—at the border. Only air freight would be an exception, and even then Laredo is the number seven air cargo handler from North America to Latin America. Any notions of a speedy bypass at the border were dashed with the heightened security measures implemented after 9/11. The additional security requirements mandated by Congress in 2003 and 2004 only further place the focus of cross-border commercial processes (federal inspection and oversight), clearance, and staging at the U.S.–Mexico border.[36]

Security considerations are coupled with the fact that the Mexican truck transportation sector does not have adequate equipment that would pass safety inspection at the U.S. border to enter into the interior. The aging Mexican truck fleet is 90 percent owner-operated with no more than one truck in the fleet. Open borders will gradually occur but will not, in spite of misinformation and media hype, bring a flood of Mexican trucks into the United States. Safe operations in all sectors of the trucking industry, to include border dray trucks, will remain paramount to the volume and regulation of cross-border shipments. Rob Harrison of the Center for Transportation Research in Austin, Texas noted: "Major U.S. trucking firms currently dominate NAFTA truck trade and they have large efficient and safe partners in Mexico. Furthermore, trucking is both conservative and highly capitalized, so responses will be cautious." Thus, there will be an increasing incremental incentive to expand both seaport and border infrastructure facilities as well as improve north- and southbound rail and truck routes to take advantage of transshipments to inland distribution hubs and U.S. ports.[37]

Historically, four primary corridors of cross-border commerce have defined nearly two centuries of trade between Mexico and the United States. These routes were little more than barren trails improved into wagon roads—dusty by the heat of summer and very poor in times of rain. There was very little intracoastal trade due to poor or nonexistent ports-of-call. While mule trains and stagecoaches were added over time, the event that opened the region to increased volumes of trade and cross-border commerce was the arrival of the railroad in the 1880s. Notwithstanding the fact that in 2005 there were over two dozen different crossings on the U.S.–Mexico border, there are today only four prime overland trade corridors between the two nations. The primary north-south overland corridor (also the oldest, spurred on by the arrival of tycoon Jay Gould's International and Great Northern Railroad in the 1880s and the completion of Interstate 35 and the Pan American Highway southward in the late 1930s) is anchored at the logistical hub of Laredo–Nuevo Laredo. From Laredo the road runs northward to San Antonio, Dallas, Kansas City, and Chicago, as well as to direct links to ports at Houston and Corpus Christi. In the detailed work by John P. McCray on the "Rivers of Trade" on North America it was concluded: "The most dominant U.S.-Mexican truck transportation corridor segment in the U.S. is on IH-35 from Laredo."[38] No other north-south corridor handles this volume of overland trade and in 2004, over 1.6 million trucks traversed this route.

Southward into Mexico this Gulf Coast corridor connects Nuevo Laredo to industrial giant Monterrey, Saltillo, Torreón, and on to Mexico City. At El Paso the central corridor connects to Dallas–Fort Worth and on to the Midwest and north. Even more significantly, over the past two decades, much of the U.S. West Coast overland logistics moves between the over five hundred maquiladora operations in the Ciudad Juarez region and a broad number of California ports, most notably Long Beach. Southward from Ciudad Juarez, road and rail connect to Chihuahua. The third historical access route is the western corridor crossing at Nogales with linkage to Phoenix, Albuquerque, Tucson, and on to Denver. Southward, this prime crossing for seasonal agricultural products connects Agua Prieta and a growing manufacturing center at Hermosillo. The final north-south connection is the Pacific corridor from San Diego northward to Los Angles, San Francisco, and on to the northwest. From San Diego this corridor is connected to Tijuana, Mexicali, and Tecate, with service to Baja California.[39]

These four corridors, while the cornerstone of cross-border business, have been expanded by decades of road and rail improvements to better link the Mexican seaports. Not since the foreign direct investment boom of the 1890s in railroad and mining has Mexico received so much private-sector attention to its infrastructure. Mexican government attention to infrastructure for most of the twentieth century was directed primarily to the needs of the Federal

District of México and to the Port of Veracruz. The prime catalyst to infrastructure enhancement in Mexico began with the expansion of the maquiladora industry and Mexico's entry into GATT in 1986, followed by the privatizations in the mid-1990s of many components affecting the infrastructure and economy. The conclusion of NAFTA in 1994 provided the final catalyst to recognizing the need to enhance the trade flows and infrastructure in both countries.[40]

Trade corridors are a key component to adding value to a region's production base. One observer of the corridor impact noted: "In and of themselves corridors do not add value, but their interaction with the adoption of just-in-time (JIT) production and distribution make an efficient transportation corridor an asset and principal component of a firm's logistics matrix."[41] The distinct border corridors are accentuated by a near void of east-west infrastructure on either side of the border. North-south corridors will be the dominant flow of commerce. Furthermore, trade corridor hubs will increasingly be more interactive given the rise of containerization and intermodal facilities. Those communities that will prosper in such clusters are locations that can best integrate land, air, and sea components—or have close, near direct access to one or all of these factors.

What has followed in the past few years is a rush to identify logistical enhancement to insure the smooth flow of goods both north and south. Overland a wave of privatized highways and railroads in Mexico in the early 1990s fell on hard times prior to the 1995 devaluation and government abandonment of these projects. The critical linkages from Laredo to Mexico City, the original Pan American Highway, survived these funding cuts and were either completed or expanded. From McAllen a new highway now links Monterrey. However, existing highways from both El Paso and San Diego, California southward into Mexico are much the same as they were a decade ago. While over 80 percent of all shipments between the United States and Mexico are by truck, in recent years the need for intermodal capacity has resulted in rail carriers becoming markedly more efficient since privatization.

Table 5-5 Components of an Intermodal Transportation Corridor

Land	Air	Sea
Motor carriers	Airports	Marine vessels
Cross dock facilities	Aviation facilities	Barges/tug service
Railroads/railyards	Airplanes	River and sea
Trucks/truck terminal	Maintenance facilities	Ports and docks
Intermodal terminals	Customs clearance	Cargo cranes
Drayage services	Foreign Trade Zones	Warehouses (bonded)
Fueling/repair services	Onsite loading equipment	Access to land transport

Source: Adapted from Boske and Cuttino, *Impacts of U.S.–Latin American Trade*

Delayed by much needed capital improvement, the Mexican train system has gradually become more cost-effective with the addition of new locomotives, better border crossing efficiencies, and crew training. There are still only five rail crossings across the Texas border—Brownsville, Laredo, Eagle Pass, Presidio, and El Paso. What has enhanced this service and will further expand trade is the need to link Mexican seaports with rail and intermodal service for transshipment of goods to the North American markets. To accomplish this old but newly articulated strategy is to better link inland ports with seaports better connecting the upstream suppliers and customers in both the United States and Mexican markets. One concern is to avoid a total collapse of inbound shipments to American distributors of Asian producers. This occurred in 2002 when the West Coast U.S. ports were closed due to the Longshoremen's strike over the introduction of new cost-saving technology to expedite shipment in the ports. All the assumptions of just-in-time inventories were shattered as the supply chain came to a near halt highlighting the exposure such a disruption can have, even in a short period, to the economy. And thus, unwittingly, the U.S. West Coast strike along with increased demand for logistical services has caused shippers worldwide to reconsider alternative means to insure access to the U.S. market by way of Gulf of Mexico ports at New Orleans, Houston, and Corpus Christi, as well as renewed interest in expanding the port facilities in Mexico at Lázaro Cárdenas, Manzanillo, and Topolobampo.[42]

Just as efficiencies in sourcing raw materials and manufacturing have transformed quality production, so too will the web of distribution and logistical centers that have risen along the border. The trend toward locating on the U.S. side of the border will continue to attract new investment and distribution hubs in numerous border cities. Efforts at inland port designations (site or terminal locations away from the U.S.–Mexico border) will prove important for regional distribution, but will not overly affect the expertise and efficiency of strategic border locations. There are a number of factors for this, including a continued lack of infrastructure in Mexico and an aging infrastructure on the U.S. side of the border. Priorities for border security will affect state and federal funding directed toward the needs of the metro areas and away from purely investing in north-south highways infrastructure. Thus, the political alternative at the state level has been to raise the question of a need for toll roads.

Plans to identify new corridors in the United States have been in development for over a decade in various federal highway legislative packages. Among those proposed is I-69, a result of national highway legislation, from Laredo to link northwestward to Houston and on to the Midwest. Another is an innovative regional effort known as the Port-to-Plains Corridor coalition initiative to link 1,400 miles of existing Texas highways from Laredo through Lubbock and on to Denver and the Northwest. And looking to the future, the state of Texas in late 2004 announced the selection of the initial $7.2 billion construction consortium for the "Trans-Texas Corridor" (TTC-35) comprising Zachary Construction Corporation of San Antonio and Cintra of Spain. The new statewide multimodal network is estimated to cost $184 billion to construct over 4,000 miles of road and rail from the key markets across the state from the Oklahoma border to the Rio Grande. This system is envisioned to be the toll road of the future, but build-out funding, right-of-ways, environmental studies, and any actual construction loom decades into the future.[43]

In an ever-growing JIT scheme of world commerce and manufacturing, regional airport hub development in Mexico will be critical to the movement of low-weight/density high-value goods and components between manufacturing/assembly centers in Mexico–the United States and offshore suppliers. Privatization on a limited scale of Mexican airports has resulted in only marginal improvements. As was the case with the seaports, the upgrade of such facilities is capital-intensive and long-term. Today the bulk of air cargo to Mexico is handled in already congested Mexico City, Monterrey, and Toluca, with secondary limited service at Tijuana, Ciudad Juarez, Nuevo Laredo, Guadalajara, and Cancun. What has happened is a fuller awareness of the significance of international trade and the infrastructure needed to address future logistical demands. "Third Party Logistics" (3PL) providers to conduct total or partial transportation management have arisen and are gaining popularity as firms outsource to improve supply-chain results. And in taking a broader look at the dynamics and importance of logistics to the bottom line, Hau L. Lee concluded, "Efficient supply chains often become uncompetitive because they don't adapt to changes in the structure of markets. The best supply chains aren't just fast and cost-effective. They are agile and adaptable, and they ensure that all their companies' interests stay aligned." This "triple-A"—adapt, align, and be agile—approach is critical to the movement of goods and materials, yet given the overall expansion of trade and the shortfall in current levels of infrastructure funding, adequate multimodal corridors will be years before fully realized.[44]

The federal and state governments of both countries have examined the increased flow of trade and the level of responsibility or role of each federal agency. In the case of the United States, there are four primary federal inspection agencies: U.S. Customs Service, Immigration and Naturalization Service (merged after 9/11 into the Department of Homeland Security), U.S. Department of Agriculture, and the Food and Drug Administration. During the next decade, the U.S.–Mexico border crossings can expect no less than an annual 12–15 percent increase in cross-border shipments.[45]

Beyond the cross-border dynamics of the U.S.–Mexico border region are concerns about the overall trade flow throughout the hemisphere. In the last ten years since NAFTA took effect, surface trade between the U.S., Mexico, and Canada has grown more than 80 percent. Overall landed exports increased 57.3 percent with top states in surface transportation to Mexico including Texas, California, Michigan, Illinois, and Ohio.[46] Given the old adage that "time is money," there will need to be added attention to the flow of

Table 5-6 Maquiladora Industry Top 10 Companies in Mexico, 2005

Company	Sector	Plants	Employment (thousands)
Delphi Automotive	Automotive	57	68.6
General Electric	Automotive	17	27.9
Yazaki	Automotive	12	27.5
Alcoa Fujikura	Automotive	21	23.0
Sanmina-Sol		6	12.0
Offshore International[1]		3	11.6
Phillips Electronics	Electronics	8	11.5
Visteon-Ford Motor	Automotive	7	11.2
Thomson Electronics	Electronics	6	10.9
Sony	Electronics	6	9.7

Source: Maquila Portal
[1]Shelter operator only. Has locations in three cities.

goods and the investment of infrastructure to make shipping possible. Today there is no coordinated assessment beyond state attempts to address local concerns, Stephen Blank concluded; in a project termed "Mapping the New North America" he highlighted the challenge:

> North American prosperity is intimately linked to the continent's economic flows, economic policy makers in the NAFTA countries continue to downplay this reality. Despite current levels of integration, few resources are devoted to managing the North American system and studying what might be expected of it in the future. The reality of an integrated North America generates challenges that cannot be ignored and opportunities that are being missed. The starting point must be the recognition that North America cannot achieve greater integration except insofar as its varied and ideologically diverse constituencies are seized with its urgency.[47]

CONCLUSION

It is now evident that a combination of trade liberalization of the 1990s with the growth of foreign direct investment in the manufacturing sector in Mexico will continue to have a sweeping impact on the delivery of logistical, technical, and professional services to the region. The fortunes for the growth of value-added offshore manufacturing in Mexico look bright. Such growth will prove a tremendous challenge to those who plan and execute economic development in the border region. The U.S.-Mexican border will remain one of the fastest growing regions in the world. As of October 2004, 61.7 percent of Mexico's 2,811 registered maquiladora plants were located in the northern border cities, and 82 percent of the overall sector was installed in Mexico's six northern border states. The challenges to support offshore business, provide adequate infrastructure, and insure the needs of the resulting urbanization are substantial. Yet despite these challenges, the future bodes well for regional manufacturing and investment.

The offshore manufacturing, logistics, and trade sector in Mexico moved into a new era with the implementation of both NAFTA and WTO. With the broader dynamics of the globalization of all areas of manufacturing and commerce there emerges an ongoing focus of priorities that will shape the economic development of the region, enhance trade corridors, and serve as a vital barometer to those engaged in industrial development in all parts of the globe. While these trends are not singularly unique, in their sum total these items will drive investment and commercial considerations during the next decade.

Benchmarks and Trends

- *Expansion of existing facilities*—Since 1999 over three hundred new maquilas were established in Mexico; however, one trend that is seldom noted is the expansion of current or existing operations. In Mexico alone, over six hundred multinational firms have expanded onsite facilities 50–100,000 square feet each. Those companies that located on sites that allowed room to expand have reaped tremendous cost savings and time-savings versus creating a de novo facility. Thus, advanced site location and planning with the option to expand is a primary consideration when locating a new facility in Mexico.
- *Where are the suppliers?*—One prime aspect of the transparency aims of the NAFTA was the need to make the Mexican market more open to suppliers who would supply not only the maquilas but also the Mexican-owned and operated companies. Historically less than 3 percent of raw materials was sourced in Mexico by offshore plants. The opening of the market as well as the treatment of duties on intercompany exports back to the parent company will precipitate the growth of more local suppliers as well as the need for suppliers to move closer to the manufacturers. Thus, in spite of limited access to credit for small-to-medium businesses, outsourcing of components and services has vastly increased the number of "participants" who have a vested interest in the final product.
- *The workforce*—Workforce development and training will increasingly become a key determinant both offshore and in the United States for all industrial, service, and commercial operations. Manufacturers as well as shippers, consolidators, brokers, and logistics planners daily require workers skilled beyond entry level. The future rests with those companies, driven by quality and productivity demands, that can identify, train, and retain employees in all sectors of their business that provide value-added skills. Furthermore, Mexico over the past decade has witnessed a significant decline in organized union activity, with union membership of the

total work force dropping over one-third from over 30 percent in 1984 to under 20 percent by 2000. Steady union decline in Mexico has occurred in transportation, warehousing, mining, electricity, and gas transmission, and thus should not pose any undue challenge in the growth of the manufacturing sector.[48]

- *Who pays the tax?*—There will need to be constant vigilance to insure an understanding and compliance with shifting tax regimes and regulations. The reduction of import tariffs and duties as well as the more interactive nature of the impact of transfer pricing on global manufacturing and sourcing has necessitated nations rethinking how best to raise and retain revenues. In the shifting treatment of operations for accounting purposes (under the permanent establishment rules or PITEX), offshore manufacturing facilities are no longer treated as "cost centers" but instead as "profit centers," thus making them more of a target for offshore taxation. If not managed properly, this could have a dramatic impact on both profitability and competitiveness. Additionally, in mid-2004, the Mexican government approved the first "Strategic Bonded Zone" (SBZ) in San Luis Potosi in the new multimodal Logistik Industrial park. The SBZ, similar in concept to the U.S. Foreign Trade Zone network, will operate as a duty-free area and is expected to attract new FDI. Sites in Nuevo Laredo and Reynosa are awaiting approval.[50]

- *Infrastructure*—Increased trade and industrialization is only as successful as the means and modes by which materials and finished goods are moved from one location to another and ultimately to the end-user. The era of cheap transport is over. With the supply chain wound as "tight" as it has been in the last decade, there will be an ongoing increased demand to insure adequate infrastructure in all areas from highways to ports to utilities. Federally unfunded mandates for ingress and egress infrastructure will continue to burden the border region. Furthermore, increasingly regions will, by competitive necessity, enhance trade corridors and turn to intermodal facilities to insure timely movement of goods as well as providing a competitive edge in attracting new business to their community. There will continue to be a mindset that "just-in-time" in today's dynamic world will never be fast enough. Expanded border security screening and profiling under such programs as BASC, CT-PAT, FAST, and US VISIT will incrementally increase the amount of commercial processing on the border while at the same time raise the cost of doing business. And both local and federal agencies, in cooperation with an ongoing public-private dialogue, will be needed to insure growth is both well planned and efficient.

6

—◦—▽—◦—

FOCUS ON THE FUTURE

The further backward you look, the further forward you can see.
—Winston Churchill

THE IMPORTANCE OF the United States' relationship with Mexico must not be underestimated or ignored. It would appear that many in the United States view Mexico from a small prism focused on immigration issues, drug trafficking, and a vacation spot in the sun. The dynamics of the binational relationship are seated deep in long-standing historical antagonisms, a factor of more importance to Mexicans than to most Americans. Mexico's keen sense of history also must account for the evolution of economic interdependence between the two countries. In the past decade the tremendous dialog about the NAFTA and its potential impact on both nations has somewhat sharpened the thinking of those for and against any particular issue that concerns the two nations. And the transition to more open government, while not necessarily the full embrace of democratic processes, has not been given its full due.

At time of the publication of this book the population of the United States very quietly passed the 300 million mark, and Mexico is approaching 110 million. In each nation the composition of the population is changing on a number of different levels—most notably in terms of age distribution (gradually older in the United States while Mexico is still young). The very nature of this age gap, which results in a shortage of jobs in Mexico coupled with demand in the United States, has driven and will continue to drive cross-border migration from south to north with or without a revision of a formal immigration policy. With the U.S. economy seventeen times larger than that of Mexico, the pent up demand for entry-level labor in the United States continues to grow. To reconcile the demand for workers with the line-in-the-sand approach by those who wish to build walls along the border will prove to be one of the biggest political challenges of this decade and beyond.

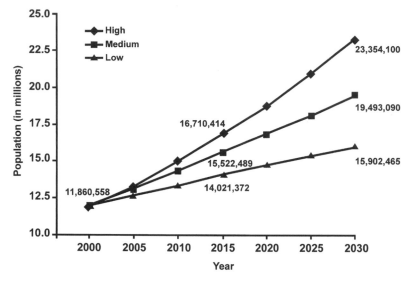

Figure 6-1 Total Population Projection for the U.S.–Mexican Border Region
Source: U.S. Census Bureau

The irony of the immigration issue is that it is one of the few topics of national scope that can have both positive and negative ramifications on both sides of the border. Mexico, regardless of U.S. congressional action and new border procedures enacted by Homeland Security or any other agency, must be a part of the solution. The view that going north is a safety valve for Mexico could hit a political mine field if the United States were to substantially enhance interdiction along the border. Mexico in many respects is much more apprehensive about the form and degree of any new immigration policy than the United States. Events or actions, both in fact or implied, that could strain U.S.–Mexico relations with regards to immigration are numerous. One response could be a heightened sense of nationalism that could slow Mexico's process toward more democratic institutions and result in the rise of an anti-American populist government determined not to be seen as close to U.S. policy objectives. However, given the expanding cross-border economic ties which involve both direct capital investment in Mexico and the rising level of billions of dollars in hard cash remittances back into the Mexican economy, such a radical government seems unlikely.

One primary reason for continued cooperation is the success of NAFTA. The very implementation of that agreement was a dramatic step toward free and open markets as well as more democratic government. In the case of Mexico, NAFTA compelled domestic corporations with multinational ties to stay competitive. Furthermore, as Mexican commercial activities become more linked with the United States there is little or no possibility they will revert to an unproductive protectionist past. Binational trade in goods and services has grown by 300 percent over the past decade. After the 1994–95 currency crisis, Mexico reduced inflation from over 50 percent to below 4 percent in early 2005. Mexico, in light of the exodus of companies to Asia seeking low-wage workers, is increasingly the place for production of value-added high-tech products and firms that understand and appreciate the importance of its strategic proximity to the North American market.

After decades of one party rule, President Vicente Fox has been a transitional chief-of-state. However, the resulting rise of a split multi-party congress in Mexico has produced gridlock and resulted in the inability of Fox to obtain critical reforms in the areas of energy, education, infrastructure expansion, judicial transparency, and health care. In large measure, due to what some term a dysfunctional democracy (but one that is better than before 2000), Fox became a very lame duck in the fall of 2004 with the prospects of little or no action during the last two years of his administration. The 2006 presidential election will be a further step in Mexico's steady political transition, spotlighting as many as ten diverse candidates from the PRI, PAN, and PRD. The proportional representation composition introduced by the de la Madrid administration in 1986 in order to further democratization has in fact created gridlock and effectively limited citizen representation. Thus, regardless of who is elected president, without a consensus in the Mexican Congress, few reforms will be accomplished short of a crisis.

Over the past three decades economic considerations and market disruptions such as the 1994 peso devaluation were all items of concern to the stability of markets and growth potential. Thus, Mexico's windfall of some $21.2 billion in export oil revenues during 2004 (27 percent higher than in 2003 and due to higher world oil prices not Mexican production capacity), could send a mixed message to those who do not fully grasp the need to improve the energy sector. Extensive investment is needed in new facilities, transmission lines, and equipment, to include additional plants to generate more electricity for a daily more urban and growing nation. Mexico is a net importer of its primary energy needs and continues to look for means to both source and transport more LNG. There are abundant natural gas reserves in the northern Burgos region, but if they are not soon developed an energy shortage is inevitable.

The irony is that there seems to be no urgency in Mexico concerning the pending shortfall of critical utilities and services. In an extensive joint report by the Centro de Investigación y Docencia Económicas and the Chicago Council on Foreign Relations, prospects of an energy shortage were not cited as a critical threat or an item for consideration as a foreign policy impediment. In reviewing the conclusions of the CIDE/CCFR report, Mexico tends to focus foreign policy concerns, as would be expected, on more global issues, such as the world economic crisis, international terrorism, world environmental problems, and China, and not on domestic issues (like the peso

Table 6-1 Critical Threats to Mexico and U.S. Vital Interests

Mexico	United States
Drug trafficking	International terrorism
World economic crisis	Chemical and biological weapons
Chemical and bio-weapons	Unfriendly countries with nuclear powers
International terrorism	AIDS, Ebola, and other potential epidemics
World environmental problems	Immigrants and refugees entering the U.S.

Source: CIDE/CCFR 2004

devaluation crisis of 1994–95) that could have regional and global consequences. In terms of foreign policy goals the focus of Mexico is directed towards protecting the interest of Mexican citizens in foreign countries, promoting Mexican products abroad, and stemming the illegal flow of drugs to the United States. In contrast U.S. priorities include protection of American jobs, combating terrorism, securing adequate energy, and curbing illegal immigration.

The goal of securing adequate energy encompasses a number of key components of the U.S.–Mexico relationship, including the political stability of the region and the ability to maintain industrial production linked to the North American market, which in the grander scheme is a key factor in regional security. The proximity of the two nations is a fact of geography and pivotal to continued good relations. The very border that joins the two countries is also a tremendous challenge. The U.S.–Mexico border region will continue to be one of the fastest growing regions in the world. Furthermore, the border will be under tremendous scrutiny as measures are increased to tighten security checks of both individuals and merchandise. Immigration control can be expected to be directly linked with border security and antiterrorism measures. The traditional means of doing business along the border will shift in parallel with the national security priorities and policies of both the United States and Mexico. And central to cross-border relations will be the response of both nations to immigration and illegal aliens.

The border is a window on the future of binational relations and interdependence given the demands and challenges created by continued urbanization. Agricultural production, infrastructure enhancements, air quality, and water rights are among the many issues that will be a growing concern to both nations. Water, water availability, water quality, and water clean-up will in fact be a key limiting growth factor for not only the border but all the U.S. Southwest and northern Mexico. The two dominant users of over 90 percent of the region's water are the growing twin-city urban centers along the Rio Grande and agricultural demands in the lower reaches of the river. Natural freshwater resources are scarce today, and thus water use in Mexico is on an unsustainable path. As this demand increases and the water table continues to drop throughout the region (and thus has a high saline content), a more focused approach will be needed to insure the viability of the region. Such issues are but a part of the larger cross-border dynamics that have been affected by global events.

Mexico was positioned to enter a new era with the United States as Presidents Fox and Bush took office at the turn of the century. However, following President Bush's first international visit to Mexico shortly after his inauguration in 2000, both Mexico and Latin America have received little attention given the overwhelming attention focused on the Middle East. The lower regional priority is a direct result of the post-9/11 war on terrorism. Nevertheless, Mexico remains among a small group of newly industrialized nations, which includes China, Brazil, Indonesia, Turkey, India, and Egypt, that have been and will be critical to the U.S. national interest. Thus, the U.S. binational relationship with Mexico will endure despite profound geopolitical and economic differences. The economic stability, prosperity, and strategic consequences of regional security of both nations and their citizens are of vital importance.

NOTES

INTRODUCTION

1. Howard F. Cline, *The United States and Mexico*, (Cambridge: Harvard University Press, 1953, 385–86.

2. Nelson A. Rockefeller, *The Rockefeller Report on the Americas: The Official Report of a United States Presidential Mission for the Western Hemisphere* (Chicago: Quadrangle Books, 1969), 39.

3. See also Sidney Weintraub, *A Marriage of Convenience: Relations Between Mexico and the United States* (New York: Oxford University Press, 1990); Peter Drucker, *Managing for the Future: The 1990s and Beyond* (New York: Dutton, 1992); Frank Tannenbaum, *Mexico: The Struggle for Peace and Bread* (New York: Knopf, 1950); and Jaime Suchlicki, *Mexico: From Montezuma to NAFTA, Chiapas, and Beyond* (Washington, D.C.: Brassey's, 1996), 189–203; Claudio Loser and Eliot Kalter, eds., *Mexico: The Strategy to Achieve Sustained Economic Growth* (Washington, D.C.: International Monetary Fund, 1992); IMF, *World Economic Outlook* (Washington, D.C.: IMF, 2004), 32.

4. Robert A. Pastor, *Integration with Mexico: Options for U.S. Policy* (New York: Twentieth Century Fund Press, 1993), 9–22.

5. John A. Adams, Jr., *Mexican Banking and Investment in Transition* (Westport, Conn.: Quorum, 1997), 2–3, 55–62.

6. W. Dirk Raat, *Mexico and the United States* (Athens: University of Georgia Press, 1992), 1–4; Francois Cheralier, *Land and Society in Colonial Mexico* (Berkeley: University of California Press, 1977), 7–183.

7. Enrique Krauze, *Mexico: Biography of Power: A History of Modern Mexico, 1810–1996* (New York: HarperCollins,1997), 43–44. See also Brantz Mayer, *Mexico, Aztec, Spanish and Republican: Ancient Aztec Empire and Civilization*, Hartford, Conn.: S. Drake, 1853; Jonathan Kandell, *La Capital: The Biography of Mexico City* (New York: Random House,1988), 95–148.

8. Bernal Díaz del Castillo, *True History of the Conquest of New Spain*, ed. and trans. A. P. Maudsley (London: Hakluyt Society, 1908); José López Portillo y Pacheco, *They Are Coming . . . The Conquest of Mexico* (Denton, Tex.: University of North Texas Press, 1992); Raat, *Mexico and the United States*, 12–31.

9. See also Frederick Peterson, *Ancient Mexico: An Introduction to the Pre-Hispanic Cultures* (New York: Putnam, 1959).

10. Colin M. MacLachlan and Jaime E. Rodriguez O. *The Forming of the Cosmic Race: A Reinterpretation of Colonial Mexico* (Berkeley: University of California Press, 1980), 36–168; Cheralier, *Land and Society in Colonial Mexico*, 7–73.

11. Henry Kamen, *Empire: How Spain Became a World Power, 1492–1763* (New York: Penguin, 2003), 88–89, 431; Kenneth Pomeranz and Steven Topik, *The World that Trade Created: Society, Culture, and the World Economy, 1400 to the Present* (London: M. E. Sharpe, 1999), 183–85.

12. Olivier Berner, *The World in 1800* (New York: John Wiley & Sons, 2000), 227–69; Raat, *Mexico and the United States*, 38–54.

13. John K. Chance, *Race and Class in Colonial Oaxaca* (Stanford, Calif.: Stanford University Press, 1978, 30–66; Lesley B. Simpson, *The Encomienda in New Spain: The Beginning of Spanish Mexico* (Berkeley: University of California Press,1966), 39–171.

14. Krauze, *Mexico*, 118.

15. Terry Pindell, *Yesterday's Train: A Rail Odyssey through Mexican History* (New York: Henry Holt & Company, 1997), 99.

16. Paul Garner, *Porfirio Díaz, Profile in Power* (Harlow, U.K.: Longman, 2001), 68–173; Eric Hobsbawm, *The Age of Capital, 1848–1875* (New York: Vintage, 1996), 64.

17. Andrés Molina Enríquez, *Los Grandes Problemas Nacionales, 1909* (Mexico City: Ediciones Era, 1978), 1–146; Enrique Krauze, "Will Mexico Break Free?" *New York Times*, July 5, 1997, Y-21; MacLachlan and Rodriguez, *Forging of the Cosmic Race*, 334–37; John Mason Hart, *Empire and Revolution: The Americans in Mexico since the Civil War* (Berkeley: University of California Press, 2002), 271–304.

18. Hector A Camin and Lorenzo Meyer, *In the Shadow of the Mexican Revolution* (Austin: University of Texas Press, 1993), 15–54.

19. Government of Mexico, *The True Facts About the Expropriation of the Oil Companies' Properties in Mexico* (Mexico City, 1940), 83. See also Lorenzo Meyer, *Mexico and the United States in the Oil Controversy, 1917–1942* (Austin: University of Texas Press, 1977).

20. Carlos Salinas de Gortari, *Mexico: The Policy and Politics of Modernization* (Barcelona: Plaza & Janes Editores, 2002), 9–36; Jorge G. Castañeda, *The Mexican Shock: Its Meaning for the U.S.* (New York: New Press, 1995), 1–8, 129–30; Andres Oppenheimer, *Bordering on Chaos: Guerrillas, Stockbrokers, Politicians, and Mexico's Road to Prosperity* (Boston: Little, Brown, 1996), 128–61.

21. Robert E. Rubin and Jacob Weisberg, *In an Uncertain World* (New York: Random House, 2004), 3–38; Adams, *Mexican Banking and Investment in Transition*, 135–76. See also General Accounting Office, *Mexico's Financial Crisis: Origins, Awareness, Assistance, and Initial Efforts to Recover*, Report GAO/GGD-96–56 (Washington, D.C.: GAO, 1996).

22. John A. Adams, Jr., "Mexico vs. China," *Laredo 2020* 4, no. 1 (2003): 1–5.

23. Salinas, *Mexico*, 657–701.

24. Alan Riding, *Distant Neighbors: A Portrait of the Mexicans* (New York: Knopf, 1985).

25. For candid observations on agricultural and environmental issues see Tom Barry, *Zapata's Revenge: Free Trade and the Farm Crisis in Mexico* (Boston: South End Press, 1995); Joel Simon *Endangered Mexico: An Environment on the Edge* (San

Francisco: Sierra Club Books, 1997); John Womack, *Zapata and the Mexican Revolution* (New York, Vintage, 1970).

26. Krauze, "Will Mexico Break Free?" Y 21; Sidney Weintraub, *Transforming the Mexican Economy: The Salinas Sexenio* (Washington, D.C.: National Planning Association, 1990), 1–61.

27. John A. Adams, Jr., "Mexico and the IMF: Regional Banking Crisis—Global Consequences," in *Banking in North America: NAFTA and Beyond,* ed. Jerry Harr and Krishnan Dandapani (Amsterdam: Pergamon, 1999), 166–82.

28. Manu Dornbiere, "La Verdad de Nuestra Democracia," *El Mañana,* May 14, 2005, 5A.

29. Weintraub, *Transforming the Mexican Economy,* 59–60.

CHAPTER 1. Agriculture: Tierra y Libertad

1. Norbert Fiess and Daniel Lederman, "Mexican Corn: The Effects of NAFTA," *Trade Notes,* no. 18, September 27, 2004, 1–7, www.worldbank.org/research/trade; Daryll Ray, "Mexico and Corn," *The Farm Press,* September 17, 2003; Tim Weiner, "Subsidized U.S. Imports Bury Family Farms," February 26, 2002; USDA, U.S. Embassy Mexico City, "Mexico Announces Support Programs for Sinaloa White Corn [as released by SAGARPA and published in *Diario Oficial,* July 30, 2004]," Mexico City: USDA, August 17, 2004.

2. Barry, *Zapata's Revenge,* 191; "Presence of Typical Mexican Food," *Mexico's Economic Situation Monthly Report,* August 2002, 4; David Luhnow, "Of Corn, Crisis and Capitol Hill," *Wall Street Journal,* March 5, 2003, A13; "The Hypocrisy of Farm Subsidies," *New York Times,* December 1, 2002, 8; "High Levels of Agricultural Support in OECD Countries: A Cause for Concern for Developing Economies," OECD, 2002, www.oecd.org.oecd; "Foundering in a Tariff-free Landscape," *Economist,* November 30, 2002, 31. Farmers in Mexico received a higher guaranteed subsidy payback in dollars per ton (Spring 2001 and Winter 2001–02 crop statistics): for example, corn—U.S. $99, Mexico 153; wheat—U.S. 105, Mexico 150; and soybeans—U.S. 169, Mexico 218.

3. Parr Rosson and Flynn Adcock, "The North American Free Trade Agreement: Deepening Economic Integration and Responses to Competition," no. 2003-3, Center for North American Studies [CNAS], Texas A&M University, July 2003); Mary A. O'Grady, "Clinton's Sugar Daddy Becomes Now Threat on NAFTA's Future," *Wall Street Journal,* December 20, 2002, A15; "A Free Trade Revival," ibid, August 15, 2002, A12.

4. Herman von Bertrab, *Negotiating NAFTA: A Mexican Envoy's Account* (Westport, Conn.: Praeger, 1997), 147–48.

5. www.era.usda.gov/briefing/mexico/trade; OECD, *Economic Survey: Mexico,* 2004, 189.

6. OECD, *Economic Survey: Mexico,* 2004, 189.

7. D. T. Nguyen and M. L. Martinez, "The Effects of Land Reform on Agricultural Production, Employment and Income Distribution: A Statistical Study of Mexican States, 1959–1969," *Economic Journal,* September 1979, 634. See also P. Dorner and D. Kanel, "The Economic Case for Land Reform," in *Land Reform, Land Settlement and Cooperatives,* ed. Peter Dorner (Madison: Wisconsin Land Tenure Center, 1971),

1:1–16; M. W. Mueller, "Changing Patterns of Agricultural Output and Production in the Private and Land Reform Sectors in Mexico, 1940–60," *Economic Development and Cultural Change* 18, no. 2 (January 1970): 252–66; Roger Bartra, *Agrarian Structure and Political Power in Mexico* (Baltimore: Johns Hopkins University Press, 1993), 19–33.

8. David Barkin, *Distorted Development: Mexico in the World Economy* (Boulder, Colo.: Westview Press, 1990), 35–36, 124–25; OECD, *Economic Surveys: Mexico*, January 2004, 189–92.

9. Jorge Carpizo, *La Constitución Mexicana de 1917* (Mexico City: UNAM, 1969), 131.

10. John Bailey, "The Bureaucracy," in *Prospects For Mexico*, ed. George W. Grayson (Washington, D.C.: Foreign Service Institute, 1988), 31.

11. Von Bertrab, *Negotiating NAFTA*, 148. See also Daniel C. Levy and Kathleen Bruhn, *Mexico: Struggles for Democratic Development* (Berkeley: University of California Press, 2001), 162–66.

12. Bartra, *Agrarian Structure and Political Power in Mexico*, 79–105; Bruce F. Johnston et al., eds., *U.S.–Mexico Relations: Agriculture and Rural Development* (Stanford, Calif.: Stanford University Press, 1987), 365–70; Nguyen and Martinez, "Effects of Land Reform," 625; Camin and Meyer, *In the Shadow of the Mexican Revolution*, 80. See also Thomas Benjamin, *La Revolución: Mexico's Great Revolution as Memory, Myth, and History* (Austin: University of Texas Press, 2000); U.S. International Trade Commission, *The Likely Impact on the United States of a Free Trade Agreement with Mexico* (Washington, D.C.: GPO, 1991), 4-3–4-17.

13. A. Yunez-Naude, "The Dismantling of CONASUPO, a Mexican State Trader in Agriculture," *World Economy* 26, no. 1 (January 2003): 97–122; Xiaodong Gong et al., "Mobility in the Urban Labor Markets: A Rural Data Analysis for Mexico," *Economic Development and Cultural Change*, October 2004, 1–36; "Mexico Case Study: PROGRESA," Annex 4(C), www.fao.org/DOCREP/006.

14. CIA, "Mexico," in *The World Factbook*, www.cis.gov/cia/publications/factbook; Stephen P. Mumme, *Apportioning Groundwater beneath the U.S.–Mexico Border* (San Diego: Center for U.S.–Mexican Studies, 1988); Helen Igram, Nancy Laney, and David Gillilan, *Divided Waters: Bridging the U.S.–Mexico Border* (Tucson: University of Arizona Press, 1995), 1–20.

15. OECD, *Economic Surveys: Mexico*, January 2004, 121.

16. Daniel Levy and Gabriel Szekely, *Mexico: Paradoxes of Stability and Change* (Boulder: University of Colorado Press, 1987), 26–30; Barry, *Zapata's Revenge*, 81, 87; Bartra, *Agrarian Structure and Political Power in Mexico*, 168–88; *Mexico Country Report* (London: Economist Intelligence Unit, 2002), 25–26. Fewer than 2,000 families owned 87 percent of the land in 1910. In the early 1990s more than 5 million ejidatarios controlled 90 percent of the land.

17. Michael J. Mazan, *Global Trends 2005* (New York: St. Martin's Press, 1999), 25–26.

18. Simon, *Endangered Mexico*, 60–61.

19. Kandell, *La Capital*, 529–71; *OECD Territorial Reviews: Mexico City* (Paris: OECD Policy Briefs, 2004), 1–7.

20. Kandell, *La Capital*, 529.

21. "Chilango Heaven," *Economist*, May 1, 2004, 39.

22. www.popcouncil.org/lao/Mexico Infant mortality rates have declined from 114 per 1000 live births in 1950 to 32 per 1000. It is estimated there are approximately 621 people in Mexico per doctor, versus 24 people per doctor in the United States.

23. Jonathan House et al., "The Quest: Spanish Bank Sees U.S. Hispanic Treasure," *Wall Street Journal*, July 8, 2004; Samuel P. Huntington, *Who Are We? The Challenges to America's National Identity* (New York: Simon & Schuster, 2004), 1–448; R. Smith, "Dilemas y perspectivas del sistema migratorio de America del Norte," *Comercio Exterior* 50 (November 4, 2000): 289–304; Michael Gonzalez, "Hispanics for Jorge," *Wall Street Journal*, November 8, 2004, A15.

24. Salinas de Gortari, *Mexico: The Policy and Politics of Modernization*, 666–70; J. Ramon Gil-Garcia, "Article 27: The Change in Mexican Agrarian Policy and the Policy Formulation Process in the Developing World," *Rockefeller College Review* 1, no. 2 (1997): 24–38; Barry, *Zapata's Revenge*, 80–86. During the 1992 ejido reform a certification and titling program (*dominio plene*) known as PROCEDE (Programa de Certificación de Derechos Ejidales y Titilación de Solares Urbanos) was in operation until the late 1990s.

25. Rosson and Adcock, "North American Free Trade Agreement"; Jenalia Moreno, "Land and Loss," *Houston Chronicle*, October 20, 2002.

26. Salinas de Gortari, *Mexico*, 693–96; Barry, *Zapata's Revenge*, 17–37.

27. Executive Office of the President, *North American Free Trade Agreement between the Government of the United States of America, the Government of Canada and the Government of the United Mexican States* (Washington, D.C.: GPO, 1993), 1: 7-1– 7-42.

28. "From Corn Wars to Corn Laws," *Economist*, September 25, 2004, 50; Edit Antal, "Who Should Tell Me What to Eat? The Case of Transgenic Maize," *Voices of Mexico*, April 2004, 113–16; S'ra DeSantis, "Genetically Modified Organisms Threaten Indigenous Corn," *Z Magazine*, July 2002, www.zmag.org/ZMag/articles/julaug02desantis.html.

29. Concerns expressed about GM corn or Bt corn draw on research that shows this variety of corn contains genes from soil bacterium *Bacillus thuringiensis* (Bt) that can produce toxins that kill certain insect pests (e.g., the European corn borer or Southwest corn borer), yet could have what the National Environmental Trust terms the "unintended consequences which include allergic reactions and plant toxicity, " as well as the possibility that, "Bt may accumulate in the soil (unlike organic spraying of Bt) and thus, the use of Bt corn will create pesticide resistance, thereby reducing the effectiveness of Bt as an organic pesticide." quoted in Frank Ackerman et al., "Free Trade, Corn, and the Environment: Environmental Impacts of US–Mexico Corn Trade under NAFTA," Global Development and Environmental Institute, working paper no. 03-06, Tufts University, Medford, Mass., June 2003, 11–12.

30. Robert Mann, "Has GM Corn 'Invaded' Mexico?" *Science Magazine*, March 2002, 1617–19; GAO, *U.S. Agencies Need Greater Focus to Support Mexico's Successful Transition to Liberalized Agricultural Trade under NAFTA*, GAO-05-272 (Washington, D.C.: GPO, 2005). The value of U.S. corn exports to Mexico in 2003 totals $651 million.

31. Barry, *Zapata's Revenge*, 244–47; "Tequila Sunrise?" *Financial Times*, March 12, 2004, 14; Bonnie Pfister, "Mexican Farmers Fear U.S. Competition," *San Antonio Express-News*, November 14, 2002.

32. Barkin, *Distorted Development*, 33, 35. See also Parr Rosson, "GMO and Biosafety Protocols: Issues and Implications for Texas Agriculture" (Center for North American Studies, Texas A&M University, 2004).

33. Fiess and Ledeman, "Mexican Corn," 2. As proof of this corn production SAGARPA in August 2004 forecast a record white corn crop of 4.2 MMT for the state of

Sinaloa, a record crop that was 41 percent higher than the previous year. Sinaloa accounts for approximately 70 percent of the fall/winter white corn production in Mexico.

34. Nora Lustig, B. P. Bosworth, and Robert Z. Lawrence, eds., *North American Free Trade: Assessing the Impact* (Washington, D.C.: Brookings Institution, 1992), 89–90, 159–67; "Floundering in a Tariff-free Landscape," *Economist*, November 30. 2002, 32.

35. David Luhnow, "Why Corona Is Big Here, and Miller Is So Scarce in Mexico," *Wall Street Journal*, January 17, 2003, B1.

36. Jack Jackson, *Los Mestenos: Spanish Ranching in Texas, 1721–1821* (College Station: Texas A&M University Press, 1986), 9–617; J. Frank Dobie, *The Longhorns* (Boston: Little, Brown, and Co., 1941), 3-42; Manuel A. Machado, *The North Mexican Cattle Industry, 1920–1975* (College Station: Texas A&M University Press, 1981), 3–12.

37. 1. Dave Price, "Let's Really Look at Free Trade," *Beef*, October 2004, 47; *Consumer Latin America: 2004* (London: Euromonitor, 2003), 296.

38. *Canadian Boxed Beef Report*, National Beef Industry Development Fund, January 5, 2004; Clint Peck, "Southern Exposure," *Beef*, July 2004, 26; www.usmef.org; "Final BSE Rules May be Postponed," *Weekly Livestock Reporter*, December 16, 2004, 1; GAO, *U.S. Agencies Need Greater Focus*, 41–44.

39. USDA, *Mexico and Sugar: Historical Perspective* (Washington, D.C.: USDA, 2004); Won W. Koo and Richard D. Taylor, "2004 Outlook of the U.S. and World Sugar Markets, 2003–2013," report no. 536 (Center for Agricultural Policy and Trade Studies, North Dakota State University, June 2004).

40. Jerilyn M. Gomez, "An Assessment of U.S. Sugar Program Sustainability: The Implication of Granting Increased Market Access to Foreign Sugar Producers," Agricultural Economics Department, Penn State University, 2004.

41. Von Bertrab, *Negotiating NAFTA*, 137–38.

42. ERS/USDA, "Sugar and Sweetener: Policy," February 5, 2003; USDA "U.S.–Mexico Sweetener Trade Mired in Dispute," *Agricultural Outlook*, September 1999, 17–20; See also GAO, *U.S. Agencies Need Greater Focus*, 30–31, 47–49.

43. Michael E. Porter, *The Competitive Advantage of Nations* (New York: Free Press, 1990), 735. See also Barkin, *Distorted Development*, 11.

CHAPTER 2. La Frontera: The Border and Immigration

1. John L. Kessell, *Spain in the Southwest* (Norman: University of Oklahoma Press, 2002), 202–14; Tom Barry, *Crossing the Line: Immigrants, Economic Integration, and Drug Enforcement on the U.S.–Mexico Border* (Albuquerque: Resource Center Press, 1994), 1, 12–13; Raat, *Mexico and the United States*, 5, 55–78. See also H. W. Brands, *Lone Star Nation* (New York: Doubleday, 2004); David S. Heidler and Jeane T. Heidler, *Manifest Destiny* (Westport, Conn.: Greenwood Press, 2003); Lawrence A. Herzog, *Where North Meets South: Cities, Space, and Politics on the United States–Mexico Border* (Austin: Center for Mexican American Studies, University of Texas, 1990).

2. Juan Mora-Torres, *The Making of the Mexican Border* (Austin: University of Texas Press, 2001), 29–125; David Montejano, *Anglos and Mexicans* (Austin: University

of Texas Press, 1987), 30–49; Gilberto M. Hinojosa, *A Borderland Town in Transition* (College Station: Texas A&M University Press, 1983), 70–122; Daniel C. Levy and Kathleen Bruhn, *Mexico: The Struggle for Democratic Development* (Berkeley: University of California Press, 2001), 180–83.

3. Ronnie C. Tyler, *Santiago Vidaurri and the Southern Confederacy* Austin: Texas State Historical Association, 1973, pp. 41–156; Thomas D. Schoonover, *Dollars Over Dominion* (Baton Rouge: Louisiana State University Press, 1978), 78–177; Robert H. Jackson, ed., *New Views of Borderlands History* (Albuquerque: University of New Mexico Press, 1988), 120–26.

4. Anita Brenner, *The Wind that Swept Mexico* (repr., Austin: University of Texas Press, 1971), 76. Brenner repeatedly labels the so-called revolutionary unrest a "civil war."

5. Charles Frazier, "The Migrant Worker and the Bracero in the U.S." *The Role of the Mexican American in the History of the Southwest*, Edinburg, Tex.: Pan American College, November 17, 1969, 24–34; Samuel P. Huntington, "The Hispanic Challenge," *Foreign Policy*, March 2004, 1–12.

6. Libson and Renteria, *The U.S. and Mexico: Borderland Development and the National Economies*, 131–32; Grayson, *Prospects For Mexico*, 212–13.

7. Kim Cobb, "Bracero-era Hardships Cast Doubt on Guest Worker Plan," *Houston Chronicle*, August 3, 2003, 1; Grayson, *Prospects for Mexico*, 149–210; "Political Tensions Aroused in Mexico," *New York Times*, September 12, 1982; "Mexico after the Fiesta," ibid., February 14, 1982. See also Gong, Van Soest, and Villagomez, "Mobility in the Urban Labor Markets," 1–36.

8. Herzog, *Where North Meets South*, 52–62, 146–63; Michael J. Mazarr, *Mexico 2005* (Washington: D.C.: CSIS Press, 1999), 79.

9. Oscar J. Martinez, "Transnational Fronterizos: Cross-Border Linkages in Mexican Border Society," *Journal of Borderlands Studies*, Spring 1990, 79–94; Raul A. Fernandez, *The Mexican-American Border Region* (Notre Dame. Ind.: University of Notre Dame Press, 1989), 32–44; 8 CFR 235.1 (f) (iii) and section (a) (15) (B); 22 Stat. 214-215; www.archives.gov/research-room/genealogy/immigrant-arrivals/mexican-border. The Arizona-Mexico border entering distance was extended to 65 miles in 1999 in hopes of promoting more retail trade with Mexico.

10. Barry, *Crossing the Line*, 9–11.

11. Charles A. Kupchan, *The End of the American Era* (New York: Vintage, 2003), xix, 331.

12. Barry, *Crossing the Line*, 25–27.

13. "Farmers: Mexico Water Debt Due," *Dallas Morning News*, August 28, 2004; Alejandro Diaz-Bautista, "Economic Growth in the Northern Border of Mexico, Recent Economic Trends along the U.S.–Mexico Border," COLEF, December 3, 2004; EPA, *Border 2012: U.S.–Mexico Environmental Program*, EPA-160-D-02-01 (Washington, D.C.: GPO, 2002). See also Fernandez, *Mexican-American Border Region*, 45–66; David J. Eaton and John M. Andersen, *The State of the Rio Grande / Rio Bravo* (Tucson: University of Arizona Press, 1987); Norris Hurdley, Jr., *Dividing the Waters: A Century of Controversy between the United States and Mexico* (Berkeley: University of California Press, 1966).

14. Bill Emmott, *20:21 Vision* (New York: Farrar, Straus, and Giroux, 2003), 261. See also Kapchan, *End of the American Era*, 99.

15. William H. Frey, "Migration Swings," *American Demographics*, February 2002, 18–21; Wayne Karrfalt, "A Multicultural Mecca," ibid., S4–S5; Guillermina Rodriquez, "Mexican Residents in the USA," in *Review if the Economic Situation of Mexico*, ed. (Mexico City: Banamex, 2004), 440–46.

16. Magazine Publishers of America, "Hispanic-Latino Market Profile," 2004, 1–17, www.magazine.org/marketprofiles; http://portal.sre.gob.mx/usa/index; Jeffery Passel, "Mexican Immigration to the US: The Latest Estimates," *Migration Information Source*, www.migrationinformation.org, accessed March 1, 2004: OECD, *Economic Survey: Mexico*, January 2004, 126–28; B. Lindsay Lowell and Roberto Suro, "How Many Undocumented: The Numbers behind the U.S.–Mexico Migration Talks," *Pew Hispanic Center*, March 21, 2003, 1–11; Jed Babbin, "Do the Math: Costs of Illegal Immigrants Outweigh Benefits," *Houston Chronicle*, April 10, 2005, E1; "Dreaming of the Other Side of the Wire," *Economist*, March 12, 2005, 27–29; "A Slip of the Tongue, Governor?" ibid., April 30, 2005, 28.

17. Frazier, "Migrant Worker and the Bracero in the U.S.," 33; Fernandez, *Mexican-American Border Region*, 67–83.

18. Ninna N. Sorensen, "The Development Dimension of Migrant Remittances," final report, Danish Institute for Development Studies, Copenhagen, April 2004, 8–10; Inter-American Development Bank, "Sending Money Home: Remittances to Latin America and the Caribbean," Washington, D.C., May 2004, 7–24. Of the over $75 billion in remittances to developing countries from nations worldwide, India accounts for 15 percent of the total, followed by Mexico, the Philippines, China, and Turkey.

19. Daniel T. Griswold, "Willing Workers: Fixing the Problem of Illegal Mexican Migration to the United States," Cato Institute, Washington, D.C., 11.

20. Richard Lapper, "Latin Americans Scale Summit of the Remittance League," *Financial Times*, March 26, 2004; Sergio Bustos, "$30 Billion Leaves the U.S." *El Paso Times*, May 18, 2004; Roberto Coronado, "Workers' Remittances to Mexico," *Business Frontier* [El Paso Federal Reserve Branch], no. 1 (2004); OECD, *Economic Survey*, 2004, 146–57.

21. Barry, *Crossing the Line*, 21; U.S. Census, 2003, "Estimates of the Unauthorized Immigrant Population Residing in the U.S."; OECD, *Economic Survey*, 2004, 131; Victor D. Hanson, *Mexifornia* (San Francisco: Encounter Books, 2003), 22–23.

22. "Immigration Reality Check," editorial, *Wall Street Journal*, May 4, 2005, A18.

23. Barry, *Crossing the Line*, 21, 25; "Dreaming of the Other Side of the Wire," *Economist*, March 12, 2005, 27–29.

24. Hanson, *Mexifornia*, 9; See also Huntington, *Who Are We?*; Julie Watts, "Mexico–U.S. Migration and Labor Unions: Obstacles to Building Cross-Border Solidarity," working paper 79, CCIS, University of California, La Jolla, June 2003, 1–35.

25. Jeffrey Davidow, *The US and Mexico: The Bear and the Porcupine* (Princeton: Markus Weiner Publishers, 2004), 112; Barry, *Crossing the Line*, 32–44; Francisco Alba, "Mexico: A Crucial Crossroads," Migration Policy Institute, Washington, D.C., March 2004.

26. OECD, *Economic Survey*, 2004, 133; *Barron's* quoted in "George Melloan, "What Pitfalls Will Bush Face in 2005?" *Wall Street Journal*, January 4, 2005, A13; Barry, *Crossing the Line*, 45–52; see also Leon C. Metz, *Border: The U.S. Mexico Line*

(El Paso: Mangan Books, 1989); Oscar J. Martinez, *Troublesome Border* (Tucson: University of Arizona Press, 1988).

27. Hanson, *Mexifornia*, 26–27; see also Riordan Roett, *Mexico's External Relations in the 1990s* (Boulder: Lynne Rienner Publishers, 1991), 237–41.

28. "The Vote Next Time," *Economist*, March 5, 2005, 39; OECD, *Economic Survey*, 2004, 151; Jorge Durand, "From Traitors to Heroes: 100 Years of Mexican Migration Policies," Migration Policy Institute, Washington, D.C., March 1, 2004; Eduardo Porter, "Fox Pushes to Cement Ties with Mexicans in U.S.," *Wall Street Journal*, March 6, 2003, A11. In 2004, Mexico had about 68.8 million registered voters.

29. Davidow, *US and Mexico*, 111, 115; see also Levy and Bruhn, *Mexico*, 228–42.

30. Timothy J. Dunn, *The Militarization of the U.S.–Mexico Border 1978–1992* (Austin: CMAS, 1996), 76–83.

31. "Dangerous Desert, Breached Border," *Economist*, January 8, 2005, 37; Pia Orrenius, "Illegal Immigration and Enforcement Along the U.S.–Mexico Border: An Overview," in *Economic and Financial Review* (Dallas: Federal Reserve Bank of Dallas, 2001). The migration of others includes aliens from Brazil, all of Central America, and Cuba, as well as reports of Romanians, Chinese, and Russians. Over 90 percent of immigrants use a coyote, which in early 2005 is estimated to cost $1,000–1,700 per person per crossing (Joel Millman, "Mexico Focuses on Brazilians amid U.S. Migrant Concerns," *Wall Street Journal*, May 10, 2005, A15).

32. "Immigration Anxiety," editorial, *Wall Street Journal*, October 25, 2004, A18; Miriam Jordon, "Arizona Limits Illegal Immigrants' Access to Benefits," ibid., November 4, 2004, A4; Donald L. Barlett and James B. Steele, "Who Left the Door Open?" *Time*, September 20, 2004, 51–66; "Dreaming of the Other Side of the Wire," *Economist*, March 12, 2005, 29.

33. Monica Verea, "A Watershed in the U.S.–Mexico Migration Debate: Closing the Borders," *World Press Review*, April 2002; "The Second 1984 Presidential Debate," *The McNeil-Lehrer Newshour*, October 28, 1984, www.pbs.org/newshour; Jason L. Riley, "Ignore the Anti-Immigrant Right. Bush Did." *Wall Street Journal*, November 22, 2004, A14; Jessica M. Vaughan, "Modernizing the Welcome Mat: A Look at the Goals and Challenges of the US-VISIT Program," CIS, Smart Borders Conference, Washington, D.C., October 26, 2004.

34. Passel, "Mexican Immigration to the US." Passel notes that the undocumented population in the United States by country and region of origin in 2002 was Mexico 57%, other Latin America 23%, Asia 10%, Europe and Canada 5%, and Africa and other countries 5%.

35. Michael A. Fletcher, "Bush Immigration Plan Meets GOP Opposition," *Washington Post*, January 2, 2005, A6.

36. 1. Executive Office of the President, House, *Economic Report of the President*, 109th Cong., 1st sess., H. Doc. 109-1 (Washington, D.C.: GPO, 2005), 93–116; "Bittersweet Trade," editorial, *Wall Street Journal*, May 13, 2005, A12; "Central America's Trade Challenge," editorial, *Financial Times*, May 13, 2005, 14.

37. Richard Schmitt and H. G. Reza, "U.S. Fears Terrorism Via Mexico's Time-Tested Smuggling Routes," *Los Angeles Times*, September 15, 2004, A16; "Dangerous Desert, Breached Border," *Economist*, January 8, 2005, 38.

38. Stephen J. Blank, *Rethinking Asymmetric Threats* (Carlisle, Pa.: SSI-U.S. Army War College, 2003); Autulio J. Echevarria and Bert B. Tussing, *From 'Defending*

Forward' to a *'Global Defense-in depth':* *Globalization and Homeland Security* (Carlisle, Pa.: SSI-U.S. Army War College, 2003); Mark Krikorian, "Keeping Terror Out: Immigration Policy and Asymmetric Warfare," CIS, Washington, D.C., Spring 2004, 1–9; Tamar Jacoby, "Borderline," *New Republic*, January 26, 2004, 18–22.

39. U.S. House of Representatives, *Intelligence Reform and Terrorism Prevention Act of 2004*, 108th Cong., 2nd sess., Report 108-796, December 7, 2004; Donald E. Schultz and Edward J. Williams, eds., *Mexico Faces the 21ˢᵗ Century* (Westport, Conn.: Greenwood Press, 1995), 125–29. See also U.S.–Mexico Binational Council, *U.S.–Mexico Border Security and the Evolving Security Relationship* (Washington, D.C.: CSIS, 2004), 1–31; "Destruye Violencia Vida de la Frontera," *El Mañana*, May 14, 2005, 1.

40. Krikorian, "Keeping Terror Out," 9. For detailed review, see Griswold, "Willing Workers," 1–24. See also James Pinkerton and Ivan Grillo, "The Fight for Nuevo Laredo," *Houston Chronicle*, May 8, 2005, 1; Olga R. Rodriguez, "Cartel Aims to Control Border Flow," Associated Press, February 13, 2005.

CHAPTER 3. Black Gold: Energy Dynamics of Mexico

1. "Into Deep Water," *Economist*, February 26, 2005, 36; Juan Rosellon and Jonathan Halpern, "Regulatory Reform in Mexico's Natural Gas Industry," World Bank Policy Research Working Paper no. 2537, January 2001, 3; Lourdes Rocha and Sergio Luna, "Energy in Mexico: Some General Reflections," *Review of the Economic Situation of Mexico*, August 2002, 322–25. The ranking of Mexico's potential level of proven reserves varies in different reports from seventh to eleventh.

2. Krauze, *Mexico*, 355–56.; Hart, *Empire and Revolution*, 73–89, 152, 154–63. See also Jonathan C. Brown, *Oil and Revolution in Mexico* (Berkeley: University of California Press, 1993); Jesús Silva Herzog, *Historia de la Expropiacion Petróleo* (Mexico City: Cuadernos Americanos, 1963); Justo Sierra, *La Evolución Política del Pueblo Mexicano* (Mexico City, 1902). While the bulk of rail expansion was built with foreign capital, the Díaz administration allowed the state to take over (nationalize) most of the railroads in 1907.

3. Daniel Yergin, *The Prize: The Epic Quest for Oil, Money, and Power* (New York: Touchstone Books, 1992), 232.

4. Pietro S. Nivola, "Energy Independence or Interdependence? Integrating the North American Energy Market," *Brookings Review*, Spring 2002, 24–27; U.S. Department of Energy, "Mexico Country Analysis Brief," November 2004, www.eia.doe.gov.

5. George Baker, "Mexico's New Upstream Philosophy," *Oil and Gas Investor*, September 2002, 53–55; Yergin, *Prize*, 231.

6. Government of Mexico, *True Facts*, 1–270.

7. John Gunther, *Inside Latin America* (New York: Harper& Brothers, 1941), 107–15.

8. Hart, *Empire and Revolution*, 431. See also Catherine E. Jayne, *Oil, War, and Anglo-American Relations: American and British Reactions to Mexico's Expropriation of Foreign Oil Properties, 1937–1941* (Westport, Conn.: Greenwood Press, 2001), 105–60.

9. Krauze, *Mexico*, 473–75, 503, 596; Hart, *Empire and Revolution*, 403, 415–17. See also Thomas E. Skidmore and Peter H. Smith, *Modern Latin America*, 5th ed. (Oxford: Oxford University Press, 2001), 236–37.

10. Adams, *Mexican Banking and Investment in Transition*, 54–56. In addition to gaining broader commercial access to over one hundred national markets, duties in

Mexico dropped from 120 percent to an average of 20 percent (pre-NAFTA) in 1993. See also Pamela S. Falk, *Petroleum and Mexico's Future* (Boulder, Colo.: Westview Press, 1987), 21, 55–59.

11. Adams, *Mexican Banking and Investment in Transition*, 67–83. See also GAO, *Mexican Oil: Issues Affecting Potential U.S. Trade and Investment*, GAO, NSIAD-92-169 (Washington, D.C.: GAO, 1992).

12. U.S. Department of Energy, "An Energy Overview of Mexico", www.eia.doe .gov, accessed October 2, 2002, 1–14; ibid., "Mexico Country Analysis Brief," November 2004.

13. "Americans Maintain Thirst for Gas Guzzlers," *Financial Times*, May 17, 2004, 11; Jenalia Moreno, "Oil Blurs Problems," *Houston Chronicle*, October 17, 2004, D1.

14. Ronald Buchanan, "PEMEX Seeks Cheer from Mexican Waves," *Financial Times*, October 5, 2004, 18.

15. Jose de Cordoba, "Mexico's Fox Wins Duel with Pemex Oil Workers," *Wall Street Journal*, October 1, 2002, A19; Bonnie Pfister, "Pemex May Invite Foreigners," *San Antonio Express News*, September 29, 2002, 1K; Tim Weiner, "Mexico Oil Contract," *New York Times*, October 1, 2002, A7.

16. North America Energy Working Group, *North America—The Energy Picture*, June 2002, 20–21, 65, 67.

17. UNDP/World Bank, *Mexico Energy Environment Review*, May 2001, 94–99; "PEMEX," *Latin Trade*, November 2002, 14; John Lyons, "An Oil Binge in Latin America," *Wall Street Journal*, November 16, 2004, A22. Latin America accounts for only about 12 percent of global oil production.

18. "Oficio con el que remite iniciativa de decreto por el que se reforman, adicionan y derogan diversas disposiciones de la ley de la comision reguladora de energia," *Gaceta Parlamentaria*, August 21, 2002, www.senado.gob.mx.

19. Krauze, *Mexico*, 657; Miguel A. Quintana, "Energy, Natural Resources and Utilities," *International Financial Law Review* 2000: 11–14; Geri Smith, "Mexico's Electric Power Struggle," *Business Week*, March 25, 2002. The first electricity in Mexico was produced by a hydroelectric plant in 1920, and the electrical industry was nationalized on September 27, 1960.

20. DOE, "Energy Overview of Mexico," October 2002; Rosellon and Halpern, "Regulatory Reform in Mexico's Natural Gas Industry," 4–12. See also Salinas de Gortari, *Mexico: The Policy and Politics of Modernization*, 495–502; Buchanan, "PEMEX Seeks Chen," *Financial Times*, October 5, 2005.

21. DOE, "An Energy Overview of Mexico," p. 3.; Nydia Iglesias, "Energy Reform on the Agenda," *Review of the Economic Situation of Mexico*, September 2002, 370–75.

22. Hil Anderson, "U.S. World Energy Demand to Grow 60 Percent," *Washington Times*, March 26, 2002; RosioVargas and Victor Rodriguez-Padilla, "The Energy Reform: A Long-tem Strategy," *Voices of Mexico*, December 2003, 15–19.

23. Angela Shah and B. M. Case, "Texas Companies May Export Gas to Mexico," *Dallas Morning News*, June 5, 2002; Mont P. Hoyt, "Cooking with Gas," *World Trade*, August 2002, 36–38; Texas Railroad Commission, "State of the Oil and Gas Industry: 2001," www.rrc.state.tx.us.

24. NAE Working Group, *North America—The Energy Picture*, 26–28; Raul Montefonte, "Gas-demand Growth Will Push Expansion in Mexican Transmission Infrastructure," *Oil and Gas Journal*, February 11, 2002, 70–75.

25. Francisco Barnes de Castro, "Contratos de Servicios Multiples: Una opcion para anmentar la oferta de gas natural en México," Secretaría de Energía, Mexico, June 20, 2002.

26. DOE, "An Energy Overview of Mexico," 10.

27. Ibid., 13–18, 35–37; OECD, *Economic Surveys: Mexico*, January 2004, 97.

28. David Shields, "Mexican Pipeline: The Future of Oil under Vicente Fox," *NACLA Report on the Americas*, February 2001, 31–37; Bob Woodward, *Maestro* (New York: Simon and Schuster, 2000), 138–44.

29. Matthew Gower, "Energizing PEMEX," *Business Mexico*, May 2002, 37–39; "Price Tag to Upgrade Mexico's Refineries: $19 Billion," *World Refining*, February 2002, 20; Kara Sissell, "The New Face of PEMEX Taking a Private-sector Approach to Business," *Chemical Week*, May 29, 2002, 20–22; Tim Weiner, "Pemex Chief Struggles to Free Energy Giant 'Lashed by Politics'" *New York Times*, February 1, 2003.

30. George Baker, "Mexican Energy Sector Reform Includes Foreign Operators' Participation in E & D," *Oil and Gas Journal*, February 11, 2002, 64–66; "Despide Fox a M. Leos," *El Mañana*, November 2, 2004, 1; Ioan Grillo, "Pemex Shakes Up Leadership," *Houston Chronicle*, November 1, 2004; "Dir. Of Mexico's State-run Oil Co. Resigns," *New York Times*, November 1, 2004. The former head of the PEMEX exploration and production unit, Luis Ramirez, replaced Munoz (David Luhnow, "Pemex Chief Says Mexican Oil Patch Needs Investors," *Wall Street Journal*, May 6, 2005, A13.

31. "Dollars by the Barrel-full: Petrodollars—What's in the Pipeline," *HSBC Economic Bulletin*, October 22, 2004, 1–18; Brian Bremner and Dexter Roberts, "China: The Great Oil Hunt," *Business Week*, November 15, 2004, 60–63.

32. "Into Deep Water," 36.

33. David Ronfeldt, Richard Nehring, and Arturo Gandara, *Mexico's Petroleum and U.S. Policy: Implications for the 1980s* (Santa Monica, Calif.: Rand Corporation, 1980), 59.

34. Carlos Guerra, "NAFTA's Impact on Border Is More than a Regional Concern," *San Antonio Express News*, December 12, 2002, B1.

35. Steve H. Hanke, "Over the Barrel," *Wall Street Journal*, October 24, 2004.

CHAPTER 4. Mexico versus China

1. Daniel Yergin and Joseph Stanislaw, *The Commanding Heights* (New York: Simon & Schuster, 1998), 364–91; John Micklethwait and Adrian Wooldridge, *The Witch Doctor* (London: Mandarin, 1997), 243–66; Kupchan, *End of the American Era*, 85–112; Geoffrey Garrett, "Globalization's Missing Middle," *Foreign Affairs*, December 2004, 84–196; Pomeranz and Topik, *World that Trade Created*, 179–239; "A World at Work," *Economist*, November 11, 2004; Jim Dolmas, "Beyond the Border: Globalization Myths and Realities," *Southwest Economy* [Federal Reserve Bank of Dallas], October 2004; Thomas L. Friedman, *The Lexus and the Olive Tree: Understanding Globalization* (New York: Farrar, Straus and Giroux, 2000.

2. William Greider, "A New Sucking Sound," *Nation*, December 26, 2001; Supachai Panitchpakdi and Mark L. Clifford, *China and the WTO: Changing China, Changing World Trade* (New York: John Wiley & Sons, 2002), 1–98; Juan Jose Ramirez Bonilla, "Asia Pacific and the Challenges for Mexico," *Comercio Exterior*, October 2002, 860–65; Ralph Watkins, "Mexico Versus China: Factors Affecting Export and

Investment Competition," *Industry Trade and Technology Review* (USITC, pub. 3534), July 2002, 11–26.

3. Adams, *Mexican Banking and Investment in Transition*, 13–86; James Bovard, *The Fair-Trade Fraud* (New York: St. Martin's Press, 1991), 306–18; William McGaughey, *A U.S.–Mexico-Canada Free-Trade Agreement* (Minneapolis: Thistlerose Publications, 1992), 26–43.

4. Bradford DeLong, C. DeLong, and Sherman Robinson, "The Case for Mexico's Rescue," *Foreign Affairs*, May 1996, 8–14.

5. "The Cuba Test," *Economist*, April 18, 2002.

6. Davidow, *U.S. and Mexico*, 97–108.

7. David Shields, "Government Indifferent as Assembly Jobs Flee Mexico," *News* (Mexico City), March 11, 2002.

8. Davidow, *U.S. and Mexico*, 242.

9. Adams, *Mexican Banking and Investment in Transition*, 50–62. For an extensive look at the impact on American investment since 1870, see Hart, *Empire and Revolution*, 2002.

10. Philip L. Martin and Michael S. Teitelbaum, "The Mirage of Mexican Guest Workers," *Foreign Affairs*, November 2001, 122–24; Scott M Schwartz, "The Border Industrialization Program of Mexico," *Southwest Journal of Business and Economics*, Summer 1987, 1–51.

11. Adams, *Mexican Banking and Investment in Transition*, 32–37; Roger Turner, "Mexico Turns to Its In-Bond Industry as a Means of Generating Exchange," *Business America*, November 28, 1983, 27-32; Martin E. Rosenfeldt, "Mexico's In Bond Export Industries and U.S. Legislation: Conflictive Issues," *Journal of Borderlands Studies*, Spring 1990, 47–65. The word maquiladora is a term that is often interchanged with maquila, twin plant, and offshore operation or plant.

12. Kathryn Kopinak, *Desert Capitalism: Maquiladoras in North America's Western Industrial Corridor* (Tucson: University of Arizona Press, 1996), 7–36.

13. James Gerber, "Uncertainty and Growth in Mexico's Maquiladora Sector," *Borderlines*, March 2001, 1; OECD, *Territorial Review: Mexico*, 165–68.

14. INEGI; Porter, *Competitive Advantage of Nations*, 11, 383–712; Ralph Watkins, "Production—Sharing Update: Developments in 2001," *Industry Trade and Technology Review* (USITC, pub. 3534), July 2002, 27–42.

15. "Maquila Scoreboard," *Twin Plant News*, August 2002, 54–55; ibid., March 2004, 54–55. For a contrarian view of domestic Mexican industry see Nichola Lowe and Martin Kenny, "Foreign Investment and the Global Geography of Production: Why the Mexican Consumer Electronics Industry Failed," *World Development*, August 1999, 1427–43.

16. Kevin P. Gallagher, *Free Trade and the Environment: Mexico, NAFTA, and Beyond* (Stanford, Calif.: Stanford University Press, 2004), 55. U.S. firms own twelve major cement plants and produce 16 percent of global cement.

17. Kopinak, *Desert Capitalism*, 115–45.

18. Chuck Owen, "Caterpillar Plant Head Touts Management Practices," *Laredo Morning Times*, February 18, 2002. In 2002 the Nuevo Laredo Caterpillar plant earned the Mexican government's *Planta Limpia* (clean plant) certification and the Caterpillar Chairman's Award for the safest plant in Caterpillar worldwide.

19. Gerber, "Uncertainty and Growth"; "Trabajadores hondureños agradecidos con empleo de maquiladoras taiwanesas," *Nacionales* (Honduras), May 22, 2001.

20. Ginger Thompson, "Fallout of U.S. Recession Drifts South Into Mexico, *New York Times*, December 21, 2001; Laura Rodriguez, "Cross-Border Manufacturing in Selected Industries: Apparel," in *Production Sharing: Use of Components and Materials in Foreign Assembly Operations*, pub. 3265 (Washington, D.C.: USITC, 1999), 3–19.

21. Kenneth W. Dam, *The Rules of the Global Game* (Chicago: University of Chicago Press, 2001), 139; Joseph P. Quinlan, "Ties That Bind," *Foreign Affairs*, July 2002, 116–26; Bill Gertz, *The China Threat: How the People's Republic Targets America* (Washington, D.C.: Regnery Publishing, 2000), xx–13.

22. W.A.P. Martin, *The Awakening of China* (New York: Doubleday, Page, and Canopy, 1910), v.

23. Sergio L. Ornelas, "Mexico's Reaction to the China Challenge," *Mexico Now*, January 2003, 17–21; "The Jobs Story" *Wall Street Journal*, September 3, 2004, A10.

24. George F. Gilboy, "The Myth behind China's Miracle," *Foreign Affairs*, August 2004, 33–48; Andrea Mandel Campbell, "Mexico Seeks Deal on China Joining WTO," *Financial Times*, August 14, 2001; Dam, *Rules of the Global Game*, 176; Ross Terrill, *The New Chinese Empire* (New York: Basic Books, 2003), 36–86; Daniel Burstein and Arne de Keijzer, *Big Dragon: The Future of China* (New York: Simon and Schuster, 1998).

25. Walter P. Webb, *The Great Plains* (New York: Grosset and Dunlap, 1931), 273–80; Stephen E. Ambrose, *Nothing Like It in the World: The Men Who Built the Transcontinental Railroad* (New York: Touchstone, 2000), 198–99, 243; Joe Cummings, "Sweet and Sour Times on the Border," *Mexico Connect*, www.mexconnect.com.

26. Terrill, *New Chinese Empire*, 1–141; Kupchan, *End of the American Era*, 278–80; Burstein and de Keijzer, *Big Dragon*, 13–51.

27. Yergin and Stanislaw, *Commanding Heights* 189–99; Gerald Segal, "Does China Matter?" *Foreign Affairs*, September 1999, 24–36; Andrew Scobell and Larry M. Wortzel, *China's Growing Military Power* (Carlisle, Pa.: SSI U.S. Army War College, 2002), 1–306; Andrew Scobell and Larry Wortzel, eds., *Civil-Military Change in China: Elites, Institutes, and Ideas After the 16th Party Congress* (Carlisle, Pa.: SSI U.S. Army War College, 2004); Susan M. Puska, *People's Liberation Army After Next* (Carlisle, Pa.: SSI U.S. Army War College, 2000), 1–327. See also Clay Chandler "Inside the New China" *Fortune*, October 4, 2004, 84–110.

28. "Hu Succeeds Jiang to Top Military Job," *China World*, September 20, 2004, 1; "China's Growth Spreads Inland," *Economist*, November 20, 2004, 13. In addition to *China World*, extensive daily coverage is available on China in a broad cross-section of newspapers: *Shanghai Daily, International Herald Tribune, Straits Times, South China Morning Post*, the *CAAC Journal*, and the *Sunday Morning Post*.

29. Hamish McRae, *The World in 2020* (Boston: Harvard Business School Press, 1994), 158; Panitchpakdi and Clifford, *China and the WTO*, 21–28; James Miles, "A Dragon Out of Puff," *Economist*, June 15, 2002, 3–10; Victor Mallet, "Power Hungry: Asia's Surging Energy Demand," *Financial Times*, May 12, 2004, 13; Brian Bremner and Dexter Roberts, "China: The Great Oil Hunt," *Business Week*, November 15, 2004, 60–62.

30. James Kynge, "China's Capitalists Get a Party Invitation," *Financial Times*, August 16, 2002.

31. "GDP per Person," *Economist*, August 24, 2002, 74; Fu Dong and Jahyeong Koo, "Latest Economic Developments in China," in Federal Reserve Bank of Dallas,

Expand Your Insight, http://www.dallasfed.org/eyi/global/0302china.html, accessed January 31, 2003; James Kynge, "Overseas Investment in China tops $53 bn, [for first 10 months of 2004]," *Financial Times*, November 16, 2004, 3; Erwan Quintin, "Mexico's Export Woes Not All China-Induced," *Southwest Economy* [Dallas Federal Reserve Bank], November 2004.

32. Peter Marsh, "Scrap Steel Turns to Gold as Global Demand Hardens," *Financial Times*, October 8, 2004; "String of Pearls," *Economist*, November 20, 2004, 43.

33. Yergin and Stanislaw, *Commanding Heights*, 194–201; See also James Kynge and Dan Roberts, "Cut-throat Competitors" *Financial Times*, February 5, 2003, 13.

34. Terrill, *New Chinese Empire*, 228, 299–301; Burstein and de Keijzer, *Big Dragon*, 229–32; "China Hits Out at Chen" *Shanghai Daily*, September 16, 2004, 4.

35. "Where Does the Buck stop?" *Economist*, November 13, 2004, 13.

36. Tom Zeller, "Beijing Loves the Web," *New York Times*, December 6, 2004; interview with Ya O Yo in Beijing, September 20, 2004. Internet usage in 2000 was less than 17 million. China's leading internet search sites include www.Baidu.com and www.Yisou.com.

37. Hugo Restall, "Behind China's Stability Lies Risk," *Wall Street Journal*, August 13, 2002; "China's Internet Illusion," editorial, ibid., August 22, 2002; Karby Leggett, "Foreign Investment Not a Panacea in China," ibid., January 14, 2002; James Kynge, "China Enjoys Trade Surplus as Direct Inward Investment Surges," *Financial Times*, August 13, 2002; Simon Cantledge, "The Other Side of China's Success Story," ibid., January 20, 2003, 11; Peter Wonacott, "China Shuns a Financial Overhaul," *Wall Street Journal*, January 28, 2003, A14. See also Minxin Pei, "China's Governance Crisis," *Foreign Affairs*, September 2002, 96–109.

38. Sara Silver, "US Sneezes, Mexico Catches Cold," *Financial Times*, February 11, 2002; Shields, "Government Indifferent"; Gerardo Bracho, "Mexico's Foreign Trade in Trouble—China's Impact," *Voices of Mexico*, April 2004, 50–55; Quintin, "Mexico's Export Woes," 2.

39. "Cemex Seeks Stable Cash Flow From Major UK Acquisition," *Global Finance*, November 2004, 55.

40. "China's Great Commodity Grab," *Asia Tomorrow*, November 2004, 10–14; "Beans to Beijing," *Latin Trade*, September 2004, 20; Marc Frank, "Hu Lends Friendship to Cuban Comrades," *Financial Times*, November 24, 2004, 3. In 2004, China consumed 25 percent of the world's steel and over 50 percent of the world's cement.

41. United Nations, *2004 Trade and Development Report* (New York: UN, 2004), 5.

42. "Latin America's Chinese Dividend," *Financial Times*, May 19, 2004; Mark Stevenson, "Chinese Premier Visits Fox," *Laredo Morning Times*, December 13, 2003; "Soft Landing?" *Economist*, July 3, 2004; Josephine Lee, "Ka-Ching!" *Forbes*, March 29, 2004, 54; "Panama Canal: Manifest Destiny Meets Democracy," *Economist*, May 1, 2004, 37; "China Builds Trade Ties With South America," *Wall Street Journal*, November 19, 2004, A12; James Kynge, "Chinese Central Bank Refuses to Be Moved," *Financial Times*, November 19, 2004, 11. In spite of the talk of "market economy" arrangements, Brazil in 2003 had twenty-three anti-dumping measures in force against China.

43. Elisabeth Malkin, "Japan to Sign a Trade Pact with Mexico," *International Herald Tribune*, September 18, 2004, 11; Davidow, *U.S. and Mexico*, 162; "Tequila Sunrise?" *Financial Times*, March 14, 2004, 14.

44. Michael J. Pisani and Wayne A. Label, "Plan Puebla-Panama: Toward FTAA or Regionalism?" *Business Horizons*, September 2003, 33–40; Eduardo Castillo, "Economic Issues Spark Meeting," *San Antonio Express-News*, November 13, 2004, 19; OECD, *OECD Territorial Review: Mexico* (Paris: OECD, 2003), 134–35, 185–89. Mexico became a member of the OECD on May 18, 1994 and is the only Latin American nation in the OECD. In the case of the PPP, Colombia was included as an "observing member."

45. OECD, *Territorial Reviews: Mexico*, 3. It is interesting to note that 'PPP' is also used to denote "purchasing power parity."

46. Ibid., 134–35, 185–88; *News* (Mexico City), February 14, 2002. See also Daniel Griswold and Daniel Ikenson, "The Case for CAFTA: Consolidating Central America's Freedom Revolution," Cato Institute Trade Briefing Papers, no. 21, September 21, 2004.

47. "Article 303," *Twin Plant News*, October 2004, 29–31.

48. Gerber, "Uncertainty and Growth"; Watkins, "Production-Sharing," *Industry Trade and Technology Review*, July 2002, 27–32.

49. World Bank, *China 2020: China Engaged* (Washington, D.C.: IBRD-World Bank, 1997), 36; "Trade Prices: How High is Up?" *Business Week*, March 8, 2004, 29–31; Fang Xinghai, "China Must Develop Stronger Capital Markets," *Financial Times*, December 11, 2003; David Pilling, "China Provides Boost for Tokyo Growth Revival," ibid., October 12, 2004; James Kynge, "The Chinese Boom Is Bound to End in Tears," *Financial Times*, March 24, 2004.

50. Sergio L. Ornelas, "Mexico's Reaction to the China Challenge," *Mexiconow*, January 2003, 16–21.

51. Gilboy, "Myth behind China's Miracle," 44; Geri Smith, "How China Opened My Eyes," *Business Week*, November 8, 2004, 66.

52. U. S. Department of Commerce, *Manufacturing in America: A Comprehensive Strategy to Address the Challenges to U.S. Manufacturers* (Washington, D.C.: GPO, 2004), 7.

53. U.S. Department of the Treasury and Federal Reserve Board data quoted in "U.S. Treasury Securities," *Economist*, November 27, 2004, 109. Japan as of September 2004 held 38.8 percent (or $720 billion in foreign investment in U.S. treasuries) followed by China at 9.4 percent ($175 billion) and Britain at 7.3 percent ($138 billion). The yuan is fully convertible only in the current account, and remains tightly controlled on the capital account, including FDI and portfolio investment. In October 2004, China's foreign exchange reserve totaled $543 billion.

54. "The Myth of China, Inc." *Economist*, September 3, 2005, pp. 54–55; Guy de Jonquieres, "China's 'New Economy' is Not Immune to a Business Downtown," *Financial Times*, September 27, 2005, p. 19.

CHAPTER 5. Maquilas, Technology Transfer, and Trade Corridors

1. Emmott, *20:21 Vision*, 25–27, 194–207; Brad Delong, "Globalization Means We Share Jobs as Well as Goods," *Financial Times*, August 27, 2003; Kenichi Ohmae, *The End of the Nation State: The Rise of Regional Economies* (New York: Free Press, 1996), 71–100; Jeff Ferry, "Flextronics: Stay Real in a Virtual World," *Strategy+Business*, Winter 2004, 64–73; Dani Rodrik, "Globalization for Whom?" *MexicoNow*, January

2003, 37–40; Porter, *Competitive Advantage of Nations*, 92–107. See also United Nations, *Trade and Development Report, 2004*, 3–18: WTO, *World Trade Report— 2004* (Geneva: WTO, 2004), xvi–xx.

2. Kopinak, *Desert Capitalism*, 3–27 Jagdish Bhagwati, *In Defense of Globalization* (London: Oxford University Press, 2004), 7–100. See also Freeman, *Lexus and the Olive Tree.*

3. Peter Cange, "Impact of the Mexican Border Industrial Program on the Texas Border Economy," *AIDC Journal*, January 1977, 7–46; J. Michael Patrick, "Maquiladoras and South Texas Border Economic Development," *Journal of Borderlands Studies*, Spring 1989, 89–99; Joel Millman, "A New Future for Mexico's Work Force," *Wall Street Journal*, April 14, 2000, 15–16.

4. BIP objectives quoted in Joan B. Anderson, "Maquiladoras and Border Industrialization: Impact on Economic Development in Mexico," *Journal of Borderlands Studies* 5, no. 1: 5.

5. Jesus Canas and Roberto Coronado, "U.S.–Mexico Trade: Are We Still Connected?" *Business Frontier* [Federal Reserve Bank of El Paso], no. 3 (2004).

6. U.S. House of Representatives. Committee on Ways and Means, *North American Free Trade Agreement (NAFTA) and Supplemental Agreements to the NAFTA*, 103rd Cong., 1st sess., Hearing by Subcommittee on Trade, September 14, 15, 21, and 23, 1993 (Washington, D.C.: GPO, 1993), 51–164; Don Nibbie, "Maquila," *Twin Plant News*, January 2000; Adams, *Mexican Banking and Investment in Transition*, 32–45: John Bailey, "The Bureaucracy," in Grayson, *Prospects for Mexico*, 15–34.

7. "Decreto para el Fomento y Operación de la Industria Maquiladora de Exportación" [referred to as the "Maquila Decree"], *Official Gazette*, Mexico City; December 22, 1989 and amended December 24, 1993; Banco National de Mexico [Banamex], "Maquiladora Industry," *Review of the Economic Situation of Mexico*, December, 1999, 471–77; Carol S. Osmond, "Maquiladoras and NAFTA Beyond the Year 2000," presentation at 14th Annual MexCon 2000 Conference, La Jolla, California, March 28, 2000; Barkin, *Distorted Development*, 90. As of early 2000, the only area of Mexico that is off-limits to maquiladora operations is the capital city or Federal District.

8. Elisabeth Malkin, "Desperately Seeking Skilled Labor," *Business Week*, March 20, 2000, 60; William T. Gavin and Kevin L. Kliesen, "Available Labor Supply," *National Economic Trends* [Federal Reserve Bank of Dallas], February 2000, 1; Lucinda Vargas, "The Binational Importance of the Maquiladora Industry," *Southwest Economy* [Federal Reserve Bank of Dallas], November 1999, 1–5. See also William J. Siembieda and Eduardo Lopez Moreno, "Expanding Housing Choices for the Sector Popular: Strategies for Mexico," *Housing Policy Debate* 8, no. 3: 651–77.

9. "Maquila Decree"; Banamex, "Maquiladora Industry," 471–77; Osmond, "Maquiladoras and NAFTA Beyond the Year 2000."

10. Malkin, "Desperately Seeking Skilled Labor," *Business Week*, March 20, 2000, p. 60; Gavin and Kliesen, "Available Labor Supply," *National Economic Trends* Federal Reserve Bank of Dallas, February 2000, p. 1; Vargas, "The Binational Importance of the Maquiladora Industry," *Southwest Economy* Federal Reserve Bank of Dallas, November 1999, pp. 1–5. See also Siembieda and Moreno, "Expanding Housing Choices for the Sector Popular: Strategies for Mexico," *Housing Policy Debate* Vol. 8, No. 3, pp. 651–77.

11. Executive Office of the President, *North American Free Trade Agreement*; Banamex, "The State of the Economy," *Review of the Economic Situation of Mexico*, October 1999, 348–64; Jonathan Friedland, "Mexico Receives Coveted Investment-Grade Rating," *Wall Street Journal*, March 8, 2000. See also Cletus C. Coughlin and Patricia S. Pollard, "State Exports and the Asian Crisis," *Review* [Federal Reserve Bank of St. Louis], January 2000, 15–30. For an extensive bibliography on NAFTA see Alan Metz, ed., *A NAFTA Bibliography* (Westport, Conn.: Greenwood, 1996).

12. "Mexico Is One of the Most Important Destinations for U.S. Ports," *Nafta Works*, October 2004, 1–2; "U.S.–Mexico Trade Activity at the Major U.S.–Mexico Border Ports," *Border Business Indicators*, July 2004, 1–8.

13. U.S. International Trade Commission, *Production Sharing: Use of U.S. Components and Materials in Foreign Assembly Operations, 1995–1998* (Washington, D.C.: GPO, 1999), 2–3.

14. Vargas, "Binational Importance," 1–5; Baker & McKenzie, "Responding to Mexico's Attempt to Tax the Income and Assets of U.S. Companies with Maquiladora or PITEX Operations," Juarez, March 1999, 1–4. See also Jay Choi and John A. Doukas, *Emerging Capital Markets* (Westport, CT: Greenwood Publishing, 1998), 285–337; "Maquiladora Downturn: Structural Change or Cyclical Factors?" *Business Frontier* [Federal Reserve Bank of El Paso] (2004): 1–8; John H. Christman, "Mexico's Maquiladora Industry Outlook: 2004–2009," report, Global Insight, Laredo, Texas, September 24, 2004.

15. Enrique D. Peters, "The Maquila Export Industry and Production Integration," *Voices of Mexico*, January 2003, 31–35; Patricia A. Wilson, "The Global Assembly Industry: Maquiladoras in International Perspective," *Journal of Borderlands Studies*, Fall 1991, 73–104; Jenalia Moreno, "Companies Price Free Trade's Cost," *Houston Chronicle*, December 8, 2004.

16. GAO, *International Trade: Mexico's Maquiladora Decline Affects U.S.–Mexico Border Communities and Trade: Recovery Depends in Part on Mexico's Actions*, Report 03-891 (Washington, D.C.: GAO, 2003), 3–29 [hereafter GAO Nafta]; Francis Williams, "WTO Forecasts Global Trade Growth of 8.5%," *Financial Times*, October 26, 2004, 9; V. G. Narayanan and Ananth Raman, "Aligning Incentives in the Supply Chains," *Harvard Business Review*, November 2004, 95–102. The July 2003 report was one of the first extensive efforts to by the GAO to look into the maquiladora sector and its impact on the border and the U.S. economy; however, they failed to visit and make a part of the report the dynamic role and impact of the number one southern port of entry since 1890 at Laredo. There is little coverage of Nuevo Laredo or its daily some one-third of the maquiladora operations, representing over seven hundred of the Fortune 1000 firms, cross goods, merchandise, and raw material via Laredo–Nuevo Laredo. Laredo daily does more cross-border trade than the next five southern border crossings combined.

17. Adams, "Mexico and the IMF: Regional Banking Crisis—Global Consequences," in Harr and Dandapani, *Banking in North America*, 166–82; Dani Rodrik, "How Far Will International Economic Integration Go?" *Journal of Economic Perspectives*, Winter 2000, 177–86; Laura Cohn, "Will the IMF Get a Dose of Its Own Medicine?" *Business Week*, October 4, 1999, 37-38. See also Dani Rodrik, *Has Globalization Gone Too Far?* (Washington, D.C.: Institute for International Economics, 1997), 1–10.

18. Ohmae, *End of the Nation State*, 88–89, 118–19.

19. "A World of Work," *Economist*, November 13, 2004, 1–20.

20. Adams, *Mexican Banking and Investment*, 39–40, 157–59; Assembly of Deputies, Romania, "Government Emergency Ordinance on Incentives for Direct Investment." Law 241/1998, Bucharest, March 4, 1988. In addition to free trade agreements with the United States, Canada, and the European Union, Mexico has agreements with Israel, Chile, Colombia, Venezuela, Nicaragua, and Costa Rica. Talks are underway with Brazil, Panama, El Salvador, Guatemala, Honduras, and Japan.

21. Leslie Alan Glick, "WTO and Seattle," *Twin Plant News*, February 2000, 16–17; "Futile Trade Fortresses," *Financial Times*, August 26, 2003.

22. Porter, *Competitive Advantage of Nations*, 735.

23. Maria L. Kun, "Latin American Banks Branch Out," *Latin Finance*, September 2004, 12–13, 42.

24. Geraldo Samor, "Latin America Warms Up to EU Trade Talk, *Wall Street Journal*, April 15, 2004; Jonathan House et al., "The Quest: Spanish Bank Sees U.S. Hispanic Treasure," ibid., July 8, 2004, C11; Mike Hall, "The Shape of Banking in Laredo," *LMT Business Journal*, October 11, 2004, 10–11.

25. John H. Christman, "Mexico's Maquiladora Industry Outlook: 2004–2009," and Ralph A. Biedermann, "Site Location—Update on Trends on the Border and Mexico," both presented at the 11th Annual LDF-LMA Manufacturing Symposium, Laredo, Texas, September 24, 2004.

26. Raul Urteaga-Trani, "U.S.–Mexico Relations: Balancing Trade, Security and Economic Integration," presentation at the Center for the Study of the Western Hemispheric Trade, Texas A&M International University, Laredo, Texas, November 10, 2003.

27. Ibid.; Sergio L Ornelas, "Mexico's Electronic Manufacturing Services (EMS) Industry," *MexicoNow*, September 2004, 22–33; Ferry, "Flexronics," 67–69. The EMS or contract manufacturing industry was developed in the mid-1980s as a reaction to the demand for the mass production of printed circuit boards (PCB). One irony of American manufacturing, as noted by Jeff Ferry, was that U.S. computer giants like IBM and HP transferred what they deemed as "low-skilled, worker-intensive activities" offshore in order to instead focus on product development. See also Richard J. Schonberger, *World Class Manufacturing: The Lessons of Simplicity Applied* (New York: Free Press, 1986); ibid., *World Class Manufacturing—The Next Decade: Building Power, Strength, and Value* (New York: Free Press, 1996); ibid., *Let's Fix It! Overcoming the Crisis in Manufacturing* (New York: Free Press, 2001).

28. Joel Millman, "Mexico Blazes Trade Success," *Wall Street Journal*, November 29, 2004, A12; Lourdes Rocha (Banamex), "The Maquiladora Export Industry: A General and Sectoral Description," *Review of the Economic Situation of Mexico*, October 2004, 404–5.

29. Gallagher, *Free Trade and the Environment*, 1–109. See also Francisco Aguayo and Kevin P. Gallagher, "Economic Reform, Energy, and Development: The Case of Mexican Manufacturing," Global Development and Environment Institute, paper no. 03-05, Tufts University, Medford, Massachusetts, July 2003; Barkin, *Distorted Development*, 41–54.

30. OECD, *Regulatory Reform in Mexico* (Paris: OECD, 1999), 11–14; Mary A. O'Grady, "Why Mexico's Nafta Boost Didn't Last," *Wall Street Journal*, October 22,

2004, A17. See also Aaron Tornell, Frank Westermann, and Lorenza Martinez, "NAFTA and Mexico's Less-than-Stellar Performance," NBER working paper 10289, Cambridge, Massachusetts, February 2004.

31. Ken Krizner, "Foreign Automakers Continue to Drive Industry South," *Expansion Management*, September 2004, 17–24; Doreen H. Michelini, "Mexico and China," *MexicoNow*, September 2004, 18–21; "An Overlooked Revolution," *Economist*, August 28, 2004, 32–33; GAO Nafta, 37–42. A survey of the World Economic Forum (WEF) on "Burden of Regulation" ranks Mexico eighty-second, the United States nineteenth, and China twenty-first. Yet in terms of "Growth Competitiveness" the WEF ranks Mexico forty-eighth, the United States second, and China forty-sixth.

32. Quoted in Jesus Canas et al., "Maquiladora Downturn: Structural Change or Cyclical Factors?" *Business Frontier* [Federal Reserve Bank of El Paso], no. 2 (2004): 3. See also David Luhnow, "As Jobs Move East Plants in Mexico Retool to Compete," *Wall Street Journal*, March 5, 2004.

33. "U.S.–Mexico Trade: U.S.–Mexico Border Continues to be Hub of Activity," *Border Business Indicators*, September 2004, 1–8; Kenneth J. Button, "Economic Development and Transport Hub," in *Handbook of Transport Geography and Spatial Systems*, ed. David Hensher et al. (London: Elsevier, 2004), 77–95; Yvonne Bontekoning and Jan J. Trip, "Rail-rail Hub-terminals as an Alternative for Shunting: An Explorative Comparative Case Study," in *Transport Developments and Innovations in an Evolving World*, ed. Michel Beuthe et al. (Berlin: Springer, 2004), 235–51; J. Michael Patrick, "Laredo: The Port of Choice in 2003," *Border Business Indicators*, April 2004, 1.

34. James Kruse, David Bierling, and Nathan Vajdos, "Analysis of Start-up Cross-Gulf Short Sea Shipping Activities with Mexico since 1990: Problems and Opportunities," Texas Transportation Institute, Texas A&M University, August 2004.

35. Josephine Lee, "Ka-Ching!" *Forbes*, March 29, 2004, 54; Leigh B. Boske, *Maritime Transportation in Latin America and the Caribbean*, no. 138 (Austin: LBJ School of Public Affairs, 2001), 138–44; Claude Comtois and Peter J. Rimmer, "China's Competitive Push for Global Trade," in *Shipping and Ports in the Twenty-first Century*, David Pinder and Brian Spack (London: Routledge, 2004), 40–62. An additional investor in the Port of Veracruz is the joint venture between Philippine-owned International Container Terminal Services, Inc. and Grupo ICA for operation of a twenty-year box terminal, jointly known as ICAVE.

36. John Kasarda, et al., "Villa XXI Multimodal District: Conceptual Description," Monterrey, May 6, 2002; Bill Mongelluzzo, "Mexican Alternative," *Journal of Commerce*, January 10, 2005, 1.

37. U.S. Department of Homeland Security (HLS), "U.S. Customs and Border Protection—Protecting our Borders Against Terrorism," fact sheet, August 6, 2004; ibid., "Free and Secure Trade (FAST)—United States and Mexico," November 12, 2004; ibid., "Under Secretary Asa Hutchinson Discusses Expansion of US-VISIT Program to Include Visitors Traveling Under the Visa Waiver Program," September 29, 2004; ibid., "Radiation Portal Monitor Systems," January 2004; HLS, Customs and Border Protection, "Required Advanced Electronic Presentation of Cargo Information: Compliance Dates for Truck Carriers," 19 CFR Part 123, *Federal Register* 69, no. 158 (August 17, 2004): 51007–9; "Revisit US-VISIT for Economy's Sake," editorial, *San Antonio Express-News*, March 25, 2004; David Hendricks, "Inland Port at Kelly USA remains Distant goal," ibid., January 6, 2005.

38. Joel Millman, "Mexico's Ports Go Global," *Wall Street Journal*, March 31, 2004; Rebecca Buckman, "Maritime Security Measures Begin," ibid., July 1, 2004, A11; Rick Alm, "KC Signs Trade Pact with Mexican Port," *Kansas City Star*, November 10, 2004.

39. John P. McCray, "NAFTA Truck Highway Corridors: U.S.–Mexico Truck Rivers of Trade," Transportation Research Board, Washington, D.C., January 11, 1998.

40. Leigh B. Boske, *Texas-Mexico Multimodal Transportation*, no. 104 (Austin: LBJ School of Public Affairs, 1993), 63–78.

41. Kopinak, *Desert Capitalism*, 28–48.

42. Leigh B. Boske and John C. Cuttino, *The Impacts of U.S. Latin American Trade on the Southwest's Economy and Transportation System: An Assessment of Impact Methodologies* (Austin: LBJ School of Public Affairs, 2001), 5.

43. Len Cheng, "US Stores See Danger on the Waterfront," *Financial Times*, June 19, 2002; Alm, "KC Signs Trade Pact"; Suzanne Marta, "Shipping by Rail Still Off Track," *Dallas Morning News*, August 23, 2004. See also Rene Gonzalez, "Critical Issues in Cross Border Trucking," LDF Special Report, Laredo, 2004; Boske, *Texas-Mexico Multimodal Transportation*, 85–100.

44. Patrick Driscoll, "State Is on Road to New Highway Era," *San Antonio Express-News*, December 17, 2004; Mike Hall, "Trade Corridor Won't Bypass Gateway City," *Laredo Morning Times*, October 27, 2004; Alison Beshur, "Area May Link to Interstate 69," *Corpus Christi Caller Times*, November 10, 2004; Dan Roberts, "Bottled Up: US Transport Infrastructure Feels Strain of Growing Global Trade," *Financial Times*, November 16, 2004.

45. Boske, *Texas-Mexico Multimodal Transportation*, 106–18; Hau L. Lee, "The Triple-A Supply Chain," *Harvard Business Review*, October 2004, 102, 104. See also Kasra Ferdows, Michael A. Lewis, and Jose A. Machuca, "Rapid-Fire Fulfillment," *Harvard Business Review*, November 2004, 104–10.

46. Banamex, "Mexico-European Union," *Review*, December 1999, 469–70.

47. Bureau of Transportation Statistics, hht://www.bts.gov/transborder/.

48. Stephen Blank, Stephenie Golub, and Guy Stanley, "Mapping the New North American Reality," Institute for Research and Public Policy, working paper no. 2004-09, 2004. See also Alan K. Fox, Joseph F. Francois, and Pilar Londono-Kent, "Measuring Border Crossing Costs and Their Impact on Trade Flows: The United States–Mexico Trucking Case," Materials for 2003 GTAP Conference in Scheveningen, Netherlands, April 30, 2003; Cletus C. Coughlin, "The Increasing Importance of Proximity for Exports from U.S. States, " *Review* [Federal Reserve Bank of St. Louis], November 2004, 1–18

49. David Fairris and Edward Levine, "Declining Union Density in Mexico, 1984–2000," *Monthly Labor Review*, September 2004, 10–18. See also Kevin J. Middlebrook, *The Paradox of Revolution: Labor, the State, and Authoritarianism in Mexico* (Baltimore: Johns Hopkins University Press, 1995).

50. "Recinto Fiscalizado Estratégico," *Diario Oficial* (Mexico City), October 8, 2003, July 22, 2004.

BIBLIOGRAPHY

PRIMARY SOURCES

Government Documents

Canas, Jesus, and Roberto Coronado. "U.S.-Mexico Trade: Are We Still Connected?" *Business Frontier* [Federal Reserve Bank of El Paso], no. 3 (Fall 2004).

Coronado, Roberto. "Workers' Remittances to Mexico." *Business Frontier* [Federal Reserve Bank of El Paso], no. 1 (2004).

Coughlin, Cletus C. "The Increasing Importance of Proximity for Exports from the U.S. States." *Review* [Federal Reserve Bank of St. Louis], November 2004, 1–18.

Coughlin, Cletus C., and Patricia S. Pollard. "State Exports and the Asian Crisis." *Review* [Federal Reserve Bank of St. Louis], January 2000, 15–30.

Dolmas, Jim. "Beyond the Border: Globalization Myths and Realities." *Southwest Economy* [Federal Reserve Bank of Dallas], October 2004.

Environmental Protection Agency. *Border 2012: U.S.-Mexico Environmental Program*. EPA-160-D-02-1001. Washington, D.C.: GPO, 2002.

Executive Office of the President. Executive Order. "Department of Homeland Security: Required Advance Electronic Presentation of Cargo Information: Compliance for Truck Carriers." 19 *Code of Federal Regulations* Part 123, August 17, 2004, *Federal Register*. 51007–9.

———. *Economic Report of the President*. 109th Cong., 1st sess., February 2005. H. Doc. 109-1.

———. *North American Free Trade Agreement Between the Governments of the United States of America, the Government of Canada, and the United Mexican States*. 2 vols. Washington, D.C.: GPO, 1993.

Gavin, William T., and Kevin L. Kliesen. "Available Labor Supply," *National Economic Trends* [Federal Reserve Bank of Dallas], February 2000.

General Accounting Office [GAO]. *Customs Service Modernization: Ineffective Software Development Processes Increase Customs Development Risk*. GAO/ AIMD-99-35. February 1999.

———. *Mexican Oil: Issues Affecting Potential U.S. Trade and Investment*. GAO, NSIAD-92-169. March 1992.

————. *Mexico's Financial Crisis: Origins, Awareness, Assistance, and Initial Efforts to Recover*. GAO/GGD-96-56. February 1996.

————. *Mexico's Maquiladora Decline Affects U.S.-Mexico Border Communities and Trade: Recovery Depends in Part on Mexico's Actions*. GAO-03-891. July 2003.

————. *Undocumented Aliens: Questions Persist About Their Impact on Hospitals' Uncompensated Care Costs*. GAO-01-472. May 2004.

————. *U.S. Agencies Need Greater Focus to Support Mexico's Successful Transition to Liberalized Agricultural Trade under NAFTA*. GAO-05-272. March 2005.

————. *U.S. Customs and Border Protection Faces Challenges in Addressing Illegal Textile Transshipments*. GAO-04-345. January 2001.

————. *U.S.-Mexico Border: Better Planning, Coordination Needed to Handle Growing Commercial Traffic*. GAO/NSAIN-00-25. March 2000.

————. *U.S.-Mexico Border: Issues and Challenges Confronting the United States and Mexico*. GAO/NSIAD-99-190. July 1999.

————. *U.S.-Mexico Trade: Survey of U.S. Border Infrastructure Needs*. GAO/NSIAD-91-228. November 1991.

General Agreement on Tariffs and Trade (GATT). *International Trade 91-92: Statistics*. Geneva: GATT, 1993.

Hall, Howard J. "NAFTA and the Geography of North American Trade." St. Louis Branch of the Federal Reserve Bank. Research Branch Working Papers, 2000-017B, November 2000.

Mexico. *Diario Oficial*. Mexico City, 2002–04.

————. *The True Facts about the Expropriation of the Oil Companies' Properties in Mexico*. Mexico City: Talleres Gráficos de la Nación, 1940.

Orrenius, Pia. "Illegal Immigration and Enforcement along the Southwest Border." *Border Economy* [Dallas Branch of the Federal Reserve Bank], June 2001, 30–36.

Phillips, Keith. San Antonio Branch of the Federal Reserve Bank. "Maquiladora Industry Outlook Meeting." Presentation in Laredo, Texas, September 24, 2004.

Quintin, Erwan. "Mexico's Export Woes Not All China-Induced." *Southwest Economy* [Dallas Branch of the Federal Reserve Bank], November 2004.

Rodriguez, Laura. "Cross-Border Manufacturing in Selected Industries: Apparel." In *Production Sharing: Use of Components and Materials in Foreign Assembly Operations*. Edited by U.S. International Trade Commission. Pub 3265. Washington, D.C.: USITC, 999.

Runyon, Jack L. "Immigration Reform and Control Act of 1986." Bulletin no. 652. Washington, D.C.: Economic Research Service, 1987.

Texas Commission on Environmental Quality [formerly TNRCC]. *State of the Rio Grande and the Environment of the Border Region—Strategic Plan: Fiscal Years 2003–2007*. Austin, 2003.

Texas Comptroller of Public Accounts. *Bordering the Future: Challenge and Opportunity in the Texas Border Region*. Austin, July 1998.

Texas Senate. Committee in International Relations and Trade. *Interim Report*. 78th Legislature. Austin, December 2, 2004.

————. Office of Senator Eliot Shapleigh. "Texas Borderlands 2005." Austin, January 2005.

Texas Workforce Commission. *Texas Labor Market Review*. Austin, January to November 2004.

United Nations. *Trade and Development Report, 2004*. New York, September 2004.

U.S. Bureau of the Census. *Profile of the Foreign-Born Population in the United States: 2000*. Washington, D.C.: GPO, 2001.

U.S. Congress. House. Committee on Ways and Means. *North American Free Trade Agreement (NAFTA) and Supplemental Agreements to the NAFTA*. 103rd Cong., 1st sess., Hearings, Serial 103-48, September 14, 15, 21, and 23, 1993.

———. *Intelligence Reform and Terrorism Prevention Act of 2004*. 108th Cong., 2nd sess., Report 108-796, December 7, 2004.

U.S. Congress. Senate. Committee on Foreign Relations. *Multinational Corporations in Brazil and Mexico: Structural Sources of Economic and Noneconomic Power*. 94th Cong, 1st sess., August 1975.

U.S. Department of Agriculture. *Mexico and Sugar: Historical Perspective*. Washington, D.C.: USDA, 2004.

U.S. Department of Commerce. *Manufacturing in America: A Comprehensive Strategy to Address the Challenge to U.S. Manufacturers*. Washington, D.C.: GPO, 2004.

U.S. Department of Energy. "An Energy Overview of Mexico." Washington, D.C. www.eia.doe.gov. Accessed October 2, 2002.

———. "Mexico Country Analysis Brief." Washington, D.C. November 2004. www.eia.doe.gov.

U.S. Department of Homeland Security. US-VISIT. "Fact Sheet: U.S. Land Borders." December 2004.

———. "Free and Secure Trade (Fast)—United States and Mexico." HLS, November 12, 2004.

———. "Radiation Portal Monitor Systems," HLS, January 2004.

———. "Under Secretary Asa Hutchinson Discusses Expansion of US-VISIT Program to Include Visitors Traveling under the Visa Waver Program," HLS, September 29, 2004.

———. "U.S. Customs and Border Protection—Protecting Our Borders against Terrorism." HLS, August 6, 2004.

U.S. Department of State. *Mexico: 1999 Country Reports on Human Rights Practices*. Washington, D.C., February 25, 2000.

U.S. International Trade Commission. *Production Sharing: Use of U.S. Components and Materials in Foreign Assembly Operations, 1995–1998*. Washington, D.C.: GPO, December 1999.

———. *The Likely Impact on the United States of a Free Trade Agreement with Mexico*. Pub. 2353. Washington, D.C.: GPO, February 1991.

Vargas, Lucinda. "The Binational Importance of the Maquiladora Industry." *Southwest Economy* [Federal Reserve Bank of Dallas], November 1999.

———. "NAFTA's First Five Years (Part 1)." In *El Paso Business Frontier*. Edited by Federal Reserve Bank of El Paso. El Paso: Federal Reserve, 1999.

Watkins, Ralph. "Mexico Versus China: Factors Affecting Export and Investment Competition." *Industry Trade and Technology Review* (U.S. International Trade Commission, pub. 3534) July 2002, 11–26.

———. "Production—Sharing Update: Developments in 2001." *Industry Trade and Technology Review* (U.S. International Trade Commission, pub. 3534), July 2002, 27–42.

World Trade Organization. *Trade and Development Report—2004*. Geneva: WTO, 2004.

Newspapers

Dallas Morning News
El Mañana (Nuevo Laredo)
Financial Times (London)
Houston Chronicle
Laredo Morning Times, 1990–2004
La Reforma (Mexico City)
News (Mexico City)
New York Times, 1950–2004
San Antonio Express-News
Wall Street Journal
Washington Post, 1990–2004
Washington Times

Magazines

Asia Tomorrow, Singapore
Border Business Indicators (Texas A&M International University), Laredo
Business Week, New York
Economist, London
Expansion Management, Cleveland
Global Finance, New York
Latin Finance, Miami
Latin Trade, Miami
MexicoNow, El Paso
Twin Plant News, El Paso, 1990–2004
Voices of Mexico, Mexico City

SECONDARY SOURCES

Books and Articles

Adams, John A., Jr. *Mexican Banking and Investment in Transition*. Westport, Conn.: Quorum, 1997.
———. "Mexico vs. China" *Laredo 2020* 4, no. 1 (2003): 1–5.
Alba, Francisco. "Mexico: A Crucial Crossroads." Migrant Policy Institute, Washington, D.C., February 2004.
Ambrose, Stephen E. *Nothing Like It in the World: The Men Who Built the Transcontinental Railroad*. New York: Touchstone, 2000.
Anderson, Joan B. "Maquiladoras and Border Industrialization: Impact on Economic Development in Mexico." *Journal of Borderlands Studies* 5, no. 1.

Baerresen, D. *The Border Industrialization Program of Mexico.* Lexington, Ky.: Lexington Books, 1971.

Baker, George. "Mexico's New Upstream Philosophy." *Oil and Gas Investor*, September 2002.

Barkin, David. *Distorted Development: Mexico in the World Economy.* Boulder, Colo.: Westview Press, 1990.

Barlett, Donald L., and James B. Steele. "Who Left the Door Open?" *Time*, September 20, 2004, 51–66.

Bartra, Roger. *Agrarian Structure and Political Power in Mexico.* Baltimore: Johns Hopkins University Press, 1993.

Barry, Tom. With Harry Brown and Beth Sims. *Crossing the Line: Immigrants, Economic Integration, and Drug Enforcement of the U.S.-Mexico Border.* Albuquerque: Resource Center Press, 1994.

———. *Zapata's Revenge: Free Trade and the Farm Crisis in Mexico.* Boston: South End Press, 1995.

Benjamin, Thomas. *La Revolución: Mexico's Great Revolution as Memory, Myth, and History.* Austin: University of Texas Press, 2000.

Bergsten, Fred C. "A Renaissance for U.S. Trade Policy?" *Foreign Affairs*, November 2002, 86–98.

Berner, Olivier. *The World in 1800.* New York: John Wiley & Sons, 2000.

Betts, Dianne C., and Daniel J. Slottje. *Crisis on the Rio Grande.* Boulder, Colo.: Westview Press, 1994.

Beuthe, Michel et al. *Transport Developments and Innovations in an Evolving World.* Berlin: Springer, 2004.

Bhagwati, Jagdish. *In Defense of Globalization.* London: Oxford University Press, 2004.

Blank, Stephen J. *Rethinking Asymmetric Threats.* Carlisle, Pa.: SSI-U.S. Army War College, 2003.

Boske, Leigh B., ed. *Maritime Transportation in Latin America and the Caribbean.* No, 138. Austin: Policy Research Project, LBJ School of Public Affairs, 2001.

———. *Texas-Mexico Multimodal Transportation.* No. 104. Austin: LBJ School of Public Affairs, 1993.

Boske, Leigh B., and John C. Cuttino. *The Impacts of U.S.–Latin American Trade on the Southwest's Economy and Transportation System.* Special Project Report. Austin: LBJ School of Public Affairs, 2001.

Bovard, James. *The Fair Trade Fraud: How Congress Pillages the Consumer and Decimates American Competitiveness.* New York: St. Martin's Press, 1991.

Brands, H. W. *Lone Star Nation.* New York: Doubleday, 2004.

Brenner, Anita. *The Wind that Swept Mexico.* Repr., Austin: University of Texas Press, 1971.

Brown, Jonathan C. *Oil and Revolution in Mexico.* Berkeley: University of California Press, 1993.

Burstein, Daniel, and Arne de Keijzer. *Big Dragon: The Future of China.* New York: Simon & Schuster, 1998.

Camin, Hector Aguilar, and Lorenzo Meyer. *In the Shadow of the Mexican Revolution.* Austin: University of Texas Press, 1993.

Carpizo, Jorge. *La Constitución Mexicana de 1917.* Mexico City: UNAM, 1969.

Cange, Peter. "Impact of the Mexican Border Industrial Program on the Texas Border Economy." *AIDC Journal*, January 1977, 7–46.

Castañeda, Jorge G. *The Mexican Shock: Its Meaning for the U.S.* New York: New Press, 1995.

Centro de Investigacion y Docencia Economicas. *Global Views 2004: Comparing Mexican and American Public Opinion and Foreign Policy.* Chicago: CCFR, 2004.

———. *México y El Mundo: Mexican Public Opinion and Foreign Policy.* Mexico City: CIDE, 2004

Chance, John K. *Race and Class in Colonial Oaxaca.* Stanford, Calif.: Stanford University Press, 1978.

Cheralier, François. *Land and Society in Colonial Mexico* Berkeley: University of California Press, 1977.

Choi, Jay, and John A. Doukas. *Emerging Capital Markets.* Westport, Conn.: Greenwood Publishing, 1998.

Cline, Howard F. *The United States and Mexico.* New York: Atheneum, 1963.

Consumer Latin America: 2004. London: Euromonitor, 2003.

Cornelius, Wayne A., and David Myhre, eds. *The Transformation of Rural Mexico: Reforming the Ejido Sector.* La Jolla: Center for U.S.-Mexican Studies, University of California, San Diego, 1998.

Cross, Harry E., and James A. Sandos. *Across the Border: Rural Development in Mexico and Recent Migration to the United States.* Berkeley: Institute of Governmental Studies, 1981.

Dam, Kenneth W. *The Rules of the Global Game.* Chicago: University of Chicago Press, 2001.

Davidow, Jeffrey. *The U.S. and Mexico: The Bear and the Porcupine.* Princeton, N.J.: Markus Wiener, 2004.

Davis, Bob, and David Wessel. *Prosperity: The Coming Twenty-year Boom.* New York: Random House, 1998.

DeLeon, Arnoldo. *Mexican Americans in Texas.* Arlington Heights, Tex.: Harlan Davidson, 1993.

DeLong, Bradford, C. DeLong, and Sherman Robinson. "The Case for Mexico's Rescue." *Foreign Affairs*, May 1996, 8–14.

Dent, Harry S. *The Roaring 2000s.* New York: Simon & Schuster, 1998.

DeSantis, S'ra. "Genetically Modified Organisms Threaten Indigenous Corn." *Z Magazine*, July 2002. www.zmag.org/ZMag/articles/julaug02desantis.html.

Díaz del Castillo, Bernal. *True History of the Conquest of New Spain.* London: Hakluyt Society, 1908.

Dobie, J. Frank. *The Longhorns.* Boston: Little, Brown, and Co., 1941.

Dorner, P., and D. Kanel. "The Economic Case for Land Reform." In *Land Reform, Land Settlement and Cooperatives*, ed. Peter Dorner, 1:1–16. Washington: Agency for International Development, 1971.

Drucker, Peter. *Managing for the Future: The 1990s and Beyond.* New York: Dutton, 1992.

Dunn, Timothy J. *The Militarization of the U.S.-Mexico Border 1978–1992.* Austin: CMAS, 1996.

Durand, Jorge. "From Traitors to Heroes: 100 Years of Mexican Migration Policies." Migration Policy Institute, Washington, D.C., March 1, 2004.

Eaton, David J., and John M. Andersen. *The State of the Rio Grande/Rio Bravo.* Tucson: University of Arizona Press, 1987.

Echevarria, Autulio J., and Bert B. Tussing. *From 'Defending Forward' to a 'Global Defense-in-depth': Globalization and Homeland Security.* Carlisle, Pa.: SSI- U.S. Army War College, 2003.

Edmonston, Barry, and James P. Smith. *The New American: Economic, Demographic, and Fiscal Effects of Immigration.* Washington, D.C.: National Academy Press, 1997.

Emmott, Bill. *20:21 Vision.* New York: Farrar, Straus and Giroux, 2003.

Falk, Pamela S. *Petroleum and Mexico's Future.* Boulder, Colo.: Westview Press, 1987.

Fernandez, Raul A. *The Mexican-American Border Region.* Notre Dame, Ind.: University of Notre Dame Press, 1989.

Ferry, Jeff. "Flextronics: Stay Real in a Virtual World." *Strategy+Business,* Winter 2004, 64–73.

Fiess, Norbert, and Daniel Lederman. "Mexican Corn: The Effects of NAFTA." *Trade Notes.* No. 18. World Bank, September 27, 2004. www.worldbank.org/research/trade.

Flynn, Dennis O. et al. *European Entry into the Pacific: Spain and the Acapulco-Manila Galleons.* Aldershot, U.K.: Ashgate Pub. Ltd., 2001.

Freeman, Tom. *The Lexus and the Olive Tree.* New York: Farrar, Straus and Giroux, 1999.

Frey, William H. "Migration Swings." *American Demographics,* February 2002, 18–21.

Gallagher, Kevin P. *Free Trade and the Environment: Mexico, NAFTA, and Beyond.* Stanford, Calif.: Stanford University Press, 2004.

Garner, Paul. *Porfirio Díaz – Profiles in Power.* Harlow, U.K.: Longman, 1st ed., 2001.

Garrett, Geoffrey. "Globalization's Missing Middle." *Foreign Affairs,* December 2004, 84–196.

Garten, Jeffrey. *The Big Ten: The Big Emerging Markets and How They Will Change Our Lives.* New York: Perseus Books Group, 1997.

Gerber, James. "Uncertainty and Growth in Mexico's Maquiladora Sector." *Borderlines,* March 2001.

Gertz, Bill. *The China Threat: How the People's Republic Targets America.* Washington, D.C.: Regnery Publishing, 2000.

Gibson, Lay J., and Alfonso C. Renteria, eds. *The U.S. and Mexico: Borderlands Development and the National Economies.* Boulder, Colo.: Westview Press, 1985.

Gil, Carlos B., ed. *Hope and Frustration: Interviews with Leaders of Mexico's Political Opposition.* Wilmington: SR Books, 1991.

Gilboy, George F. "The Myth behind China's Miracle." *Foreign Affairs,* August 2004, 33–48.

Giugale, Marcelo M., et al. *Mexico: A Comprehensive Development Agenda for the New Era.* Washington, D.C.: IRBD-World Bank, 2001.

Gong, Xiaodong, Arthur Van Soest, and Elizabeth Villagomez . "Mobility in the Urban Labor Markets: A Rural Data Analysis for Mexico." *Economic Development and Cultural Change,* October 2004, 1–36.

González Casanova, Pablo. *La Democracia en México.* Mexico City: Universidad Nacional de Mexico (UNAM), 1965.

———. *Democracy in Mexico.* Translated by Danielle Salti. New York: Oxford University Press, 1970.

Grayson, George W., ed. *Prospects for Mexico.* Washington, D.C: Foreign Service Institute, 1988.

Greider, William. "A New Sucking Sound," *Nation*, December 26, 2001.

Griswold, Daniel T. "Willing Workers: Fixing the Problem of Illegal Mexican Migration to the United States." CATO Institute, Washington, D.C. October 15, 2002.

Grunwald, Joseph and Kenneth Flamm. *The Global Factory: Foreign Assembly in International Trade*. Washington, D.C.: Brookings Institution, 1985.

Gunther, John. *Inside Latin America*. New York: Harper & Brothers, 1941.

Hamel. Gary, and C. K. Prahalad. *Competing for the Future*. Boston: Harvard Business School Press, 1994.

Hanson, Victor D. *Mexifornia: A State of Becoming*. San Francisco: Encounter Books, 2003.

Harr, Jerry, and Krishnan Dandapani, eds. *Banking in North America: NAFTA and Beyond*. Amsterdam: Pergamon, 1999.

Hart, John Mason. *Empire and Revolution: The Americans in Mexico since the Civil War*. Berkeley: University of California Press, 2002.

Heidler, David S., and Jeane T. Heidler. *Manifest Destiny*. Westport, Conn.: Greenwood Press, 2003.

Hensher, David A., et al. *Handbook of Transport Geography and Spatial Systems*. London: Elsevier, 2004.

Herzog, Lawrence A. *Where North Meets South: Cities, Space, and Politics on the United States–Mexico Border*. Austin: Center for Mexican American Studies, University of Texas, 1990.

Hinojosa, Gilberto M. *A Borderland Town in Transition*. College Station: Texas A&M University Press, 1983.

Hobsbawm, Eric. *The Age of Capital 1848–1875*. New York: Vintage, 1996.

Huntington, Samuel P. *Who Are We? The Challenges to America's National Identity*. New York: Simon & Schuster, 2004.

————. "The Hispanic Challenge." *Foreign Policy*, March 2004, 1–12.

Hurdley, Norris, Jr. *Dividing the Waters: A Century of Controversy between the United States and Mexico*. Berkeley: University of California Press, 1966.

Igram, Helen, Nancy Laney, and David Gillilan. *Divided Waters: Bridging the U.S.-Mexico Border*. Tucson: University of Arizona Press, 1995.

Inter-American Development Bank. "Sending Money Home: Remittances to Latin America from the U.S." May 2004, Washington, D.C.

————. "Remittances Senders: Tracking Transactions Methods Used." 2003, Washington, D.C. www.iabd.org.

International Monetary Fund. *World Economic Outlook*. Washington, D.C.: IMF, 2004.

Jachimowicz, Maia. "Bush Proposes New Temporary Worker Program." Migration Policy Institute, Washington, D.C., February 1, 2004.

Jackson, Jack. *Los Mestenos: Spanish Ranching in Texas, 1721–1821*. College Station: Texas A&M University Press, 1986.

Jackson, Robert H., ed. *New Views of Borderlands History*. Albuquerque: University of New Mexico Press, 1998.

Jacoby, Tamar. "Borderline." *New Republic*, January 26, 2004, 18–23.

Jaffe, Amy Myers, and Robert A. Manning. "The Shocks of a World of Cheap Oil," *Foreign Affairs*, January 2000, 16–29.

Jayne, Catherine E. *Oil, War, and Anglo-American Relations: American and British Reactions to Mexico's Expropriation of Foreign Oil Properties, 1937–1941*. Westport, Conn.: Greenwood Press, 2001.

Johnston, Bruce F., et al., eds. *U.S.-Mexico Relations: Agriculture and Rural Development*. Stanford, Calif.: Stanford University Press, 1987.

Kamen, Henry. *Empire: How Spain Became a World Empire 1492–1763*. New York: Penguin, 2003.

Kandell, Jonathan. *La Capital: The Biography of Mexico City*. New York: Random House, 1988.

Karrfalt, Wayne. "A Multicultural Mecca." *American Demographics*, February 2002, S4–S5.

Kennedy, Paul. *Preparing for the Twenty-First Century*. New York: Random House, 1993.

Kessell, John L. *Spain in the Southwest*. Norman: University of Oklahoma Press, 2002.

Kopinak, Kathryn. *Desert Capitalism: Maquiladoras in North America's Western Industrial Corridor*. Tucson: University of Arizona Press, 1996.

Krauze, Enrique. *Mexico Biography of Power: A History of Modern Mexico, 1810–1996*. New York: HarperCollins, 1997.

———. "Will Mexico Break Free?" *New York Times*, July 5, 1997.

Krikorian, Mark. "Keeping Terror Out: Immigration Policy and Asymmetric Warfare." CIS, Washington, D.C., Spring 2004.

Kupchan, Charles A. *The End of the American Era*. New York: Vintage. 2002.

Leiken, Robert. "With a Friend Like Fox." *Foreign Affairs*, September 2001, 91–104.

Levy, Daniel, and Gabriel Szekely. *Mexico: Paradoxes of Stability and Change*. Boulder, Colo.: Westview Press, 2nd ed., 1987.

Levy, Daniel, and Kathleen Bruhn. *Mexico: The Struggle for Democratic Development*. Berkeley: University of California Press, 2001.

López Portillo y Pacheco, José. *They Are Coming . . . The Conquest of Mexico*. Denton: University of North Texas Press, 1992.

Loser, Claudio, and Eliot Kalter, eds. *Mexico: The Strategy to Achieve Sustained Economic Growth*. Washington, D.C.: International Monetary Fund, 1992.

Lowe, Nichola, and Martin Kenny. "Foreign Investment and the Global Geography of Production: Why the Mexican Consumer Electronics Industry Failed." *World Development*, August 1999, 1427–43.

Lowell, B. Lindsey, and Roberto Suro, "How Many Undocumented: The Numbers Behind the U.S.-Mexico Migration Talks." Pew Hispanic Center. March 21, 2003.

Lustig, Nora, B. P. Bosworth, and Robert Z. Lawrence, eds. *North American Free Trade: Assessing the Impact*. Washington, D.C.: Brookings Institution, 1992.

Machado, Manuel A. *The North Mexican Cattle Industry, 1920–1975*. College Station: Texas A&M University Press, 1981.

MacLachlan, Colin M., and Jaime E. Rodriquez O. *The Forging of the Cosmic Race: A Reinterpretation of Colonial Mexico*. Berkeley: University of California Press, 1980.

Magazine Publishers of America. "Hispanic-Latino Market Profile." 2004. www.magazine.org/marketprofiles.

Manke, Richard B. *Mexican Oil and Natural Gas: Political, Strategic, and Economic Implications*. New York: Praeger Publishers, 1979.

Mann, Robert. "Has GM Corn 'Invaded' Mexico?" *Science Magazine*, March 2002, 1617–19.

Martin, Philip L., and Michael S. Teitelbaum. "The Mirage of Mexican Guest Work-ers." *Foreign Affairs*, November 2001, 122–24.

Martin, W.A.P. *The Awakening of China*. New York: Doubleday, Page, and Canopy, 1910.

Martinez, Oscar J. "Transnational Fronterizos: Cross-Border Linkages in Mexican Border Society." *Journal of Borderlands Studies*, Spring 1990, 79–94.

———. *Troublesome Border*. Tucson: University of Arizona Press, 1988.

———. *U.S.-Mexico Borderlands: Historical and Contemporary Perspectives*. Wil-mington: Scholarly Resources, 1996.

Mayer, Brantz. *Mexico, Aztec, Spanish and Republican: Ancient Aztec Empire and Civilization*. 2 vols. Hartford, Conn.: S. Drake, 1853.

Mayer, Frederick W. *Interpreting NAFTA: The Science and Art of Political Analysis*. New York: Columbia University Press, 1998.

Mazarr, Michael J. *Mexico 2005: The Challenges of the New Millennium*. Washington: D.C.: CSIS Press, 1999.

———. *Global Trends 2005*. New York: St. Martin's Press, 1999.

McGaughey, William. *A U.S.-Mexico-Canada Free-Trade Agreement: Do We Just Say No?* Minneapolis: Thistlerose Publications, 1992.

McRae, Hamish. *The World in 2020: Power, Culture and Prosperity*. Boston: Harvard Business School Press, 1994.

Metz, Alan, ed. *A NAFTA Bibliography*. Westport, Conn.: Greenwood Publishing, 1996.

Metz, Leon C. *Border: The U.S.-Mexico Line*. El Paso: Mangan Books, 1989.

Meyer, Lorenzo. *Mexico and the United States in the Oil Controversy, 1917–1942*. Austin: University of Texas Press, 1977.

Meyers, Debrorah. N. "Does 'Smart' Lead to Safer? An Assessment of the Border Accords with Canada and Mexico." *Insight*, January 2002. Migration Policy Institute, Washington, D.C.

Mexico-U.S. Migration: A Shared Responsibility. Washington, D.C.: Carnegie Endow-ment, 2001.

Micklethwait, John, and Adrian Wooldridge. *A Future Perfect: The Challenge and Hidden Promise of Globalization*. New York: Crown Business, 2000.

———. *The Witch Doctor*. London: Mandarin, 1997.

Middlebrook, Kevin J. *The Paradox of Revolution: Labor, the State, and Authoritar-ianism in Mexico*. Baltimore: Johns Hopkins University Press, 1995.

Mines, Richard, and Alain de Janvry. "Migration to the United States and Mexican Rural Development." *American Journal of Agricultural Economics*, August 1982, 444–54.

Molina Enríquez, Andrés. *Los Grandes Problemas Nacionales, 1909*. Mexico City: Ediciones Era, 1978.

Molinski, Michael. *Investing In Latin America*. Princeton, N.J.: Bloomberg Press, 1999.

Montefonte, Raul. "Gas-Demand Growth Will Push Expansion in Mexican Trans-mission Infrastructure." *Oil and Gas Journal*, February 11, 2002, 70–75.

Montejano, David. *Anglos and Mexicans*. Austin: University of Texas Press, 1987.

Mora-Torres, Juan. *The Making of the Mexican Border*. Austin: University of Texas Press, 2001.

Mueller, M. W. "Changing Patterns of Agricultural Output and Production in the Private and Land Reform Sectors in Mexico, 1940–60." *Economic Development and Cultural Change* 18, no. 2 (January 1970): 252–66.

Mumme, Stephen P. *Apportioning Groundwater beneath the U.S.-Mexico Border*. San Diego: Center for U.S.-Mexican Studies, 1988.

Nader, Ralph, et al. *The Case Against Free Trade: Gatt, NAFTA, and the Globalization of Corporate Power*. Berkeley: North Atlantic Books, 1993.

Naim, Moises. "Mexico's Larger Story," *Foreign Policy*, Summer 1995, 112–30.

Narayanan, V. G., and Ananth Raman. "Aligning Incentives in the Supply Chains." *Harvard Business Review*, November 2004, 95–102.

Nguyen, D. T., and M. L. Martinez. "The Effects of Land Reform on Agricultural Production, Employment and Income Distribution: A Statistical Study of Mexican States, 1959–69." *Economic Journal*, September 1979, 624–35.

Nivola, Pietro S. "Energy Independence or Interdependence? Integrating the North American Energy Market," *Brookings Review*, Spring 2002.

North America Energy Working Group. *North America—The Energy Picture*. June 2002.

Ohmae, Kenichi. *The End of the Nation State: The Rise of Regional Economies*. New York: Free Press, 1996.

Oppenheimer, Andres. *Bordering on Chaos: Guerrillas, Stockbrokers, Politicians, and Mexico's Road to Prosperity*. Boston: Little, Brown, 1996.

Organization for Economic Cooperation and Development. *Information and Communication Technologies and Rural Development*. Paris: OECD, 2001.

———. *OECD Economic Surveys: Mexico*. Paris: OECD, 2004.

———. *OECD Territorial Reviews: Mexico*. Paris: OECD, 2003.

———. "Public Spending in Mexico: How to Enhance its Effectiveness," Economic Department Working Paper, no. 288. OECD, Paris 2001.

———. *Regulatory Reform in Mexico*. Paris: OECD, 1999.

Panitchpakdi, Supachai, and Mark L. Clark. *China and the WTO: Changing China, Changing World Trade*. New York: John Wiley & Sons, 2002.

Papademetriou, Demetrios G. "The Mexican Factor in US Immigration Reform." Migration Policy Institute, Washington, D.C., March 1, 2004.

———. "The Shifting Expectations of Free Trade and Migration." In *NAFTA's Promise and Reality*, Washington, D.C.: Carnegie Endowment for International Peace, 2004.

Pastor, Robert A. *Integration with Mexico: Options for U.S. Policy*. New York: Twentieth Century Fund Press, 1993.

Patrick, J. Michael. "Maquiladoras and South Texas Border Economic Development." *Journal of Borderlands Studies*, Spring 1989, 89–99.

Peck, Clint. "Southern Exposure." *Beef*, July 2004.

Peterson, Frederick. *Ancient Mexico: An Introduction to the pre-Hispanic Cultures*. New York: Putnam, 1959.

Pindell, Terry. *Yesterday's Train: A Rail Odyssey through Mexican History*. New York: Henry Holt & Company, 1997.

Pinder, David, and Brian Stack. *Shipping and Ports in the Twenty-first Century*. London: Routledge, 2004.

Pomeranz, Kenneth, and Steven Topik. *The World ThatTtrade Created: Society, Culture, and the World Economy, 1400 to the Present*. London: M. E. Sharpe, 1999.

Porter, Michael E. *The Competitive Advantage of Nations*. New York: Free Press, 1990.

Price, Dave. "Let's Really Look at Free Trade," *Beef*, October 2004.

Puska, Susan M. *People's Liberation Army After Next*. Carlisle, Pa.: SSI U.S. Army War College, 2000.

Quinlan, Joseph P. "Ties That Bind." *Foreign Affairs*, July 2002, 116–26.

Raat, W. Dirk. *Mexico and the United States: Ambivalent Vista*. Athens: University of Georgia Press, 1992.

———. *Revoltosos: Mexico's Rebels in the United States, 1903–1923*. College Station: Texas A&M University Press, 2000.

Ramirez Bonilla, Juan José. "Asia Pacific and the Challenges for Mexico," *Comercio Exterior*, October 2002, 860–65.

Ray, Daryll. "Mexico and Corn." *Farm Press*, September 17, 2003.

Riding, Alan. *Distant Neighbors: A Portrait of the Mexicans*. New York: Knopf, 1985.

Roberts, Paul C., and Karen L. Arauyo. *The Capitalist Revolution in Latin America*. New York: Oxford University Press, 1997.

Rocha, Lourdes, and Sergio Luna. "Energy in Mexico: Some General Reflections." *Review of the Economic Situation of Mexico* (Banamex), August 2002.

Rockefeller, Nelson A. *The Rockefeller Report on the Americas: The Official Report of a United States Presidential Mission for the Western Hemisphere*. Chicago: Quadrangle Books, 1969.

Rodrik, Dani. *Has Globalization Gone Too Far?* Washington, D.C.: Institute for International Economics, 1997.

———. "How Far Will International Economic Integration Go?" *Journal of Economic Perspectives*, Winter 2000, 177–86.

Rodriquez, Guillermina. "Mexican Residents in the USA," *Review if the Economic Situation of Mexico* (Banamex), 2003.

Roett, Riordan. *Mexico's External Relations in the 1990s*. Boulder, Colo.: Lynne Rienner Publishing, 1991.

Ronfeldt, David, Richard Nehring, and Arturo Gandara. *Mexico's Petroleum and U.S. Policy: Implications for the 1980s*. Santa Monica, Calif.: Rand Corporation, 1980.

Rosenbaum, Robert J. *Mexicano Resistance in the Southwest*. Austin: University of Texas Press, 1985.

Rosenfeldt, Martin E. "Mexico's In Bond Export Industries and U.S. legislation: Conflictive Issues." *Journal of Borderlands Studies*, Spring 1990, 47–65.

Rubin, Robert E., and Jacob Weisberg. *In an Uncertain World*. New York: Random House, 2004.

Ruiz, Ramon Eduardo. *Triumphs and Tragedy: A History of the Mexican People*. New York: W. W. Norton, 1992.

Salinas de Gortari, Carlos. *The Policy and Politics of Modernization*. Barcelona: Plaza & Janes Editores, 2002.

Salvatore, Dominick. "International Trade Policies, Industrialization, and Economic Development." *International Trade Journal*, Summer 1996, 21–47.

Sanders, Sol. *Mexico: Chaos on Our Doorstep*. Lanham, Md.: Madison Books, 1989.

Schonberger, Richard J. *Let's Fix It! Overcoming the Crisis in Manufacturing*. New York: Free Press, 2001.

———. *World Class Manufacturing: The Lessons of Simplicity Applied*. New York: Free Press, 1986.

———. *World Class Manufacturing—The Next Decade: Building Power, Strength, and Value*. New York: Free Press, 1996.

Schoonover, Thomas D. *Dollars Over Dominion*. Baton Rouge: Louisiana State University Press, 1978.

Schultz, Donald E., and Edward J. Williams, eds. *Mexico Faces the 21ˢᵗ Century*. Westport, Conn.: Greenwood Press, 1995.

Schwartz, Scott M. "The Border Industrialization Program of Mexico." *Southwest Journal of Business and Economics*, Summer 1987, 1–51.

Scobell, Andrew, and Larry M. Wortzel. *China's Growing Military Power*. Carlisle, Pa.: SSI U.S. Army War College, 2002.

———, eds. *Civil-Military Change in China: Elites, Institutes, and Ideas After the 16th Party Congress*. Carlisle, Pa.: SSI U.S. Army War College, 2004.

Segal, Gerald. "Does China Matter?" *Foreign Affairs*, September 1999, 24–36.

Siembieda, William J., and Eduardo Lopez Moreno, "Expanding Housing Choices for the Sector Popular: Strategies for Mexico." *Housing Policy Debate* 8, no. 3: 651–77.

Sierra, Justo. *La Evolución Política del Pueblo Mexicano*. Mexico City: Universidad Nacional de Mexico (UNAM), 1902.

Silva Herzog, Jesús. *Historia de la Expropiación Petróleo*. Mexico City: Cuadernos Americanos, 1963.

Simon, Joel. *Endangered Mexico: An Environment on the Edge*. San Francisco: Sierra Club Books, 1997.

Simpson, Lesley B. *The Encomienda in New Spain: The Beginning of Spanish Mexico*. Berkeley: University of California Press, 1966.

Skidmore, Thomas E., and Peter H. Smith. *Modern Latin America*. 5th ed. Oxford: Oxford University Press, 2001.

Sorensen, Ninna N. "The Development Dimension of Migrant Remittances." Final Report. Danish Institute for Development Studies, Copenhagen, April 2004.

Suchlicki, Jaime. *Mexico: From Montezuma to NAFTA, Chiapas, and Beyond*. Washington, D.C.: Brassey's, 1996.

Tannenbaum, Frank. *Mexico: The Struggle for Peace and Bread*. New York: Knopf, 1950.

Terrill, Ross. *The New Chinese Empire*. New York: Basic Books, 2003.

Turner, Roger. "Mexico Turns to Its In-Bond Industry as a Means of Generating Exchange." *Business America*, November 28, 1983, 27–32.

U.S.-Mexico Binational Council. *U.S.-Mexico Border Security and the Evolving Security Relationship*. Washington, D.C.: CSIS, 2004.

Vanderwood, Paul J. *Disorder and Progress: Bandits, Police, and Mexican Development*. Lincoln: University of Nebraska Press, 1981.

Vasquez, Josefina Z., and Lorenzo Meyer. *The United States and Mexico*. Chicago: University of Chicago Press, 1985.

Verea, Monica. "A Watershed in the U.S.-Mexico Migration Debate: Closing the Borders." *World Press Review*, April 2002.

Von Bertrab, Hermann. *Negotiating NAFTA: A Mexican Envoy's Account*. Westport, Conn.: Praeger, 1997.

Webb, Walter P. *The Great Plains*. New York: Grosset and Dunlap, 1931.

Weiler, Stephen, and Becky Zerlentes. "Maquila Sunrise or Sunset? Evolution of Regional Production Advantages." *Social Science Journal*, 2003, 283–97.

Weintraub, Sidney. *Free Trade between Mexico and the United States?* Washington, D.C.: Brookings Institution, 1984.

————. *A Marriage of Convenience: Relations between Mexico and the United States.* New York: Oxford University Press, 1990.

————. *Transforming the Mexican Economy: The Salinas Sexenio.* Washington, D.C.: National Planning Association, 1990.

Wilson, Patricia A. "The Global Assembly Industry: Maquiladoras in International Perspective," *Journal of Borderlands Studies,* Fall 1991, 73–104.

Womack, John. *Zapata and the Mexican Revolution* New York, Vintage, 1970.

Woodward, Bob. *Maestro.* New York: Simon & Schuster, 2000.

World Bank. *China 2020: China Engaged.* Washington, D.C.: IBRD-World Bank, 1997.

————. *Global Economic Prospects: Overview and Global Outlook, 2005.* Washington, D.C.: IBRD-World Bank, 2005.

————. *Think Globally, Act Locally: Decentralized Incentive Framework for Mexico's Private Sector Development.* Washington, D.C.: IRBD-World Bank, 2002.

Yergin, Daniel. *The Prize: The Epic Quest for Oil, Money, and Power.* New York: Touchstone Books, 1992.

Yergin, Daniel, and Joseph Stanislaw. *The Commanding Heights: The Battle for the World Economy.* New York: Simon & Schuster, 1998.

Yunez-Naude, A. "The Dismantling of CONASUPO, a Mexican State Trader in Agriculture." *World Economy* 26, no. 1 (January 2003): 97–122.

Yusuf, Shahid, M.A. Altaf, and Kaorv Nabeshima. *Global Production Networking and Technological Change in East Asia.* Washington, D.C.: World Bank, 2004.

Zedillo Ponce de Leon, Ernesto. "The Mexican External Debt: The Last Decade." In *Politics and Economics of External Debt Crisis: The Latin American Experience,* edited by Miguel S. Wionczek and Luciano Tomassini, 294–324. Boulder: Westview Press, 1988.

Unpublished Manuscripts, Proceedings, and Reports

Ackerman, Frank et al. "Free Trade, Corn, and the Environment: Environmental Impacts of U.S.-Mexico Corn Trade under NAFTA." Working Paper no. 03-06. Global Development and Environment Institute, Tufts University, June 2003.

Aguayo, Francisco, and Kevin P. Gallagher. "Economic Reform, Energy, and Development: The Case of Mexican Manufacturing." Working Paper no. 03-05. Global Development and Environment Institute, Tufts University, July 2003.

Border Trade Alliance. "Border Trade Alliance: Southwest Border Infrastructure Initiative Final Report". Laredo, Texas, February 1993.

————. "Maquiladora Impact Survey: Findings and Conclusions." Department of Marketing, University of Texas at El Paso, El Paso, July 1987.

Chiquiar, Daniel, and Gordon H. Hanson. "International Migration, Self-Selection, and Distribution of Wages: Evidence from Mexico and the United States." University of California, San Diego, September 2002.

Dias, Vivianne V., and Jose D. Lima. "Production Sharing in Latin American Trade: A Research Note." United Nations, International Trade and Integration Division, Santiago, Chile, December 2001.

Gomez, Jerilyn M. "An Assessment of U.S. Sugar Program Sustainability: The Implication of Granting Increased Market Access to Foreign Sugar Producers." Agricultural Economics Department, Penn State University, 2004.

Gonzales-Anaya, Jose A. "Why Have Banks Stopped Lending in Mexico since the Peso Crisis in 1995." Paper no. 118, Center for Research on Economic Development and Policy Reform, Stanford University, April 2003.

Griswold, Daniel, and Daniel Ikenson. "The Case for CAFTA: Consolidating Central America's Freedom Revolution." Cato Institute Trade Briefing Papers, no. 21, September 21, 2004.

Koo, Won W., and Richard D. Taylor. "2004 Outlook of the U.S. and World Sugar Markets, 2003–2013." Report no. 536, Center for Agricultural Policy and Trade Studies, North Dakota State University, June 2004.

Kruse, James, David Bierling, and Nathan Vajdos. "Analysis of Start-Up Cross-Gulf Short Sea Shipping Activities with Mexico since 1990: Problems and Opportunities." Texas Transportation Institute: Texas A&M University, August 2004.

Laredo Chamber of Commerce. "Laredo 2000 and Beyond: Legislative Priorities." Laredo, Texas, March 2000.

Laredo Development Foundation. "Proceedings of the 11th Annual Manufacturing in Mexico and on the U.S. Border Symposium." Laredo, Texas, September 22–24, 2004.

McCray, John P. "NAFTA Truck Highway Corridors: U.S.-Mexico Truck Rivers of Trade." Transportation Research Board, Washington, D.C. January 11, 1998.

North American Energy Working Group. "North America—The Energy Picture." June 2002.

Rosellon, Juan, and Jonathan Halpern. "Regulatory Reform in Mexico's Natural Gas Industry." World Bank Policy Research Working Paper, no. 2537, January 2001.

Rosson, Parr. "GMO and Bio-safety Protocols: Issues and Implications for Texas Agriculture" Center for North American Studies, Texas A&M University, 2004.

———. "U.S. Market Integration in North America: Potential Roles of the WTO and Trade Agreements." Center for North American Studies, Department of Agricultural Economics, Texas A&M University, 2004.

Rosson, Parr, and Flynn Adcock. "The North American Free Trade Agreement (NAFTA): Deepening Economic Integration and response to Competition." No. 2003-3, Center for North American Studies, (CNAS), Texas A&M University, July 2003.

Urteaga-Trani, Raul, Economic Counselor, Embassy of Mexico. "U.S.-Mexico Relations: Balancing Trade, Security and Economic Integration." Presentation, Center for the Study of Western Hemispheric Trade, Texas A&M International University, Laredo Texas, November 10, 2003.

U.S.-Mexico Bilateral Council. "U.S.-Mexico Border Security Relationship." Center for Strategic and International Studies, Washington, D.C., April 2004.

Van Waas, Michael. "The Multinationals' Strategy for Labor: Foreign Assembly Plants in Mexico's Border Industrialization Program." PhD diss., Stanford University, 1981.

Vaughan, Jessica M. "Modernizing the Welcome Mat: A Look at the Goals and Challenges of the US-VISIT Program." Center for Immigration Studies, Smart Borders Conference, Washington, D.C., October 26, 2004.

Watts, Julie. "Mexico-U.S. Migration and Labor Unions: Obstacles to Building Cross-Border Solidarity." Working Paper no. 79, Center for Comparative Immigration Studies, University of California, San Diego, June 2003.

INDEX

Adams-Onis Treaty of 1819, 5, 10
agriculture, 17–39
Aztecs, 5–7

Baker, George, 64
Barry, Tom, 17, 53
beef production, 29–32
border affairs, 41–60
Border Industrial Program, 45,
   80–81, 100
Border Liaison Mechanism
   (BLM), 46
Bracero Program, 44, 51, 53,
   80, 100
Bush, George W., xi, 41, 58, 125
Business Anti-smuggling Coalition
   (BASC), 120

Canada Free Trade Agreement
   (CFTA), 33
Cárdenas, Cuauhtémoc, 13
Cárdenas, Lázaro, 63
Castañeda, Jorge, 79
Central America Free Trade
   Agreement (CAFTA), 58, 96
Central American Bank of Economic
   Development (CABED), 92
China, 14, 73, 77–98, 123

Christman, John, 109
Churchill, Winston, 121
Cline, Howard, 3
Clinton, William, 55–56, 84
Cold War, xi, 84, 86
Columbus, Christopher, 5–6
corn (GMO maize), 27–28, 34
Cortés, Hernán, 5–8, 14

Daíz, Porfirio, 5, 11, 22, 61–62, 73
Davidow, Jeffery, 56, 79

Echeverría, Luis, 20
Economic Commission for Latin
   America and the Caribbean
   (ECLAC), 92
ejido system, 14, 20–22

Fox, Vicente, 5, 16, 17, 71, 75, 90,
   93, 123, 125
financial crisis of 1994, 13–16

General Agreement on Tariffs and
   Trade (GATT), 26, 79, 82, 84,
   104, 106, 108, 115
González, Carlos de Icaza, 41

Gould, Jay, 43
Grayson, George W., 3, 54

Hanson, Victor D. 55
Harrison, Rob, 113
Hart, John Mason, 63

Illegal Immigration Reform and
  Immigrant Responsibility Act
  (IIRIRA), 56
immigration, 50–60, 124; "Texas
  Proviso," 54
Immigration and Nationality Act of
  1924, 44
Immigration Reform and
  Control Act of 1986 (IRCA),
  53, 57
Intelligence Reform and Terrorism
  Prevention Act of 2004, 59
Inter-American Development Bank
  (IDB), 51, 92
International and Great Northern
  Railroad (I&GN), 43
International Boundary and Water
  Commission, 49
International Monetary Fund (IMF),
  13, 15, 107
Iturbide, Agustín, 5, 10

Jintao, Hu, 86
Juárez, Benito, 11

Kandell, Jonathan, 23
Kennedy, Paul, 3
Krauze, Enrique, 6

Laredo (Texas), 43, 69, 104, 109,
  111–16
Louisiana Purchase, 10

Manifest Destiny, 11
maquiladora, 99–129
McCray, John P., 114
Mexican Constitution of 1917,
  12, 21; Article "27," 12, 21, 25,
  61–63, 72
Mexico City (Tenochtitlán), 6–8, 10,
  13, 19, 22–25, 45–46
Mexico–European Union Free
  Trade Agreement, 92, 108
Mexico–Japan Free Trade
  Agreement, 96
Monroe Doctrine, 10
multiple service contracts
  (MSC), 72

New Spain, 6–8
North America Free Trade
  Agreement (NAFTA), xi, 4, 13, 16,
  18, 26–29, 31–33, 48, 63, 78,
  81–84, 94, 97, 100, 103–8, 113,
  115, 117–19, 122

Ordaz, Gustavo Díaz, 80
Organization for Economic
  Cooperation and Development
  (OECD), 15, 22, 23, 67–68, 71, 93,
  106, 111
Organization of American States
  (OAS), 78
Organization of Petroleum Exporting
  Countries (OPEC), 16, 67

Partido Revolucionario
  Institucional (PRI), 12–13, 15, 21,
  25, 78, 123
Patrick, J. Michael, 112
Peso-value (Mexico), 91, 103
Petróleos Mexicanos (PEMEX),
  62–64, 67–68, 87
petroleum (oil), 11, 61–76, 123

Plan Puebla-Panama (PPP),
   92–93, 96
Porter, Michael E., 39, 108
Port-to-Plains Corridor, 116
Prescott, William H., 1, 7

remittances, 51 52, 55
Rio Grande (Rio Bravo), 6, 8, 18, 22,
   24, 29, 42–43, 48–50, 72, 117, 124;
   zona libre, 43, 75
Rockefeller Report on the Americas,
   The, 3
Roosevelt, Franklin D., 63, 80

Salinas, Carlos, 4, 13–15
Santa Anna, Antonio López de,
   10–11, 42
si dios quiere, 4
Silver, 8, 10
Special Economic Zones (SEZ),
   87–88, 93
Strategic Bonded Zone (SBZ), 120
sugar and HFCS, 30–33

Trans-Texas Corridor (TTC-35), 117
Treaty of Guadalupe Hidalgo, 42

Union Pacific Railroad, 43
United Nations (UN), 91
Urteaga-Trani, Raul, 99

U.S. Border Patrol, 44, 54, 56, 59
U.S.–Canadian Free Trade
   Agreement, 26, 33
U.S. Department of Energy, 70
U.S. Department of Homeland
   Security, 46, 117, 122
U.S. Department of Treasury, 13
U.S. Mexico Border Treaties and
   Agreements, 47–48
U.S. Strategic Petroleum
   Reserve, 76
U.S. VISIT, 57, 60, 120

von Bertrab, Herman, 18

Weintraub, Sidney, 16
Win Jiabao, 90
World Bank (IRBD), 15, 28, 32, 107
World Trade Organization (WTO),
   18, 26, 77, 81, 83–84, 86, 89, 91,
   95, 100, 106–8, 119

Xiaoping, Deng, 87

Yergin, Daniel, 62, 88

Zapata, Emiliano, 20
Zedillo, Ernesto, 4, 15, 71, 79
Zinser, Aquilar, 79

ABOUT THE AUTHOR

JOHN A. ADAMS, JR. is President and CEO of Enterprise Florida Inc., a public-private partnership responsible for leading Florida's statewide economic development efforts. For over twenty years he has been actively involved in international trade, with a specialty in Latin America and an emphasis on emerging industrial and financial markets in Mexico. He has served as a delegate to the GATT negotiations in Geneva, an advisor to the World Trade Organization, Chairman of the Industry Sector Advisory Council for trade policy review at the U.S. Department of Commerce, and has provided Congressional testimony on U.S.–Mexico border infrastructure issues. An adjunct professor of international banking and finance at Texas A&M International University in Laredo, Texas, he speaks widely to industry, government, international trade, and economic development groups around the world, and is the author of many articles, chapters, and books, including *Mexican Banking and Investment in Transition* (Quorum, 1997).